HISTORICAL DEVELOPMENT OF AGRICULTURE AND FOOD IN BENGAL

HISTORICAL DEVELOPMENT OF AGRICULTURE AND FOOD IN BENGAL

Nilangshu Mukherjee
Avik Mukherjee

GenNext Publication

A

ISBN: 978-93-8022-267-7
Price : ₹ 900

First Published, 2015

Published by

GenNext Publication
5, Ansari Road,
Darya Ganj
New Delhi-110002
Mob: 9811692060
E-mail: gennext@hotmail.com

Printed at : G. Print Process, Delhi

Cataloging in Publication Data—DK
Courtesy: D.K. Agencies (P) Ltd. <docinfo@dkagencies.com>

Mukherjee, Nilangshu, 1940- **author.**
Historical development of agriculture and food in Bengal / Nilangshu Mukherjee, Avik Mukherjee.
pages cm
Includes bibliographical references (pages) and index.
ISBN 9789380222677

1. Agriculture—India—Bengal—History. 2. Food—India—Bengal—History. I. Mukherjee, Avik, author. II. Title.

DDC 338.1095414 23

Contents

1

Introduction

Historical Development of Agriculture and Food in Bengal

Agriculture is primarily a land based activity of humans leaving aside very little activities on other surfaces like water or so. The earth was created through miraculous celestial movements in the solar system. Evolution of living organisms and their further evolution to humans and their skill development made doing agriculture possible. Progress in our scientific knowledge has helped us understand how life was created in water. Similarly the stepwise evolution of primates to modern humans and their becoming bipeds by practicing standing on two legs making hands free to engage in creative activities is amazing. All these developments were preceeded by development of the land surface. Thoughts of some great persons of this land generated a corpus of knowledge and subjecting these to constant scrutiny and reappraisal, they actually inspired taking an initiative.

1.1 Land surface development

(a) The present structure of the earth as we see now is as old as 40,000 lakh years. It was built up in *Hadean* period i.e. 4600 million to 3800 million years ago. Through most modern methods of testing the rocks that make the surface of the earth is as old as 39800 million years. Again the first arrival of living organisms in sea-water in the form of microorganism is 40000 to 25000 million years back. Irfan Habib suggests that life was being expressed through evolution of different forms of life at a time when earth's surface was continuously changing. Earth was expanding to larger size by reducing its density, and separating its continents bringing in seas and oceans in between. This led to development of the idea of *Gondowana* supercontinent breaking up into India, Australia, Antarctica, Africa and South America at the end of *Jurassic age* i.e. 1440 lakh years back. In *Eocene epoch* (580-370 lakh years back), the continent that held India started moving and joined *Eurasia* continent. All these happened due to movement of tectonic plates, one of which holding India, Australia and Indian Ocean (Indian plate). On its West-African and its south Eurasian plates – all the time striking each other leading to change of earth's surface going up or down. In the process during *Eocene* period chains of Himalayan mountains started raising its head like a garland of rocks from east to west separating Indian continent from rest of Asia. This event caused change of the atmosphere of Indian continent providing it with number of mighty rivers. Basham told of two great rivers – *Sindhu* and *Ganga* but it is three to include '*Brahmaputra*' also. Indus basin was separated from Ganga basin by a desert of Rajasthan (*Thar*) and by some small bills. The western half of *Ganga* plain from around Delhi to Patna includes the land between *Ganga* and its great tributary river *Yamuna* (or *Doab*) that has been the '*Aryabarta* of India (land of *Aryans*). As such its foundation is on rock of carboniferous era (3200 to 2860 lakh years old) developed in *Archaean eon* to Pleistocene period for over 300 crore years. It is established that this *Gondowana*; rock show i.e. fossils of land organisms Dinosaur that are absent in *Deccan-rock*. Again *Himalayas* and Bengal coastal saline soils have evidences of sea life of *Cambrian* period (5700 lakh years back). This indicated some early physical relation of the Himalayas with sea may be through *Tethys*. Sea fossils of *Mesozoic period* (650 lakh years back) have been detected on Himalayas.

(b) Talking about the land surface of Bengal Sankarshan Roy, 1979 stated that 100 crore year back one Volcano on the spot now occupied by *Dalma hills* erupted producing *lava* that rolled down upto Medinipur to create the oldest rocky surface. This rocky surface is spread upto '*Rarh*' area in Bengal. Ashoke Kr. Bose, 2002 called this as 'Bengal Trap' that actually made the foundation of the land of Bengal on which layers of other materials has made this land surface. This eastern part of Indian continent has always the *Himalayas* in the north and *Bay of Bengal* in the south, both created in *Archaean eon*.

The land called 'Bengal' has in its northern border Sikkim, another Indian state and the *Kanchengunga* hills of the Himalayas, northern districts being Darjeeling and Jalpaiguri. On the west of these two districts of Bengal is Nepal and on the east is Bhutan. On the east of Bengal river *Brahmaputra* was on the northern end, *Garo, Khasia* and *Jayantia* hills at the center and *Lusai*, *Chattogram*, and *Arakan hills* on the southern end. After the creation of *Bangladesh* (seventh decade of 20th cent) it lies on the east of West Bengal, *Ichhamati* river being the eastern border on the lower part. On the west is the hilly tract of Manbhum of Jharkhand lying west of Bankura district. Sanontal Parganas touch the northern Birbhum and West Medinipur adjoining Baleswar of Orissa and Singhbhum of Bihar. Southern border is Bay of Bengal touching East Medinipur and South 24-Pargana coastal area having large number of islands. The *Ganga delta* (largest in the world) is situated in between the rivers *Bhagirathi*, *Ganga-Padma* and *Meghna* covering 1.5 lakh square kilometer area.

(c) The oldest rocky mass that is on the surface or as foundation is volcanic in origin. That it is 100-200 crore year old *micacyst* and *granite* is established through most modern geological examinations and are *Archaeojoic* in class. On this foundation was layed on Cambrian (50 crore years back) and *Parmean* (22 crore year back) rocks. Some such rocks are Quartzite in *Sushunia*, sand stone in *Beliatod*, Dolomite and limestone in *Jalpaiguri* – all deposited 50-100 crore years back. In some other places like Raniganj and Asansol coal layers were deposited thereafter (20-25 crore years back).

(d) Then started the phase of 'plain' development. Bengal of any time or period and dimension is essentially a plain built up by silting of the river *Ganga – Bhagirathi* and large number of other rivers. South of Bengal is considered lower Gangetic Plain and northern part was built by other rivers like *Tista, Torsa, Mahananda, Jaldhaka* and others. Rivers are the founder of the fertile land-flat that is the delta of Bengal. Some 5-10 thousand years ago Bay of Bengal used to touch *Rarh plataeu, Rajmahal hill* and *Srihatta hill* indicating that the silted surface of the foundation rock raised its fertile back from within the sea water. The *Rarh* area spread over Bankura, Purulia, Birbhum, Barddhaman and Medinipur was inhabited first by early *'Bengalis'*. Similarly *Barendrabhumi* spread over North Bengal districts and *Pragjyotishpur* now in Assam were also inhabited in early days. Beyond anyone's eye huge quantity of broken and weathered rocks of the great *Himalayas* was carried through river water-flow. In course of this long journey they are further ground into silt and clay, deposited in sea-water to slowly raise newer land in the coast pushing back the sea. Thus the largest delta of the world is taking its shape over a very long period of time.

As per geophysiography of land and soils Bengal has three distinct areas namely – (i) *Uttaranchal Hills and Plains*, (ii) *Paschimanchal plateau or Rarh bhumi* and (iii) *Dakshinanchal – Ganga Plains*.

(i) *Uttaranchal Hills and plains* – includes hilly areas in three subdivisions of Darjeeling Kalimpong and Kurseang and plain land areas in Siliguri sub-division and district of Jalpaiguri, Coochbehar, Uttar and Dakshin Dinajpur and Maldah. While the hilly area is a part of *Himalayas*, the slightly undulating plains are created through silting of rivers. Eastern Maldah and Eastern Dakshin Dinajpur are relatively older lands and termed *Barendrabhumi*. The characteristics of this undulated reddish brown and yellowish land area is interspersed with raised lands (*tila*). Again the plains for natural reasons developed partly into *Tarai* and *Ganga Brahmputra-Doab* besides *Barendrabhoomi*. South of Darjeeling, parts of Jalpaiguri and Coochbehar and the *Doab* together forms *Dooars*. In *Doab* area low-lying *Taal* areas full of water-bodies are present in southern Coochbehar, entire

Uttar and Dakshin Dinajpur and north Maldah. In *Mahananda* bed (Maldah) large silted land areas (*Diara*) are quite common.

(ii) *Paschimanchal-plateau or Rarh bhumi* : Rows of hills lined in the west of the districts – Puruliya, Bankura and Paschim Medinipur lying close to *Chotonagpur plateau* and *Rajmahal hills* and continuing toward *Ghatshila, Musaboni* upto *Baheraguda*. This *Rarhbhum* and *Manbhum* of Jharkhand are mostly (75 per cent) built with components of volcanic materials like niece, granite, quartzite etc. rocks and the important hills are *Ajodhya, Biharinath, Joychandi, Sushunia* etc. Over long period erosion of rocks created rolling or wave-like surface of the land with reddish, lateritic mixed with old alluvium soil of shallow depth. The acidic soil in rich is iron and full of sand or pebbles. Land areas here carry designations like *Senbhum* (Asansol adjoining area), *Gopbhum* (Barddhaman–Durgapur area), *Shurbhum* (land between *Damodar* and *Dwarakeswar* rivers), *Mallabhum* (Bankura and Bishnupur), *Dhabalbhum* (right bank of *Kansai* river) and *Tungabhum* (Jhargram adjoining area) among local people. Ancient people in *Plaeocene* epoch developed these land area and settled here. These areas in Paschim Medinipur, Purulia, Bankura and West Barddhaman and Birbhum developed much earlier (53-25 lakh years back) than the districts on the east of river *Ganga*.

(iii) *Dakshinanchal the Ganga delta plains* : Southern part of Bengal – a delta developed partially on marine rocks that extended southward at the time of drifting of continents, cooling and drying of atmosphere, growth of ice-sheets on *Antartica*, formation of *Arctic ice cap* resulting in decline in sea-water level exposing rocks in continents of India, China and Africa. The delta is dead in Murshidabad area, mature in Hugli, Haora, Barddhaman and Purba Medinipur and active in Uttar and Dakshin 24-Parganas, Active delta is continuing its land development activities. Rivers *Ganga, Bramhaputra* and *Meghna* brings about 100 crore tons of silt every year. High and low tides in *Bangoposagar* (Bay of Bengal) pushes silt in opposite direction. This effected new land development on the rocky surface.

(d) The slope of northern land in Bengal is toward south, western land toward east and rest toward south-east, rivers following these slopes. The areas now known as *Paschim Banga* (West Bengal) of India and *Bangladesh* developed 20-25 lakh years back (Plaeocene epoch under Paleocene period of Cenzoic era). During this period the atmosphere was already oxygenated, photosynthesis by plants has started (earlier) and vertebrate land animals have evolved.

Mukerji, 1901 found surface geology of Bengal, a part of Indo Gangetic basin to be mostly alluvial plain. Except in lower hills of Sikkim, Bhutan, Nepal down to a height of 3000 feet above sea-level glacial boulders and morains are not represented but deeper studies (Sankarshan Roy) revealed otherwise. In the west, a band of *Cuddelore* group of rocks, sandstones, (tertiary) grits and clays underlying laterite was mentioned. In *Chattogram, Tripura, Garo and Manipur* hills elevated in post-tertiary age eosin sandstones, nummulitic limestones, cretaceous rocks and pre-tertiary states and sandstones are detected. *Jurassic system* is represented in Rajmahal hills and upper *Panchet* series of rocks. *Rajmahal rock* is basalt or trap consisting of dark coloured *Dolerite*, interstratified with hard white and gray carbonaceous shale, white and gray sandstones and hard quartzose grit. *Gondowana rocks* (both upper and lower) appear in Bengal's *Damodar valley* and Chotonagpur. Then comes typical *Barrakar rocks* (*Damuda*) of carboniferous system. Lastly *Archaean rocks*, result from metamorphic and sub-metamorphic transition (*Vindhayan*). Trap dykes are rare in Bengal gneiss.

Bengal today is the product of a long process of geotypical formation. Widespread marine transgressions and regressions with consequent uplifts featured its geologic history down to *Pleistocene time*. The beds forming western half of *Bengal delta* have very low dips, presumably developed at number of different stages in the geologic history of the basin. Quaternary sediments deposited by *Ganga – Bramhaputra* rivers and their numerous streams and distributaries made the large alluvial basin. *Rajmahal hills* bordering north-west and west of the 'basin' is composed of traps and is *lower Jurassic* of the upper *Gondowana* system. On the north-east of the basin the *Garo*, *Khasi*, and *Jayantia* hills make the boundary. This boundary is actually plateau with *Shillong* or *Assam* on them at 4500-6000 ft. elevations. On the basement rocks are overlaid horizontally sandstone and nummulatic limestone. On the east of basin boundary are *Tripura hills* to the north and *Chattogram hills* to the south, now in *Bangladesh*. The land as a whole has its own characteristic ambience choosing the life on it.

1.2 River systems of Bengal

(a) Long after creation of the earth when ice-age came to an end in *Pleistocene period* i.e. about 18 lakh to 10 thousand years back started *Holocene period* of ice melting time. In the ice-age oceans and seas became smaller in size. During 'Holocene' melting of ice caused the oceans and seas with increased water and this phase is continuing for last 8-10 thousand years. This size-increase of seas and oceans encroached huge land area. The islands of *Ganga-Bramhaputra* river system are either disappearing under water or shrinking in size. The sea coast-lines are changing and oceans and seas are occupying more and more coastal land often overflowing during high-tide turning agricultural land saline and uncultivable.

Silting of the rivers has also changed the spatial characters. Prosperity and decline of river ports namely, *Tamralipta*, *Saptagram*, *Kolkata* and *Haldia* one after the other speaks about this change. The same process of silting created the vast alluvium land area. R.D. Oldham suggested that long before creation of this alluvium a rocky island existed at the coast. In fact under the sea-water small rocks existed from the days of creation of the Bay. They may be part of ancient *Gondowana* that dipped under water due to plate shaking.

There are 96 rivers in 'Paschim Banga' part of '*Bangla*' (Asoke Kr. Basu, 2002) and they originate generally from the hills of north Bengal and western Plateau and flow toward south and south-east.

(b) Uttaranchal rivers

Number of mighty rivers like *Tista, Torsa, Jaldhaka, Mahananda* and others are shaping the northern alluvial plain through six districts. From *Tista-Thangse glacier* (6400 m) at North Sikkim and confluence of two rivers – *Lachen* and *Lachung* in Himalays, river *Tista* has originated. After touching Rongpo town of east Sikkim it entered *Paschimbanga*, passed through Darjeeling and Jalpaiguri districts and entered *Bangladesh*. It has number of tributaries in both right and left banks in Darjeeling and Jalpaiguri namely, Lish, Sebakkhola, Ramam, Rangit and Jaldhaka. They deposit large rocks and pebbles reaching the plains. Thus developed *Tarai* or *Dooars* that is full of big trees, damp with large number of rivers passing from north to south. Some other rivers are Chel, Kolka, Dhorla, Neorakhola, Karotoa, Raydak and Sankosh. *Torsa* and *Sankosh* entered Bangladesh to reach *Bramhaputra*.

Uttar and Dakshin Dinajpur are also having large number of rivers. From Purnia (Bihar) comes *Mahananda* along border of Dinajpur and merges with river *Nagar* near Mukundapur. *Nagar* coming along *Bangladesh* border merges in *Mahananda*. *Kulik* comes from Bangladesh and feeds *Nagar*. *Tangan, Punarvaba*, and *Atrayee* are also important rivers of these districts. *Maldah* is also served by rivers like *Mahananda, Pagla, Kalindi, Tangon*, and *Punarvaba* in addition to *Ganga*. *Mahananda* has divided the district. These together supplies water to the district of Maldah. At the end they entered Bangladesh to merge in Bramhaputra.

Paschimanchal plateau area rivers : Rivers of four districts namely, Purulia, Bankura, Barddhaman and Birbhum presents an altogether different geophysiography, topography and atmosphere. Land of Purulia is full of hills, low hills, '*tila*' and rolling surface, the highest point being *Ajoddha hills*. *Panchet hills* in north-east border highland in the east continued to Bankura and triangular *Barahabhum* in south is extended to Medinipur.

Subarnarekha comes from *Palamou* hills and runs along the west and southwest border of the area and tributaries like *Sankha, Salda, Rupai* etc. *Kansai* (*Kangsabati*) originated from *Jhabor* forest and entered Bankura and merged with *Kumari* river covering about 100 km. *Damodar* in the northern border receives water from *Gobai* river originating from *Hazaribag* hills and passing over *Panchet* hills. *Kumari* is on the eastern slope of *Ajodhya* hills, and covered 64 km in Purulia to reach *Kansai* in Bankura. A lake that grew in between *Adra* and *Hura* gives rise to river *Dwarakeswar* (*Dhol-kishore*) river to enter Bankura. *Sushunia* hills are on the west of Bankura or in between Bankura and Purulia. Another hill in north-west corner of the district is *Biharinath*. Mighty *Damodar* passing on the border of Barddhaman, enters the district after *Indus* town. However, *Damodar* is vast only during monsoon. *Shilai* (*Shilaboti*) receives *Joypanda* and *Purandar* rivers before it enters Medinipur. *Kansai* also passes through Barddhaman before entering Medinipur. *Ranibandh* is plateau having a forest. Water flowing from this upland forest makes *Bhairab river* that converges with *Tarafeni*. *Damodar* river is 538 km long and 228 km of it is in Bihar rest being in *Bengal*. Before it enters West Bengal it receives huge volume of water from *Agar, Bokaro, Konar, Barakar* rivers. After it has crossed *Puruliya* it turns left, touches *Barddhaman* to reach *Bankura-Barddhaman* border and flows downward.

Thereafter it passed through Hooghly and Howra to reach river *Hooghly* near *Shibganj* village. With progress of time its branch *Mundeswari* turned main course of *Damodar* henceforth. Actually *Damodar* started changing its course of flow since 15th century. It continued to change its course number of times taking different names e.g. *Khori, Banka, Behula* etc. Its width increased excessively in its 70 km flow from *Panagarh* to *Shaktigarh* and raised number of '*Char*' islands in its bed that resulted in excessive flood in districts like Hooghly, Howra and Barddhaman. Damodar Valley Corporation was created and four bund's were erected at different places and times. They are *Tilaiya, Konark, Barakar* and *Panchet*. Main object was to prevent floods by controlling and storing excess water during rains. In addition the stored water was used for irrigation of crops in Bihar and West Bengal. One barrage was also erected at *Durgapur*. Another four 'bunds' were to be erected as per plan but were not erected and as a result floods could not be stopped and the project failed to deliver as per expectations. *Ajay* river (120 km) passed over the border of Barddhaman and Birbhum and flew in west to east direction. Being heavily silted *Ajay* remains full only during monsoon even though it receives water from *Kunur and Tumni* rivulets. Most of the rivers in Birbhum are coming from *Rajmahal hills* and *Chotonagpur plateau*. Important rivers are *Ajay* and *Mayurakshi*, but they dry up during summer. *Pagla* coming from Bihar passed through Birbhum and reached Murshidabad. Besides, rivers like *Kopai, Bakreswar, Hinglo* and *Kalindi* also passes in Birbhum. *Dakshinanchal rivers* are mainly *Ganga-Bhagirathi-Hooghly* and others around passing through Hooghly, Howrah, East Medinipur, Murshidabad, Nadia and North and South 24-Parganas. *Ganga* comes out of *Gomukh* at 4000 meters above and upto *Debprayag* it is known as *Bhagirathi*. After this it merges with *Alakananda* to become *Ganga* by name. It comes down to plains after *Haridwar* and flows eastward. During this part of its journey it receives water from *Yamuna, Gomati, Shone, Gandak, Kushi* and many others. In the stretch known as *Hooghly river* huge quantity (40 crore ton/year) of silt is deposited. In fact tributaries like *Banshloi, Ajay, Damodar, Rupnarayan, Haldi, Jalangi, Churni*, and others are possibly contributing more silt than water to it. As a result the river at its mouth has become wide (20 km) but shallow. Breaking of both the banks added to the silt stock and further loss of depth. The eastern tributary originating at *Tribeni* i.e. *Yamuna* has been silted up at many places of its course before it reached *Ichamati*. Similarly *Vidyadhari* is also silted up, though it remains wide and shallow after *Canning*. Here onward in North and South 24-Parganas many tributaries namely *Saptamukhi, Thakuran, Raymangal, Gosaba, Jhilla, Bartala* and *Adi Ganga* coming out of the Hooghly and reaches the Bay of Bengal. In the coastal East Medinipur rivers like *Shilabati, Kangsabati, Keleghai, Subarnarekha, Dulung, Rasulpur* and others are important tributaries of Hooghly river. *Shilabati* comes from Bankura and reaches finally to *Rupnarayan* and *Keleghai* comes from *Kangsabati* merges with *Keleghai* to form *Haldi* which in its turn merges to Hooghly river. *Keleghai* comes from *Jhargram* while *Subarnarekha*, a branch of *Dulung* has come from Bihar and Orissa.

Most important aspect is the fact that the entire position of lower Gangetic plains is slowly but definitely changing. The rivers are changing their course, direction and some are disappearing. The geophysical changes in the land-shape is possibly the only permanent feature of the earth's surface in this part of the earth. Rivers the boon of nature is turning to become bane as *Damodar* – one time a river of misery or *Padma* – the 'Kirtinasha' has lost their infamous call names. The maps of Bengal drawn by Ptolemy in 15th Century, Zao-De-Baos in 16th century, Van Darboke in 17th or Rennel in 18th give different impressions. In the days earlier to 15th century *Bhagirathi's* main course was through *Hawra* with the name *Saraswati*, now almost dried up. In last 100 years the main course of great *Ganga* has taken a south-east bend and passed through present Bangladesh with name *Padma* to reach the Bay of Bengal and the erstwhile main course *Bhagirathi* has become weaker. In 15th century *Bhagirathi* or *Hooghly* R. was the main river. Again from Kolkata the main course of *Bhagirathi* has become very weak and on the way disappear with name *Aadi Ganga*. This changing pattern of land surface of Bengal (Bangla) has influenced the agriculture of the land. Kalikrishna Mandal studied many articles obtained from *Harinavi* and *Rajpur* area in South 24 Parganas and claimed that the Delta was built up 7000 years back. This questions the claim of Ashoke Basu that *Ganga Bhagirathi* river system is 5000 years old. Pranab Naskar examined some articles excavated from 50 ft depth of *Dhopagachi*, South 24-Parganas, a newly formed land piece and established them to be 6125 ± 125 years old. At the end of the day the ancient nature of this so long known new land surface speaks of its ancient nature undoubtedly.

The river network has adorned the land with most precious of capital stocks, the stock of sweet water, so precious for life.

1.3 Weather and climate of Bengal

Due to its location in tropical area with Himalayas in the North and Bay of Bengal in the south Bengal enjoys tropical and subtropical moderation of temperature, humidity, winds, solar radiation, rainfall round the year having no extremes so to say. Indian subcontinent reached its present location (37°N to 8°N) some 200 lakh years back in Pleistocene period. Bengal being located between 2°N and 27°N enjoys subtropical, a moderate climate of course with a good figure of annual rainfall. The entire situation round the year is quite favourable for all living organisms plants, animals and humans. Though the land being the largest delta in the world, is essentially plains, it has Darjeeling hills in the north, high plateau in the west and coastal saline tract in the south touching Bay of Bengal.

The thick forest of big trees in the hills and foothills in north and deep green of the '*Dooars*' and *Tarai* has a positive direct and indirect influence on the agriculture of Bengal. Denuded and degraded forest in the western plateau deserved the attention it started gaining since late seventies of the last century. The unique protection of mangrove forest in the coastal south is heavily taxed since independence to accommodate homeless people-East Bengal refugees and others.

Evidently besides two polar regions *Himalaya* had a large ice cap full of glaciers that attracted some early humans to settle. The moderate climate in the lower plains is a gift of this hilly range and its snowline. The vast sea belt of Arab sea, Indian ocean and the Bay of Bengal covering west to east of the sub-continent also greatly contributes toward the comfortable living of organisms and favoured agriculture in so many ways. They all regulated the arrival and departure of summer, monsoon and south-east monsoon as also the north-west rains.

This monsoon empire (*mausumi samrajja*) is said to be 20 lakh year old. But this 'empire' also functions under the influence of the alternate 'ice-age' and 'melting age' cycle that regulates the entire earth-surface. Ice-age freezes water into ice withdrawing seas and oceans with decreased rains while 'melting age' increases rains, floods, water bodies (seas and oceans) decreasing landed areas. This is the way through which existed the cycle of 'dry' and 'wet' periods on the earth some 2000 years back. Newer addition to this is the removal of green cover of the earth that has reduced absorption of C_2 from air increasing the atmospheric temperature. This having profound effect on plants and animals, influences agriculture as a whole.

As the Flemingoes get their bright pink colour from the shrimps they eat, the land and the life on it get the soothing, soft character from its climate.

2

Origin and Evolution of Life

2.0 Origin of living cells and its evolution to organisms is a universal event that is very dynamic. The characteristics of the earth for a long period has been moving and species migration has been common all over the earth's surface crossing the barriers of atmosphere and geography. Naturally evolution of life or its evolution to different species could not have any area demarcation so that one could mention any part of it separately to have taken place in India or Bengal excepting the latest stage of origin of species.

It is now clear that the lightning in the atmosphere created enough heat for hydrogen and nitrogen to combine and produce NH_3 which dissolved in a subsequent rain and reached sea-water. Reactions between different inorganic chemicals in water led to formation of organic compounds from which cells with duplicating abilities were created in stages over a long period of time. During Archaean eon at least 40,000 – 25,000 lakh years back possibly life was created in sea for the first time in the form of primitive cyano-bacteria or Blue Green algae. This stage of developments continued for a very long period to enter Cambrian period. Oldest known fossils (35,000 lakh years old) originated in hostile environment of the earth as recorded from Shak Bay (Australia), Bahamas and Indian Ocean. Stromatolites maintain homeostasis of the earth rendering the biosphere heritable for all other life. They maintain and recycle the atomic ingredients (O_2, C, N) of proteins that are essence of life. Following cyanobacteria the next life that appeared on earth is again photosynthetic and 25000 lakh years back (Proterozoic era). Fossil of Vendian biota or Ediacara fauna (appeared like Cnidarians, worms etc.) detected in white sea (Russia) 6500 lakh years back are the first animals on earth. Sea animals appeared 5,700 lakh years back (Cambrian period) and ancient land plants and insects appeared 5480-4080 lakh years back (Silurian period). Fern and mosses appeared in lower Gondowana rocks under Indian sub-continent. Flowering plants (Angiosperm) appeared 4800-3600 lakh years back (Devonian period). These were the ancestors of food crops of present time. Some such crop plants actually appeared 1440 lakh years back (Cretaceous period) and this is the time when tall trees appeared in the upper Gondowana rocks. Primitive grasses (parents of food crops) appeared 550-380 lakh years back. Possibly at the beginning of Pleistocene the food crops were similar as we find now.

Thereafter the cycle of 'ice age' that started increasing snowfall and seas turning smaller and 'melting age'- that melts down polar ice-shelf and takes upward snowline on the mountain peaks. All these led to natural growth of plants in the high and moderate rainfall areas and in low or scanty rainfall areas minimum growth of vegetation. Thus dense forest and vegetation areas in some part of the earth and dry tracts with low vegetation developed in its own way. This way 2130 lakh years back (Jurassic period) appeared birds and ancient mammals on earth. As an example at the end of Tertiary period and Pleistocene era there were possibly 17 species of elephants of which two that survived are Indian and African elephants. Wild horses of that time are extinct now as is the fate of Ostrich in India. The earth has passed through 'five species extinction cycle' before arrival of humans on earth and present period is considered to be in sixth cycle.

2.1 Arrival of humans and evolution

Anatomical and genetic data and paleontological, morphological and development-biological studies revealed a possible line of arrival of *Homosapiens sapiens*. Great apes

(Hominidae) speciated from the ancestors of gibbons or lesser apes 150 lakh years ago. Thereafter Homininae ancestors speciated from the ancestors of orangutan (130 lakh years back) and Hominini from ancestors of Gorilla (100 lakh years back), and Hominina from ancestors of Chimpanzees (70 lakh years back). *Ardipithecus* is a very early Hominin genus. Left foot prints on volcano ash in Kenya (39-29 lakh years ago) was of *Australopithecus afarensis*. Genus *Homo* was ancestral to this species. *Humans* developed to their present form during *Pleistocene* and the hominid species found was *Homo erectus* that migrated through old world, variations of humans taking place all along. In middle and late Paleolithic period new types of humans (*Modern*) appeared to develop elaborate tools. They migrated and spread all over the ice free world during late Pleistocene. *H. erectus* inhabited Asia and *H. neanderthalensis* Europe. All modern humans are *Homo sapiens* (from 4 lakh years ago).

Two models of anthropogenesis are proposed of which "Out of Africa hypothesis" is dominant. "Multiregional hypothesis" has not been widely accepted. *H. sapiens sapiens* (modern man) appeared in south of Africa (1.5 lakh years back). They migrated to different places and to Indian continent 75,000 years back and slowly ousted *H. erectus*.

Archaeological Survey of India reported (News, Vol. 9; p. 7; March 1978) the fossil of the lower jaw of human skull obtained from *Sijua* near *Kansai-Tarafeni* confluence, Binpur PS, West Medinipur and claimed this to be of *Holocene* period (10,000 BC) and earliest human fossil of India. *Saontal, Shabar* and *Kheria* living in West Medinipur are heirs of *Austro-Asiatic* races and are living in this part of the country for no less than 10,000 years and this land surface of '*Bangla*' (Bengal) exists for at least 1.4 lakh years.

One important event in human development was achieving the skill of standing on two legs by Peking man (*H. erectus*) that helped humans to make their two hands free to engage in so many other works including tool making and agriculture. The transformation of 'locking knees' and separate existence of "foramen magnum" in human body made this possible.

2.2 In search of food

Coming out of the forest and getting used to plain land without trees took *Pithecanthropus erectus* (appeared like monkeys) and their predecessors lakhs of years. They used to walk on two legs along river beach in search of stones etc. suitable for making weapons. Then appeared *Hydelbarg Man* and later *Neanderthal Man* who appeared like humans sacrificing the exposed *molar* in their dentation. This evolution over 10 lakh years brought modern humans in the scene. While their freed hands and fingers through prolonged use became more skillful.

Living on the trees while collecting fruits and nuts as food their hands gained increased efficiency. Coming down they learnt use of sticks etc. to unearth insects, rhizomes, tubers etc. and crack hard nuts with stones to eat.

When they brought themselves breaking the 'chain of jungle-living' they had to face problems of security and food.

After *Pithecanthropus, Sinanthropus* started using stone-weapon to cut open flesh of hunted or otherwise dead animals. Women nearby used to make pieces of the flesh before eating. For arranging food they had to be engaged for 24 hours minus the sleeping hours since the quantity they collected every time was very small. But most important point was the kind of tools or weapons they required to complete their work with the object of 'food collection' that could be conveniently done with them or similar weapons. Sticks and such others used in tilling land gradually took the shape of a 'spade' for their intense reach or efforts to get the right tool. At this stage their list of food contained – fruits, roots and modified stems, nuts, snails, rats, panicle of plants, insects etc. It was difficult to kill large animals with only sticks and stones. So they remained contended with small animals or even large animals – dead due to some reasons like predator attack or climatic hazard.

2.3 In search of food

Coming out of the forest and getting used to plain land without trees took *Pithecanthropus erectus* (appeared like monkeys) and their predecessors lakhs of years. They used to walk on two legs along river beach in search of stones etc. suitable for weapon-making. Then appeared 'Hydelbarg Man' and later 'Neanderthal Man' who after sacrificing the exposed 'molar' in their dentation appeared like humans. This phase of evolution over 10 lakh years brought modern humans in the scene. Their freed hands and fingers through prolonged use became more skilful.

When on trees their hands and fingers gained strength and skill while collecting fruits, nuts etc. Coming down on land they learned use of sticks etc. to unearth insects, tubers, rhizomes etc. They used stones to crack nuts and eat. For all these they spent the entire day for gathering enough quantity of food from these sources. Thus they brought themselves breaking the chain of 'jungle-living' to overcome problems of food and security.

After *Pithecanthropus*, *Sinanthropus* started using stone-weapons to cut open the flesh of hunted or otherwise dead animals. Women nearby made the flesh into pieces before eating. In spite of all these the quantity of food collected every time was very small. The kind of tools and weapons required to meet their food-need in a shorter time was the one they were in search. The stick etc. used to till land turned into a spade-like weapon. The intense search for right type of tool progressed. Their list of food contained fruits, nuts, roots, snails, rats, insects as also panicles of plants. It was difficult for them to kill large animals with only stick and stones. They remained contended with small animals and large animals also when that is dead due to some predator attack or climatic hazard.

2.4 Weapon making and their use : Paleolithic era

That humans settled in Bengal in ancient times is proved by the tools and weapons made of Paleolithic stones that have been excavated from Bankura, Birbhum, Barddhaman and Medinipur (Sur, 1986). Baghore-1 in *Shone Valley* offered evidences of presence of modern man (Irfan Habib, 2004) there 25-10.5 thousand years back and knife blades with back and handicrafts made of fossilised trees obtained from East Bengal (now Bangladesh) and Tripura (11-4.5 thousand years old) are also made by modern man. In India only fossil of human, skeleton (10 thousand BC old) that has been unearthed is in Sijua, Ramarh,

Medinipur (eastern bank of Kangsabati) by State Archaeology Department, West Bengal in 1978. Atul Sur, 1986 claims that the period of living of 'modern man' in this area is an event earlier to *Harappa-Mahenjodaro*. Moreover fossil of human skeleton has also been obtained in *Sushunia hills*, Bankura. Paleolithic weapons and tools have been obtained by excavation in many places in Bengal like *Orgonda, Shilda, Astajuri, Shahari, Bhagbandh, Kukradhupi, Chilkigarh*, of Medinipur, *Kolla, Lalbazar, Manhar, Bon, Osuria, Shaharjora, Kankradara, Bauridanga, Shusunia* and *Joypanda* of Bankura, *Gopalpur, Satkhania, Bilgova, Sagardanga, Aara* and *Khurupi* of Bardhaman and *Jhalda* and *Helamu Guha* of Puruliya. Some are obtained in present 'Bangladesh'. Rakhaldas Bandyopadhyay, 1914 recollects the statement of Koginbrown. 'Paleolithic activities in India is contemporary of similar activities in Europe. Most of the weapons obtained from North Bengal and in south-east and south-west border are quite modern. V. Ball, 1867 obtained such weapons from *Kunkun* of Hooghly district. Such weapons have been unearthed in coalmines of *Jharia* and *Bokaro*. These places yield neolithic weapons also. Later ASI detected weapons and tools in 1954-1957 at *Birvanpur*, Barddhaman handles of those are made of wood, bones and horns of animals. Earlier bull, buffalo, sheep, goat, turtle and birds were hunted using bows and arrows. During this period while preparing tools by breaking stones sparks out of it created fire on nearby heap of dry leaves and humans learnt to create fire and burning with it. At the end of this period they started burning animal flesh before consuming. However domestication of animals like cattle, sheep, goat etc. was not yet started. Clay pot making also did not start. Grinding grains with stone blocks, later developed into 'grinder' ('*Jnata*', '*Haman-Dista*' like stone bodies obtained) and using animal skin or hide as garments has started. Cultivation of crops was yet to start and grains were simply collected. Life was very hard as is evident from examination of dead bodies from below the earth. People usually lived a very short life of 19-28 years only. The progresses mentioned took place in Indian subcontinent between 8000 BC (Sarai Nahar, UP) to 2000 BC (Langhonaj, Gujarat) and in Bengal sometimes at the end of Paleolithic era.

2.5 Food gains attention

It appears that due to their coming out of the bonds of jungle-life, learning to generate fire, ability to develop stone-weapons with their hands and living in groups, they survived even the great species destruction phase during ice-age and progressed further to become more skillful and fit.

Hunter-gatherer-forager humans depended on wild plants, small animals and caracasses of otherwise dead animals as food. They were not capable of actual hunting till they had bows and arrows much later. *Homo erectus* employed hunting and gathering as subsistence strategy 1.8 million years ago and *H. sapiens* 0.2 million years ago and continued with almost similar practice. It remained the way of their arranging food even upto the end of Mesolithic period some 10,000 years ago. Actually Neolithic revolution (10,000 years ago) brought an end to this very laborious practice of food-gathering with beginning of '*agriculture*', one of the all time greatest achievement of the humans on the earth. This appeared in several different areas on the earth namely middle east, asia, mesoamerica and andes. Side by side along the jungle clad riverbanks and in wet foot-hills of monsoon regions, *forest gardens* were developed by protecting fruit trees and vines and eliminating others as a food production system.

'Fire' was an accidental invention by humans while sharpening one 'stone-tool' by striking with one another. Possibly a spark flew to some heap of dried leaves to produce fire. Early humans started burning animal body parts and found it better than raw flash to taste.

3

Neolithic Revolution and the Beginning of Agriculture

3.1 The beginning

To come out of a 25,000 years monotony of hunting and food-gathering with only small and crude tools, a major change within a short period occurred in the course of development of humans. Polished and sharper weapons were developed. Many different tools were prepared. Archaeological excavation at Mehergarh, Baluchistan (west bank of river '*Sindhu*') and also in Medinipur, Bankura and Barddhaman, from the same sites and places of discovery of Paleolithic and Mesolithic tools were obtained. While different human populations in different places were introducing novelty to existing tools and techniques, the immediate and local needs were determinants of the type of tool made. At this stage sticks with one bent-end like a 'primitive spade' was in use. The soil opening end of the stick was made very sharp to make the soil pulverized and soft. Some other tools like fish-hook ('*Bondsi*'), bone-needle etc. were developed. Gordon Child, 1930 felt that this phase of development of humans should be considered as '*Neolithic Revolution*'. The stone-hack was made more effective and useful for felling trees in forest and clearing more land. Humans developed 'stone-sickle' with bitumen handle and used in jungle clearing.

During 1954-57 Indian Archaeology Department obtained Mesolithic tools from *Birbhanpur*, Barddhaman establishing a link between Paleolithic and Neolithic culture in Bengal. Mesolithic era started in India about 10,000 years back at the end of *Holocene period*. On the Indian continent first group of farmers (agriculturists) was formed possibly during 7000-4000 BC may be on its western border. India being a vast land surface, had humans in its different areas trying to solve their problems in their own way independent of each other. So the tools and methods used had typical regional characteristics. Evidently needles, buttons etc. made showed similarities while 'fish-trap' ('*Ghuni*'), fishing-rod ('*chhip*'), fishing net ('*Jaal*') or sickle ('*Kaste*') made in different periods or grinder ('*Jnata*'), primitive spade or plow ('*Kodal*' or '*Langol*') obtained in Bengal were different and new varieties.

Records of human activities in lower Ganga basin area obtained suggest a parallel course of progress of human civilisation in this area with those in western border. In Bengal, places producing Paleolithic tools also produced Neolithic articles like *Core polishing stones, Ring stones, Boucher* or *Celt, Flake disc, Grain grinder* stone etc. as were discovered in 1886 from '*Chattogram hills*' and later from other places like valleys of *Damodar, Kangsabati, Subarnarekha* and *Ajay* rivers. Based on evidences from *Tamluk* and *Bamol* of Medinipur, *Amria, Kachinda* and *Joyponda* valley of Bankura. Rakhaldas Bandyopadhyay, 1914 felt that these areas were full of Neolithic activities and culture. Paresh Chandra Das Gupta collected nearly 1000 tools or articles and based upon his experience claimed that foot-hills of *Sushunia Hills*, Bankura was inhabited by ancient people one lakh years back. Fossils of elephants, horses, buffaloes and cattles obtained in *Sushunia Hills* area were of 40,000 BC as per their C_{14} analysis.

Neolithic revolution include two more places of humans acquiring skill and going ahead. (1) They experienced the advantage of storing flowing water by raising an obstacle placing stones, mud etc. to use for growing plants and (2) Arranging reed ('*khori*') or such other plant (creeper) stems up and down alternately to get a net form (basket) is the primordial idea of weaving in them. These ideas with older one of generating spark and fire are also components of Neolithic revolution. Side by side they made sharper weapons to get greater success in hunting. Possibly women collecting fruits from jungles and grains from river banks observed how grains cropped on moist soil of river bank germinated to produce a new plant to bear grains again. They repeated the process and success made the beginning of agriculture. This has been the story of rice cultivation in lower *Ganga valley* (silty bank) and of wheat cultivation on '*Sindhu*' *valley*.

Among the various plants and animals around the humans nature has selected and allowed to continue only useful and sustainable ones. Through growing some plants (agriculture) humans obtained another source of food nearby that slowly changed the lifestyle of the Neolithic people from '*nomadic*' to '*settled*' groups. This primitive agriculture was revolutionary. Thus 'agriculture' inspired these humans to change their lifestyle, tame and domesticate animals like cattle, goat, sheep etc. Over long period of time these domesticated animals like cattle, goat, sheep and others became smaller in size compared to their wild ancestors.

Examining cultural practices of such humans or '*Proto-australoids*' while burying dead bodies of seniors, fixed a chiseled, round top ('*Birknar*') in open field. The same practice is continuing in Medinipur, Bankura and Hooghly fixing a wooden-log (*Brishakastha*') in such occasions. Atul Sur, 1963 has drawn attention to continued use of stone articles like '*Jnata*' (Grinder), '*Haman Dista*' (small grinder) and '*Shil Nora*' (Paste maker) or cane or bamboo made articles like '*Dhama*' (Basket), '*Chubdi*' (small basket), '*Kunke*' (small measuring pail) and '*Jhnapi*' (covered basket) in different areas of Bengal. Wooden utensils like '*Barkosh*' (Plate), '*Ketko*' (Pail), '*Chaki-Belun*' (Flat Roti maker) are reminiscents of *Neolithic culture* of this land. Regarding agriculture in lower Ganga basin, NG Mukerji, 1901 based upon existence of series of wild rices in the coast and the unique transplanted rice culture claimed that rice is indigenous to east India. Another revolutionary act was possibly pasting of mud inside such basket to make it leak-proof for grains that continues as a practice in '*Adibasi*' areas of Bengal – another evidence of Neolithic culture. "Examining large number of teeths (skeletons) obtained in 1st and 2nd stages at *Mehergarh* (considered as early cultivators of Indian continent) showed greater similarity with South and Southeast Asians than West Asians". (Irfan Habib, 2002). This conclusion of Habib indicated the course of history of Indian agriculture. In *Neolithic* era only few crops were grown and animals like dog, sheep and goat were reared. Cattle and pig rearing started in S.W. Asia in 9000 BC. Along with seasonal or permanent settlements, the culture of using earthen pots started separately in regions with some unique characters. Discovery of large number of Paleolithic stone articles from a vast region (Birbhum to West Medinipur) of Bengal confirmed the Paleolithic background of the Neolithic period in Bengal. The actual places of such ancient development according to Gopal Chandra Sinha, 2009 were "*11-mile*" of Birbhum-Barddhaman border and *Jibdharpur-Kankuredanga Ajodhya Hills, Biharinath, Shushunia Hills, Kangsabati* zone of *Khatra Mukutmanipur, Nakabnidhi of Gopiballavpur, Tarafeni Bhairabbanki Valley* of Shilda-Belpahari. All these establish that *Homo erectus* the near-humans lived in these areas and engaged in hunting with paleolithic stone weapons. These nomads over a long time built temporary settlements in these hills, river banks and forest periphery. They lived together but no social system developed.

Heirs of these people in Mesolithic period made smaller and sharper weapons for use. They were food gatherers but reared animals and sown seeds casually here and there. In *Sindhu* valley Neolithic period was followed by Heliolithic or Chalcolithic period about 7500-5000 years back. Availability of metals like copper etc. was poor and use of stone articles continued along with. But metal user humans were in advantage in fighting and agriculture too during 4000-3200 BC. In Bengal also use of copper helped humans in hunting, fishing and cultivation in achieving success. Heliolithic articles obtained in Bengal 4000 years back are strong evidences of progress of heliolithic agriculture in Bengal. With its larger territory Bengal was rich source of copper in those days and it was exported also from Medinipur. A. Sur, 1986 said that the Neolithic village civilisation in Bengal gradually changed to heliolithic culture in different spheres of life including agriculture using it in making plow and other articles. The weapons of paleolithic period used 20 thousand years back in Medinipur, Bankura, Bardhaman and '*Sagardighi*' in Bengal are ancestors of the people later called 'bengalis' in this land. Hence these people were living in this area later known as Bengal for at least 10,000 yearss or more. In those days also they were ruled by regional rulers named "*Pundraraj Basudev*", "*Bangoraj Samudra Sen*" and "*Sukshma Raj*" (Atul Sur, 1986). These people used to communicate in '*pre-Aryan language*' that is "*Austric*" or "*Austro Asian*" language. Remnants of that language is now pesent in "*Saontal*", "*Kole*", "*Bhil*", "*Shabar*" and "*Pulinda*" dialects. "*Saontal*", "*Munda*" and "*Bhumij*" people lived in "*Rarhbhumi*" (Western Bengal) for long. In "*Paundra desh*" (north Bengal) lived "*Pundra*" and "*Karbot*"s. "*Kirat*", "*Kaibarta*", "*Paundra*" groups of pre-Aryan people lived in central and south-west of Bengal. "*Pods*" lived in lower part of east and south of Bengal and "*Mech*" lived in "*Tarai*" area of north Bengal. *Vedic people* (Aryans) coming from out of India used to call them non-Aryans (*Anarya*), in their literature as "*Dasyu*" (Dacoits) and in Sanskrit as "*Nishad*". But these are the earliest humans living in this land (rightly called "*Adibasi*" and main ancestors of "*Bengalis*". The civilisation, culture, language, art and craft and skill of these ancient people was extraordinary and unique in all respect. After a long gap with all these, Aryans came in India and could not proceed upto Bengal in the east possibly learning about the land full of river and rivulets, and strong foundation and culture of the people living in the land later known as Bengal.

There '*austric*' speaking people possibly started growing plants and first to settle. They are the people who for the first time fixed sharp-stone piece at the top of a stick to open soil. One has to note that the words "*langol*" (plow), "*Khnuti*" (peg) "*Chanch*", "*Bekhari*" or "*Boroj*" (loose roof structure) are austric in origin and these articles or structures are used in agriculture in Bengal. All these clearly indicated that ancient 'austric' speaking Bengalis used to cultivate rice, betel, banana, arecanut etc. that are characteristics of Bengal agriculture. After all these happenings some "*Davidian*" people came to this land from south India with their culture and characteristics. A cultural mixing took place subsequently and Bengal agriculture is also a recipient. In the seventh sitting of "*Bangiyo Sahitya Sammelan*" (Bengali Literary Conference) the president *Haraprasad Shastri* observed that before the Aryans could reach Punjab from Central Asia, Bengal was enough civilised, cultured and progressed a lot.

3.2 Agriculture from Neolithic to Heliolithic era (7500-5000 BC)

As was reported from Mehergarh, Baluchistan on west bank of *Sindhu* river use of polished and sharper tools in agriculture and rearing of animals in house is a progress (Gordon Child, 1930). Impression of oat grains – wild and cultivated on mud was also recorded. From burnt cotton seeds it appeared that cotton was also a crop there during 4000-5000 BC. Use of water in cultivation was another achievement. Similarly changes from Neolithic culture to Heliolithic culture was revolutionary. Atul Sur, 1986 claims that Neolithic villages of Bengal slowly learnt use of copper that was available in Bengal in ample quantities. Those days copper was even exported from Medinipur via water transport. The evidences of these activities were obtained in Bengal from '*Pandurajar Dhibi*' included 'painted earthen pots', tube like outlet fitted pail or vessel or half-burnt, jet-black earthen pot. The '2000 BC make' of the earthen pots are made by mixing rice-husk with mud. This '*Dhibi*' excavation exposed smaller weapons and copper-pails, white paintings on 'black' elephant and 'red' earthen pots and stone-engraved book, comb made of the tusk of elephant and terracotta idols. All these proved that the humans living in Bengal were first class, skilled community. At this stage use of potters' wheel in clay work also reached Bengal confirming nearly parallel development. Development of agriculture particularly paddy-rice cultivation progressed in greater Bengal including '*Chirand culture*' (present Bihar). Cultivation of so many crops like paddy, wheat, barley, mung, lentil etc. indicated progress of agriculture (Gopal Chandra Sinha, 2009). These people however lived in huts made of reeds. They were used to boat-like water transport evident through the structure of a boat unearthed from 45 depth in '*Pannagram*', Medinipur. Heliolithic era in Bengal had beginning 4000 years back when '*Dravid*', *Tibbat-Burmese*' and '*Austro-asian*' people reached this land and slowly settled down. Mixed population character of Bengal started gaining ground. Through practical experience people who used copper learnt that these weapons are sharper and gives sharp-cup. The metal was however soft and these people made efforts to harden it by melting together with tin to get a harder material called bronze. The copper-axe was excavated out in '*Jhatiboni*', Medinipur in 1883. It is true that Veda, composed 5700 years back mentioned tilling of land and some other issues of agriculture of north-western India but the evidences unearthed later from Barddhaman, Bankura, Birbhum and Medinipur like stone-weapons, stone grain-grinders proved of similar earliness of Bengal-agriculture. Nihar Ranjan Roy 1949 after elaborate discussion based on strong evidences said that ancient Bengal had three main ways of building up resources and wealth of which first and the most important one was agriculture. Other two namely industry and trade were largely dependant on agricultural produce. More specifically rice was the main wealth and main industry-produce were cotton and silk cloth.

3.3 Paddy agriculture of Bengal

From ancient times in pre-Aryan period rice is related deeply with culture, religion, language, literature, music and what not of the '*bengalis*' and the land Bengal. Be it a folk tale or a village ritual or any festival or any households daily life one can not imagine a spot or a moment without '*Dhanya*', '*Dhan*', '*Chaal*', '*Bhat*'. From very olden days Bengali life is woven with 'rice' in all directions.

Now '*Dhan*' or paddy as a species of plant has some unique characteristics, found in no other plant known. Tolerance to high water pressure (deep water), tillering ability, seed-shattering habit, self and cross pollination ability, high-silicon body, and germination ability or dormancy of seeds and their dependence on or independence from atmosphere, floating habit, rooting from upper nodes, striking roots in any situation etc. have made the plant species unique. It's centre of origin or the place where its cultivation started first are debated. Hiroko Morisima, 2000 and G.S. Khus *et al.*, 2001 claimed that two species namely *Oryza sativa* and *O. glaberima* are grown in most areas of Asia and in West Africa respectively as common cultivated species. Besides *Oryza* has five wild species namely *O. rufipogon*, *O. longistaminata*, *O. barthi, O. glumipatula*, and *O. meridionalis*. Among these *O. sativa* and its ancestor species *O. rufipogon* commonly occur in tropical and sub-tropical areas of Asia and many other places. Different strains of these species are named according to their spread and geographical location. Those occurring in Indian subcontinent are named *O. sativa indica*. While those in Japan, China and adjoining areas are *O. sativa japonica*. Great *Vavilov* opined that their first cultivation was at *India* and *Mayanmar*. Other records claim that they were first cultivated in *Korea* 15 thousand years back. Third view is that their first cultivation was in China 122 thousand years back. US-genome research data also suggest that it took place first on the *Yangate* river valley in China. Historian Ascopar Pola claims that rice cultivation spread to different areas from *Ganga* valley. T.K. Adhya of CRRI supported this theory of first cultivation in lower *Ganga basin*. Presence of rice in 1800 BC is mentioned and *Yajur veda* (1500-400 BC) also mentioned rice for the first time. Ancient *austric* people living in Ganga basin appear to be the first to cultivate *Rice*. Vavilov in his article "Origin, variation, immunity and breeding" published in "Chronica Batanica" suggested that although for the first time cultivated food crops and fruits, but rice was first grown in Ganga basin in the east of India and from there it reached China. Nene, 1998 also expressed doubt about the rice grain obtained in "*Non Nok Tha*", Thailand (5500 years back) may not be from the first cultivated crop.

Mukerji, 1901 has discussed in his "Handbook of Indian Agriculture" about different strains of *O. sativa*. He mentioned *O. granulata* that is a perennial species with stem as hard as wood growing in upland. *O. bengalensis* ('Uri Dhan') produce slender grains within a white husk. Usually awned grain varieties are often scented. Husks of '*Kalojira*' and '*Dadkhani*' varieties are coloured. Classification by Roxberg has also failed to include some Bengal varieties e.g. '*Bilan*' group which possibly arrived from '*tree rice*' ("Tarudhan") species. Generally, red grain varieties are from *O. rufipogon* and black grain varieties from *O. abuensis* (Mukerji, 1901), Basu, T. 1993 stated that *O. perenis* and *O. spontaneous* developed in wetlands of China. Again *O. officinalis* is a tall, perennial species having leaves with many veins, collar zone of stem hard (less than wood) and many branched panicle. *Uri rice*, *O. bengalensis* (shattering type) is a wild variety which appears to be ancestor of both *aus, aman* and *boro* varieties. Practically the lower Gangetic plains of Bengal has been the land giving rise to natural breeding and selection of many more species, varieties and strains of rice. Some more varieties are awned variety – "*Karpurkathi*" giving very fine grains. '*Jirakathi*' is another fine grain variety. '*Hatisal*' variety has very large grains producing 45-50 maund/acre. Many other local varieties are '*Otirang*', '*Sadaora*', '*Dhuki-Lata-Mal*', '*Uri*', '*Lakshmibilas*', '*Sindurtupi*', '*Bhut Kaurabi*', '*Rati Ramsal*', '*Kaloboyra*', '*Panikalma*', '*Sholapana*', '*Aman*', '*Nadanghata*', '*Sambara*', '*Kalashal*', '*Metekuji*', '*Nilkantha*' and some *aus* paddy of short duration namely '*Kele*', '*Nitali*', '*Ashwingota*' and '*Kartiksal*' that can be grown in *aman* season also. Sometime back Dr Watt identified more than 4000 varieties.

Some more varieties that are scented but not slender-grain are '*Paramannasal*', and '*Randhunipagol*', and for popped rice '*Harinakhuri*', '*Bankehur*', and '*Kanakchur*'. Fine-grain scented variety are '*Gobindabhog*', '*Khaskhani*', '*Benafuli*', '*Kamini*', '*Banshkathi*', '*Dadkhani*', '*Badshabhog*' etc. and '*Sitashal*' has excellent taste. '*Pakshiraj*' seeds have wings with medicinal properties (Mukerji, 1901). Grains of '*Dudheswar*' are bent, and '*Tulaipanji*' produce cooked rice as white as a heap of cotton. Bold grain varieties (called '*Bogra*') of Bengal are – '*Dular*' *(red husk)*, '*Dhariyal*', '*Patnai*' are liked by farm labours. '*Jugal*' variety produce two rice grains within one husk. There are many more. This vast array of diverse varieties can arrive only in a very cozy environment. With all these local and naturally bred varieties on one side and continuously growing wild rice ('*Dhani ghas*') on newly deposited mudflat in the coast on the other, newer varieties are being bred naturally and selection is taking place for thousands of years. The microfossil of paddy obtained in '*Chirand*', Bihar (a part of greater Bengal) are 3500 years old, carbon dating of which has proved it to be older than the microfossil obtained in China. Considering all these Basu, 1993 rightly claimed that in Bengal (including present Bihar and Orissa) paddy cultivation had its beginning in 4000-3000 BC or earlier. This claim was strongly supported by Kaundel, Burkhill and others. Some others opposed this claim. Huke and Huke, 1990 suggested that the centre of origin and the course of its spread is yet to be decided finally.

The evolution of paddy varieties may have followed a general course i.e. from 'awned' to 'awnless', pigmented to pigment-free husk, and perennial (wild rice) to annual varieties. That is why in the original coast of *Ganga* ('*Sundarban*'), wild rices are continuing to grow for thousands of years. D. Chatterjee, 1948 suggested that most of species of *Oryza* obtained in this part of the earth have mostly originated from this wild rice source. The varieties available upto mid twentieth century were studied by Hector and noted that they belong to five classes like (1) Rice grain is translucent or not, (2) Rice is glutinous or not, (3) Grain is 'awned' or 'awnless', (4) Grains in the panicle are in cluster or separated and (5) One or two rices per grain.

Lower Gangetic plains in coastal area pre-Aryan humans, possibly women (used to grain picking) marked the rice plants growing out of shattered grains and repeated the process by sowing seeds in coastal soft mud (silt) flat to make the great beginning of rice cultivation on earth.

3.4 Food preparation earthen pot and fire

Like Indus-valley civilisation people, pre-historic people were living in '*Panduraja*' civilisation, Barddhaman. Besides fruits, nuts etc. gathered, included new items as their food. Proto-australoid were trying to include news items to overcome the shortfall in food. Earlier they included panicles of some grasses (*Ghas Bij*) giving very small grains which hey found sweet by biting. By then they started grinding such grains between two stones to get sweet powder as a new addition to their small list of food-items.

This source of food was strengthened by their untiring and revolutionary way of growing such grains into plants to produce grains again. In wet and marshy situation existing in eastern India, particularly in coastal Bengal it was from grasses, to wild rice and to rice that were evolved naturally in unlimited number of kinds. Even the other day in mid twentieth century, people in extreme food scarcity went for grass seeds (*'Ghas Biz'*), as suggested by their accumulated ancestral knowledge. Side by side and food reservoir was located in rivers and different inland waterbodies producing fishes. We are not sure whether humans of this region later identified as Proto-australoid speaking in *Austric* language were used to taking uncooked fishes as we found the other day south-east-Asians took uncooked or later once boiled fish as food. But there is a positive likelihood since prehistoric ancients, we have shown started taking uncooked animals including insects, rodents etc. as food.

The beginning of boiling rice in water was possible since earthen pots were developed by that time and as per Niharanjan Ray, 1993 rice was the main if not only produce and *'Bhat'* (boiled rice) was the food of prehistoric Bengalis. Bengali literature of middle-ages, so far the only published evidence have very distinctly described the details of multistep (*'Jotil'*) cooking done by Bengali women to achieve a desired 'taste' and 'savour' of cooked food that is a very important characteristic of Bengali food. Since beginning, cooking must have began much earlier to reach this perfection. Niharranjan strongly felt that ancient Bengali's engaged all of their imagination and intelligence in cooking also. There were different methods of cooking rice among 'rich' and 'poor' Bengalis but Bengalis failed to imagine a life without *'Bhat'* (boiled rice) like - ***"Hanri o Bhat Nahi', Niti Abeshi"***. All these are assumed from the articles used for food preparation, obtained in these days. Since existence of no direct proof is possible the earliest recorded literature is used analytically to find out what happened and when.

It is not very evident as to when *'Bengalis'* first started consuming fish and other aquatic animals like *'shamuk'* (snail), *'googli' 'Chingri'* (prawn) and others. After achieving the skill of *'weaving'* basket or net, like things to catch fishes possibly they could gather such animals and tasted fresh or cooked. In all likelihood this happened in Neolithic age. Pottery production preceeded agriculture and we find they were in use (*'Hanri'*, *'Koda'*) in Bengal. The publication in 'Nature's 4th April, 2013 reports detection of lipids deposited due to fish cooking compels us to think of fish cooking in Bengal in those days.

3.5 Bengal agriculture in pre-historic era

Jute like wheat, rice is also one pre-historic crop (Tapas Basu, 1995). Prehistoric humans of lower Ganga delta accidentally came across panicle on longer grass like plants among grasses. They possibly tested one hard grain from such panicle within incisor teeth and tongue and charmed with sweet taste of it. First identification of the plant as consumable happened this way followed by the idea of growing it. Scientists think that natural crossing of wild rice-grasses or specifically of *Oryza perenis* and *O. spontania* has resulted in arrival of new species. *Oryza sativa*. In Indian sub-continent *Ganga coast* has always been wet silt welcoming continuous growth of self-sown wild rices till today. Botanists Kaundel, Vavilov or I.H. Burkhill emphasised this environment although Huchinson felt that rice was cultivated in Saurastra. Ethnobotanists like Goreman, 1969, Sole Hume, 1967, G. Kurien, 1945, Vandeer, 1951 and many others strongly felt that paddy-rice is a food crop of the land of Ganga valley (Tapas Basu).

In rural Bengal from pre-historic period women folk used to celebrate three *'Lakshmipuja's* (Goddess of Wealth) in a years namely in *'Falgun'* (February-March) before seed sowing, in *'Aswin'* (September-October) for ripening of grains and in *'Agrahayan'* (November-December) after rice harvest. In the evening they used to chant *'Panchali'* (verses) talking about paddy-rice. In fact it is a settled fact that the ancient *'Australs'* speaking in *'austric'* language are the first to do agriculture as also live a community life with civilised practices. These are the people who fixed sharp wood-piece in 'plow', and grew rice, betel, banana and arecanut. They have left some of their words and dialects in *'bengali'* language, some such words being *Khnuti*, *'Chhnach'* (template), *bekhari* etc. mentioned earlier. The growth of agriculture based villages in Bengal are their contribution, realising the great prospect of growing food in this area many more pre-historic human races besides *Austrics* came to this land including '*Saontal*', '*Munda*' (Rarh area), '*Ho* and *Dravid*' (West part of Bengal), *Bagi* (Birbhum), *Bauri, Pode, Hari, Dome* (northern part of Bengal), *Alpine* and *Kirat* (Mongoloid), *Koche* and *Mech* (tarai) etc. whose life style, culture and 'gene' resulted in different admixing on this land that justifies the say – "Bengali is a mixed culture".

3.6 Pre-Aryan Bengalis

Pre-Aryan settlements in Bengal were very much like 'tribal communities'. '*Pundra*', '*Gour*', '*Rarh*', '*Sukshma*' and '*Bongo*' were some such communities and settlements (Bhaskar Chattopadhyay, 2003). These societies did not have any class or any caste divisions. These very ancient groups of people were simply groups of 'austric' people called in different names according to their place or region of settlement. These societies and their cultures were altogether different from those of *Aryans*. Atul Sur, 1986 has clearly stated that the pre-historic 'Bengalis' were 'austric'–speaking, '*pre-Dravid*', *Proto-Australoid* people in anthropological term who were called "*Nishadh*" in ancient *Aryan* literature and they include "*Saontal*" etc. groups or 'tribes' and 'Hindus' called them "*Antaja*". But these are the ancient Bengalis or ancestors of Bengalis. From this stage 'Bengalis' slowly over long period turned into a 'mixed community' as has been already discussed.

Among '*Aryans*' two groups existed – '*Nordik*' and '*Alpian*'. Alpians with short forehead were called '*Asur*' and they actually came to Bengal later. The other group '*Nordik*'s could reach upto '*Varanasi*' after *Punjab* and '*Kashmir*'. The '*Aryans*' that came to '*Bengal*' used to initially hate pre-Aryan Bengalis but later mixed with them. Bhaskar Chattopadhyay, 2003 also mentions that in "*Arya Manjusri*" book of eigth Century that the tribal settlements like '*Gour*, '*Magodh*', '*Mithila*', '*Anga*', '*Bango*', '*Sukshma*', '*Kalinga*', '*Kamrup*' – etc. together earned the name '*Gourchakra*' because over long period of mixing they were very close both anthropological, language and culture points of view.

Two tribal settlements. '*Bango*' and '*Pundra*' were close to the vedic Aryan group that reached Bengal. These names of settlements have been mentioned in the Sanskrit classic '*Mahabharata*'.

These groups or communities were food gatherers and hunters in Paleolithic era and turned into tribal societies in neolithic era. From this period they started cultivation of some crops in very primitive way and did some animal rearing.

3.7 Villages and 'haats' in Bengali

Any family or '*class*' among the primitive '*Bengalis*' usually selected the place in a jungle after clearing it. The criteria of selection were – some cultivable land, some non-cultivable, some portion of forest and a source of water (Basu, 1995). This way number of families developed their settlements close to each other and a village community ('*Gram samaj*') grows up. In case of a '*Saontal*' community there is one leader ('*Majhi*') to settle any clash of opinions or quarrels. '*Munda*'s also settled similarly. A person skilled in use of metal, particularly iron is called '*Kamar*' (blacksmith). '*Majhis*' slowly gathered influence and power. But '*Kamar*'s role in making sharper weapons ultimately increased production and 'surplus' produce concept peeped in the minds of these people. The places are where copper and bronze articles were excavated, iron articles were obtained in upper layers while excavating. But in some places like '*Mangolkote*', '*Pandurajar Dhibi*', *Bharatpur* and *Baleswardanga* of Barddhaman, *Mahishadal, Haraipur, Bahiri* and *Kotasur* of Birbhum, *Dihar, Tulsipur* at Kumari-Kangsabati river confluence of Bankura produced no copper but *iron*. This resulted in production increase that in their turn brought epoc-making change in those societies and the '*Majhi*' or '*Kaumapati*' became '*Rajan*' and such title was adopted.

In the pre-Aryan period the culture of women in the society centered round '*Alpana*' (floor and wall painting) which they did by grinding ('*Shil-Nora*') rice, soaked overnight, dissolving it in water ('*Pituli*') and draw different things on floor or wall with fingers using the white suspension. Drawings included 'foot of

Goddess 'Lakshmi', creeping stem, leaves and inflorescence (mainly paddy), *'Konch'* (*'Sankha'*), *'Kolka'* (a design) etc. All these were by the women members of *'Bagdi'*, *'Bauri'*, *'Kaibarta'*, *'Pode'* and such other families. These are original, primitive ancestors of *Bengalis* who could not accept gracefully the concerned faction of *Aryans* who reached Bengal much later and slowly became a part of mixed *'Bengali'* culture and agriculture. Some of these primitive *Bengalis* later chose hills and forest and migrated for peaceful living.

4

Heliolithic to Iron Era

4.0 Context

In West India during *Sindhu-Harappa civilisation* (2000-1500 BC) rice was cultivated during *kharif* season only. Earlier during 3000-2500 BC there was plow and bullock-cart in the northern part of the valley (Habib, 2005). People there engaged bullocks initially in pulling cart and later for plowing. In the *'Hacra'* commodity business in Punjab the well known farmer and animal rearing community used to settle and live in small groups. Their main crops were Barley and wheat. They initially tilled land with only harrow and later for tilling larger land area they started using plow.

In the second phase i.e. *Vedic era* (1500-700 BC), Vedic culture was spread from *Hindukush mountain range* in Afghanistan to the *'Ganga-Yamuna Doab'* in west of Uttar Pradesh. The first *Veda*-Rk. Veda (1500-1000 BC) has described agriculture of the area in pages. Tilled land was called *'Kshetra'* and plow was called *'Hala'* and the tip of the plow – *'Fola'*. Use of water from dug well was started but use of any pulley to lift water is not mentioned. Crops were *'Godhum'* or *'Gom'* (wheat), *'Brihi* (*'Dhan'*) (Paddy) etc. Livelihood depended on animal rearing. As a result pasture (*Gostha*) were developed. *Aryans* were fond of cow-milk. Besides there were professionals like *'Sutradhar'* (*'Chhutar', or carpenter*), 'Karmakar' *('Kamar') or blacksmith and 'Chikitsak'* (*'Vishaj'*) or physician in the society.

In the subsequent *Vedic*-period upto 700 BC their settlement spread toward south-east to '*Vas*' (North-east UP) and '*Ushinor*' (North Bihar). While they were proceeding through *Ganga Valley* fighting the local non-Aryans ('*Anarya*') with horse-drawn chariots and bows was common. Actually after 800 BC they started using iron in arms; alongwith they started using iron in agriculture. After '*Dushadbati*' river dried up Aryan farmers crossed river '*Yamuna*' to reach other side i.e. *Ganga valley* blessed with good rainfall. This was a time when people used to clear jungle with fire.

In eastern India bullock's were domesticated before 1500 BC, but for pulling plow and cart they were used later. In Bengal, sticks and '*nirani*' (hand hoe) were used for tilling land. Plow was made and used later. Irfan Habib, 2005 said that in '*Bharatpur*', '*Mahishadal*' and others of present Medinipur articles made in copper-stone age (1770-795 BC) and used in agriculture were excavated to be sufficient evidences. Carbon-dating of the articles have also confirmed this. Evidently that potters' wheel has also reached these places was revealed through red and black earthen pots obtained from these places. Those people also domesticated and reared cattle that they used for different purposes.

Starting from *Rk. Veda* period to '*Atharveda*' period society accepted four casts or groups among the people namely – '*Bramhan*', '*Rajanya*', '*Baishya*' and '*Shudra*'. After agriculture developed and got established in Aryan society, life and elsewhere, animal rearing and hunting lost importance. As described in '*Mahabharata*' in Heliolithic era in Bengal '*Pundra King*' was '*Basudev*', *Bongo King*' was '*Samudrasen*' and '*Sukshmaraj*' and *Aryans* met these '*Bango* and '*Pundra*' people in *Vedic* era (A. Sur, 1968). '*Bangrid*' race referred is possibly related to '*Gangaridae*' kingdom in south Bengal.

4.1 '*Pandurajar Dhibi*' (1200-1000 BC)

'*Pandurajar Dhibi*' or the raised piece of land known by this name is situated in '*Ausgram*', Barddhaman that is close to *Bolepur-Santiniketan* on the bank of river *Ajoy*. The archaeological articles obtained here is a symbol of city civilisation of *Harappa Mahenjodaro era*. According to Atul Sur, 1986 as he has stated that PD on excavation presented civilisations of four different ages through different archaeological evidences. Ancient Bengalis for the first time settled here in 2000 BC who built houses with '*Kankrapeta*' or '*Morum*' pieces. They used to make red, black and gray earthen pots in potters' wheel and also cultivated paddy-rice. After this first phase of settlement it was flooded and deserted. In the *second phase* people settled were in Heliolithic era when they developed well-planned houses, city, roads and even built forts. They used copper for different purposes. Their economy was agriculture and trade based. They produced paddy and other crops, reared animals and did pottery work. They used red and black coloured earthen wares, many good-looking pitchers and other utensils. They made copper knives, bone-weapons, copper ornaments and used spindle made of burnt clay. They weaved white cloth with cotton from silk-cotton trees. Carbon dating established the time to be 1020 + 120 BC. This second phase was most prosperous and glorious (Atul Sur, 1986). They had trade relations with Crete island and Mediterranean countries. The commodities for trade included spices, cotton, cloth etc. in addition to gold, silver, copper, ivory etc. Atul Sur feels that '*Gur*' (non-purified sugar) and sugar were also exported. A kind of clay-label was tied to basket ('*Jhudi*') to identify the content of the basket and some accountings. In the *third phase* there were heliolithic axe, carbonised iron weapons and black polished earthenwares. Use of red and black earthen wares continued. They had furnace for melting and casting iron. A destructive fire destroyed all these and the place was deserted. In the *fourth phase* i.e. during '*Maurya rule*', people again started habitating this place. They tried to continue with the earlier achievements particularly in the areas of agriculture and trade with agricultural commodities.

4.2 Gangaridae Civilisation (400-300 BC)

'*Gangaridae*' or '*Gangarastra*' civilisation according to Suniti Kumar Chattopadhyay is the land that is enriched with '*Ganga*' river ('*Ganga wriddha*'). Plini, 23-79 AD in his volume – 'Natural

History' explained that the place where river '*Ganga*' finishes its long journey merging in Bay of Bengal a civilised, prosperous group of people called '*Gangaridae*' lived with a sovereign powerful civilisation as existed in 400 BC. Ptolemy, 150 AD and Periplus (first cent) further described this state, its city, sea-port etc. that were glorious. Greek and Latin authors like Curtias (41-45 AD) in his 'History of Alexander', or Plutark (46-120 AD) in his "Life of Alexander" claimed that in fourth century AD, there was a sovereign and powerful state called '*Gangaridae*' in the east of India. In fact in 326 BC after defeating small kingdoms in Punjab, Alexander was planning to proceed to rest of India, the news of *Prasioi* ('*Magadh*') and '*Gangaridae* (east India) the two powerful kingdoms joining hands to oppose reached him. As a result Alexander did not cross river '*Bipasha*' and returned back. Later the glory, strength and trade of '*Gangaridae*' has been described by Romans and people of Egypt.

This kingdom was situated at the coastal end of mighty river '*Ganga*' where its sea-port '*Gange*' was functioning. Evidences obtained in '*Pandurajar Dhibi*' suggest that before first century BC Mediterranean traders used to enter heart of '*Gour-Banga*' for trade purpose through '*Gange port*'. In the hills of Crete island '*Shiblinga*' (idol of Lord '*Shiva*') used by Bengali ladies was obtained and in '*Pandurajar Dhibi*' as evidences of visit of *Mediterranean* traders a round-shaped seal in Crete script were uncovered. A long trade relationship of Bengal with Mediterranean countries is evident (Atul Sur, 1986). Excavations at *Chandraketugarh*, *Aatghora*, *Hariharpur, Mallikpur, Harinarayanpur, Boral, DeGanga, Deulpota, Pakurtala*, *Mandirtala, Pukurberia* in 24-Parganas and *Tilda, Panna, Kanthi* and *Tamluk* in Medinipur included archaeological articles, burnt-clay dolls and plates. All these evidences proved the existence of a strong trade relations of '*Gangaridae*' with Greek and Roman world both before and after Christ.

4.3 Women and '*Rannaghar*' (separate cooking space)

Mostly thatched '*haats*' – '*dochala*' or '*charchala*' with space ('*Varanda*') under extended roof on one / two / all sides to provide additional space for family members to use in different purposes.

The two important purposes for which such 'space' was used are – for cooking (called '*Rannaghar*' when the space is separated from others with thatched walls often with a door) and a fuel store. The '*Rannaghar*' was generally located in the '*Varanda*' that is on the north-south side of the living room(s) so that 'smoke' goes out. The 'hut' was built with bamboo etc. by some people (later called '*Ghorami*'). Usually an oven ('*Unun*') was dug out on the earthen floor of the space provided. It contained generally three raised portions on its periphery to hold the cooking-ware on it and one big hold in front to push fuel (dry wood pieces, leaves etc.) in the oven.

Earthen pots made by some villagers (later called '*Kumor*') were used as container on which the raw food material is placed and heated from below. Later a special shaped, deep, medium-mouth earthen container ('*Hanri*', '*Tijel*') was used for cooking '*Bhat*' (boiled rice grains) while '*Kadai*' (a flat open container) was used to prepare other food items like pulse soup ('*Daal*'), curries or fries.

Niharranjan says that 'Bengalis' generally ate cooked rice ('*Bhaat*') with boiled or roasted (later fried) vegetables particularly creepers ('*lota*') and pot herb ('*shak*') e.g. '*Nalita*' (jute). They prepared other vegetable curries also. In '*Naishadh Charit*' the food in the 'feast' ('*Bhoj*') for '*Damayanti's* marriage (well off family) has been described. Cooked rice ('*Anna*') was soft, tasty, milky white, fine (grains) releasing excellent flavour. '*Ghee*' (boiled butter) put (sprinkled) on steaming rice ('*bhat*') was generally served on banana leaf as food. The last course is sweet dish made with rice, milk and country sugar ('*Gur*') called '*Payas*' (later called '*Paramanna*'). '*Prakrita Paingal*' book published in the end of 14th century says – "*Oggara Bhatta Gaik Ghitta*" meaning wet ('*Safen*') cooked hot rice sprinkled with cow's boiled butter ('*Goghrita*). Again in the same book in another place it says – "*aggara Bhatta Rambha Patta Gaik Ghitta Dugdha Sajukta* / "*Moili Mochha Nalita Gochha Dijjoi Kanda Khai* (i) *Punabasta*" – suggesting "hot rice with '*Ghee*' or milk on a banana leaf alongwith '*Maurala*' fish' as food is taken by Bengalis.

The earliest book was '*Prayaschitta–Prakaran* " by Bhatta Bhavadev (11th cent) in regard to recorded evidence of Bengali food in early days.

Sugarcane juice, coconut water, milk of cows and goat after boiling, sap or juice from date palm (*Khenjur*) and palmyra palm ('*taal*') and honey were popular drinks of Bengalis. Such materials fermented into different kinds of '*wine*' were also common although their preparation procedures were different. '*Charshageeti*' has also talked about '*Shoundikalaya*' or '*Sunrikhana*'. Rice cooked and packed and sealed in earthen pot ('*hari*') and cover ('*sora*') and stored in dark, sealed chamber produced '*haria*' a very common drink. Houses of such alcoholic drink sellers were slapped with a symbol that invited clients in the evening to visit sellers' ('*sunri*') premises ('*Sunrikhana*') where usually wife of seller served the drink. '*Charshageeti*' later recorded that these women used to mix powdered bark (root) of a tree to make the 'drink' flavoured and tasty. Juices of palm trees collected in earthen pots hanged on the tree fermented naturally when they are brought down late in the day time (not early morning or evening). Jaggery made from sugarcane juice (obtained by crushing) was also fermented to get drinks. Bhabadev Bhatta's book "*Paayaschittakaran*" has mentioned about such liquors/beverages. Tribals ('*aadibasi*') used to ferment *Mahua* (*Madhuca*) flowers into alcoholic drink although these flowers were also used as such as food of humans and animals. It is amasing to know that '*austric*' speaking people that are "*aadi-australian*' is the mother of the words – '*begun*' (brinjal), '*lau*' (bottle gourd), '*Kumro*' (sweet gourd), '*Jhinga*' (ridged gourd), '*Kankrol*' (spinegourd), '*Kochu*' (swamp taro) now in Bengali language. Evidently these vegetables are cooked as their food from olden days. This is tracing history through the development of Bengali language. Through different other ways we can trace the use of '*palta*' (pointed gourd leaves), leaves of sweet gourd and bottle gourd leaves, (jute leaf use started much earlier), '*note*' (Amaranthus), '*gandal*' (*Geodaria* leaves), '*thankuni*' (*Centella asiatica*) leaves, leaves of '*neem*' (*Azodirachta* leaves), '*siuli*' (*Nyctanthus arbortristis*) leaves on the one hand and flowers of '*Kumro*' (sweet gourd), '*sajina*' (Drumstick), '*bok*' (*Sesbania* sp.), fig. ('*Dumur*'), banana ('*Mocha*'), '*shapla*' stalk (*Nelumbia*) etc. on the other.

Among fruits '*aam*' (mango), '*Kanthal*' (Jack fruit), '*Pempe*' (papaya), '*Bael*' (Aegle), '*Koetbael*' (elephant apple *Limonia acidissima*), '*Panifol*' (water chest nut), '*aata*' (custard apple), '*nona*' (*Anona* sp.), '*Kaglichu*' (indigenous litchi), '*piyal*' (*Buchanania angustifolia*), '*aansfol*' (*Manilkara kauki*), '*sabeda*' (sapota), '*chalta*' (elephant apple, *Dillenia*), '*tentul*' (Tamarind) were consumed. From the ancient paintings and sculpures in 'terrakota' of Bengal, the fruits are identified by older people having interest in these aspects. Many other plant parts like '*thore*' (stalk of the inflorescence of banana), '*loti*' (modified creeping branches of a kind of swamp taro), '*hatisnur*' (a species of fern), basella seeds, twigs of '*senji*', etc. are cooked and eaten.

5

Maurya and Post-Maurya Period (322-262 BC)

'Maurya's ruled over some parts of '*Gaur-Bongo*' from fourth to third BC. They ruled North Bengal. *Bimbisar* (544-491 BC) and *Ajatshatru* (491-460 BC) left a well administered and powerful rule that helped to build a favourable situation for agriculture in Bengal too. During that period '*Maurya*' rulers used to control land ownership. '*Manu Samhita*' has mentioned that the king is the primary owner of land and gets a part of the produce as protector of land (Akshay Kumar Maitreya, 1912). *Kautilya* in his '*Arthashastra*' expressed that forest, water, land and '*Ghat*' (river jetty) are centralised under state control. That is why land allotment required issuance of '*patta*' (permanent right) stating a serial number and method of sale or transfer. Regarding agriculture of that time '*Kautilya*' felt requirement of more number of '*Sudra*'s (lower caste) in villages that were more or less one *crose* away from each other and each of them had 100-500 houses. Radhakumud Mukhopadhyay, 1958 told that in case a villager allowed agricultural land to go fallow King had the authority to transfer that land to a different farmer. This generated one 'middle class' who got their land cultivated by any poor villager. Result was generation of 'farm labour' ('*Khset majur*') or share cropper ('*Bhagchashi*').

5.1 Agriculture and Villages

In the third century the records in '*Brahmi*' and '*Prakrita*' languages obtained from '*Mahasthan*', Bagura reveals that one staff called '*Mahamatya*' used to protect or preserve crops from flood, fire or pest attack. Villagers who underwent loss are offered paddy and other cereals and cash (currency '*Gandak*' or '*Kakonik*'). This distribution duty was assigned to '*Sumatra*'- another staff. The period from '*Maurya*' to the beginning of '*Gupta*' '*Bangarh*' excavation under leadership of Kunjagobinda Goswami unearthed second to first century BC punch marked silver and copper coins and third to second Cent. BC *terracotah* idol and cast coin in Tamluk. Such archaeological evidences are obtained also from *Berachampa* or *Chandraketugarh* of South 24-Parganas. Along with these, progress of agriculture land use gradually entered in a complex process in the way that after King a new tier of Jamidar class, besides land tilling farmer, farm labour and share-cropper class arrived. Actually after '*Mauryas*' Bengal was divided into small, self-ruled areas having no central rule for Bengal. Following the pattern agricultural fields were also divided along with their rights and activities on land. The geophysical condition in Ganga Valley area was favourable to initiate progress in trade and commercial activity as is evident from development of trade-route, currency development and quality of utensils. The evidences of art and craft category also speaks of people's resources and wealth generated through agriculture. The '*Kauma*' conscious Bengali groups in those days developed and progressed with their separate characteristics in lifestyle, agriculture, and animal husbandry without growth of any common Bengali culture. In subsequent '*Gupta rules*' for over two centuries some amount of commonness developed along with the caste system of Aryans. Emperor Ashok banned '*cut and burn*' agriculture or scaring away of the wild animals from jungles, and clear them to extend cultivation area. Habib, 2006 however mentioned that these steps were not followed by encouragement or incentive for agriculture. According to the '*Arthashastra*' declared policy, King usually arranged to immigrate '*Shudras*' for doing agriculture. On condition of their stay living in the villages for agriculture they were offered on loan seeds, cattle, and cash. At this stage use of bullock, iron-share of plow and sickle in plowing is mentioned. These indirectly proved through the increased production dependent huge export business which included agricultural produces. Besides *kharif* paddy, sesame and linseed some vegetables like Amaranthus, Basela, swamp taro, '*Shapla*' was quite natural in *kharif* season and in Rabi season pulses, sugarcane, mustard, safflower growing was quite possible in those days. *Mahasthan* scripts ('*Prakrita*') of *Bogura* (Third Cent. BC) tells, when people suffered loss for flood, fire or pests, they were offered paddy. This system was in vogue in Second cent BC also act as evidence from '*Bramhiilipi*' on copper plates in Berachampa and Tilda (Paresh Ch. Dasgupta and Kunjagobinda Goswami). Such evidences were mentioned in the '*Arthashastra*, preserved in Mysore (200 BC). '*Bastu*' or land for residence, '*Kshetra*' or agricultural land, 'Gochari' or grazing field, are described. Similarly '*Ushar*' or fallow land, '*Gopath*' or way for cattle movement, '*Pushkarini*' or water body, '*Bitapi*' or forest etc. helped understand the land use pattern. '*Dronemukh*' was a centre from where about 400 villages were controlled. '*Sthaniyo*' meant residences of 800 villages. All these established that village life centered round agriculture. However sometimes village ultimately developed into big trade centre. In some of the villages – 'Sea Port' or '*Bouddha Vihar*' were in the centre. Extraction of juice from sugarcane and boiling that to '*Gur*' (molasses) was developed.

Use of bullock in plowing and rearing goat, pig, poultry, duck and sheep was in practice. People had fishing-net and '*Ghunii*' (trap) in their house for fishing and even fishing on a boat was in practice. Broken boat was unearthed in *Kalibongan*' village. In those days field crops were paddy, sugarcane, sesame, cotton etc. and fruit crops were Date palm, Pomegranate, Melon etc. *Megasthenes* listed five livelihood groups of which second was agriculture and third animal rearing. Trade (sale and purchase) with animals was common. They used to consume milk and meat. '*Mahua*' was grown in '*Pundrabardhan*' which provided food and drink.

5.2 Agricultural Marketing

During post-'*Maurya*' period paddy-rice was the main commodity for sale and the primary wealth of Bengal. From north-west of India number of groups of people came (first to fifth cent, Kushan period) to '*Chandraketugar*' and established so-called peoples rule (*Janarajya*) and later kingdom to rule the land (Bratindra Mukhopadhya; Gopal Sinha). The royal seals and terracotta obtained from *Chandraketugarh* revealed all these. Names of rulers known are King Juju, Sri Rajajdhan, Tajta, Lodhpe and others. In the caves of *Shushunia*, Bankura one '*Brahmilipi*' of fourth cent AD showed the name of King Chandrabarman. Some years before the birth of Christ a running trade system between China and India developed into a steady and smooth cultural relation. Moreover, silk cloth of China was sent to Rome through Indian ports that include '*Ganga*' or '*Gange*' (near *De-Ganga*) and '*Tamralipta*' (Gopal Sinha, 1996). Later from the beginning of middle era '*Saptagram*' of Hooghly district. At this point of time trade of India including Bengal was for spices from south east Asian countries like Java, Sumatra and Cambodia. These import-export business has been described in 'Perilus of the Erithrian Sea'. 'Natural History' of Pliny and 'Geographicon' of Ptolemy. Chinese book '*Tai Ping-Yu-Lan*' has mentioned import of spices from Malay, Java, Sumatra, and Cambodia using water transport, name of one of the large ship was '*Kolandia*'. These informations suggest prosperous state of agriculture production. Countries of east and south Europe and Island countries of Asia used to send ships for trade. From Bengal the route was along the Deccan coasts upto '*Bhrigu-Kachha*'. Domestic trade followed river routes in addition to road-routes. Agricultural produces like Bay-leaf, *Pippal*, Cardamom, *Priyangu*, Mustard and Chilli was exported to many countries like Egypt, Rome and many Asian countries. Cotton and silk cloth, '*Patrorna*' and '*Khoumabastra*' were also exported.

Bengal used to produce '*Dukul*' (fine cloth) and relatively thick '*Khoumobastra*' and '*Patrorna*'. Besides '*Patrorna*' cloth like '*Muga*' and '*Endi*' were also produced. '*Dukul*' from Bengal was soft and white, from '*Pundradesh*'-ash coloured and smooth, and from '*Kamrup*' (*Subarnakudya*) like rising sun. 'Kautilya' mentioned in '*Arthasastra*' that Bengal clothes were exported to China, Italy, Greece, Rome, and Egypt. Pearl of Ganges origin was admired for its best quality (*Periplus*). Greek authors Eilion, Lukan and others spoke high of the indigenous honey (boiled sugarcane juice) produced in Bengal.

Oldest-Bengali scripts are of third and second century BC. They contained many words concerning trade and commerce in Bengal. Words '*Aapon*' (shop), '*Biponi*' (shop), '*Byapari*' (Businessman), '*Hotta*' (Haat, weekly market), '*Hottika*' (small 'Hat') etc. '*Hattopati*' (market chief) was the manager of the entire system of marketing. Some more staff employed by ruler like '*Shoulkik*', '*Tarik*' were also there. In Bengal sale of fruits, flowers, mango, jackfruit, *Mahua* etc. between villages was very regular. '*Mahasthanlipi*' on rocks in *Bogura* on the bank of river '*Karatoa*' contained the order of '*Maurya*' emperor to '*Mahamatya*' of '*Pundranagar*' to distribute paddy to seriously affected Bengali people ('*Sangbangiyo*'). They were also to be given some cash ('*Gandak*') as loan. A vivid picture of the situation in villages is evident – in both distress and affluence.

5.3 Bengali Food : early diversifications

The land was good and fertile to produce large number of food-crops including food grains (not pulses), vegetables and fruits that were selected from natural flora of this 'fertile delta' round the year.

Vegetables like brinjal ('*Begun*'), sweet gourd ('*Kumdo*'), ridged gourd (*'jhinga')*, bitter gourd (*Kasula, Karola*) etc. were cooked producing tasty food preparations eaten with cooked rice ('*Bhaat*'). Fishes of different kinds were prepared with different spice combinations as already mentioned. Sweets made from coconut ('*nadoo*', '*chaaba*') and milk were also sweet dishes in those days. Preparation of '*gur*' (country sugar) and its use in cooking or consumption has been long practiced in Bengal. 'Chira' (boiled, pressed and dried rice, '*khoi*' (popped paddy), '*muri*' (dry-fried rice) were already in the list. Different kinds of drinks from different sources (raw materials) namely '*Kalbibek*' and '*Krityatattarnab*' books narrated that in the month of '*Aswin*' on the night of '*Kojagor Purnima*' there was custom of consuming '*Chipitak*' ('*chira*') with sweets made from coconut. Family members used to consume '*Khoi*' and '*muri*' made from rice.

6

Agriculture in Gupta and Post-Gupta Period (Fourth Cent. 320-547 AD)

In ancient Bengal the province under regular administration and rules was called '*Bhukti*', a district under administrative rules was called '*Bishoy* and *Mondol*' and further subdivisions were '*Beethi*'. But exceptions were there. The scripts of 'Gupta period' mentioned three '*Bhukti*'s namely '*Pundrabardhan*', '*Barddhaman*, and '*Subarnabeethi*'. Bengal in those days was divided into five states namely – '*Kajangal*' (Uttar Rarh), '*Pundrabardhan*', '*Karnasubarna*', '*Tamralipti*' and '*Samatat*'. This is the time when a radical change in Bengali society took shape. The long standing clash between *Pre-Aryan* society and cultures of various '*Kaumas*' or communities with '*Aryan*'-'*Bramhanya*' society and culture was very much live. The clashes were resulting in genesis of newer society and culture that ignored supercilious variety of Aryan culture and sectarian outlook of pre-Aryans. Including '*Drabid*', '*Bouddha*' and '*Jain*' characteristics also an altogether new inclusive, progressive culture was taking shape.

6.1 Land, village and habitations

Established in fourth cent AD by first *Chandragupta*, Gupta kingdom included '*Gour*' and '*Rarh*' (Rakhaldas Bandyopadhyay, 1914). His gold coin *Dinarius* has been obtained in *Moshagram*,

Barddhaman. Samudragupta (350-375 AD) extended the border of his empire upto west Bank of *Bhagirathi*, *Samtat* on the east bank remaining independent. Chinese traveler *Fa Hien* came to India in 399 AD to see the progress of Buddhism. In his six years stay in India he came to *Tamralipti* in the later part of his stay before he left for Sri Lanka. He claimed that during that time people did not slaughter animals or drink wine etc. People did not consume onion or garlic but cultivated these crops. During *Vikramaditya's* rule the area was prosperous for success in agriculture. The costly silk cloth used as ceiling and essence and flowers used in different religious festivals indicated resources in agriculture. Kings and rich people used to donate freely to the monks and religious people. *Fa Hien* visited Buddhist temples at *Kapilavastu*, *Shrabasti*, *Rajgriha* and *Gaya* – all in the east. Capital *Pataliputra* was called '*City of flowers*'. All these progress was in the neighbouring areas of Bengal. *Gupta* rule and prosperity spread also to *Bengal* as is evident from the detection of *Gold coins* from *Madhabpur*, Jahanabad Sub Div., Hooghly district, *Kalighat*, Kolkata and *Mohammadpur, Jasohar* (now Bangladesh). Agriculture being the only way of earning wealth at that time, appears to be highly productive. Fa Hien's description of agriculture is of an area, adjoining Bengal and as such helps to understand Bengal-agriculture in those days. The scripts of fifth to seventh century AD do not show any mention of agriculture does not mean that agriculture was insignificant in the society. Historians feel that this is due to society giving not much importance to either '*Kshetrakar*' or agriculture. But the description of paddy threshing by trampling with cattles clarifies the position.

Information on sale of land is available from permission circular's ('*Shasan*') inscribed on copper plaques. One example for setting some '*brahmins*' in one '*Kulbyap*' land purchased by one villager to donate in *Damodarpur* village in Dinajpur is cited. This happened in 411-482 AD as per Radhagobinda Basak. Guptas used to cease land that is not cultivated by the farmer concerned or land not yet distributed by ruler and distribute among villagers the cultivated part. '*Gunaighar script*' of Bainyagupta (507-508

AD) describes land given for *'Noudandak'* or *'Noukaghat'* for harbouring small to large boats and ships which was very important for trade through seas. The water transport was very much developed in 'Bengal' and *'Haraha script'* of *Ishan barma* (Sixth cent) called the land *'Samudrashayan'* i.e. it depended on sea-transport based trade. Regarding demand for land (fifth-seventh cent copper plaque) it was more for *'Khilkshetra'* (for cultivation) than *'Bastukshetra'* (for house building) having in some cases demand for both cultivation and housing.

Lands were designated with the purpose of it like *'Aprada'* or not yet distributed, *'Aprahata'* or not cultivated, *Astamba* or no plants grow, *'Khil'* or fallow, *'Apratikar* or taxfree, *'Utpratikar'* or not yet surveyed and *'Samudaybahya'* or does not pay anything to the King, etc. Other way the designation of land was like *'Kshetra'* (cultivable), *'Japkshetra'* (no irrigation required), *'Bastu'* (habitable), *Bagicha* (Garden), *Charanbhumi* (grazing land), *Sechnala* (irrigation channel). *Kalidash* (fifth cent) in his *'Raghubangsha' Kabya* has described paddy transplanting *'Utkhat pratiropita kalam'*. In fact transplanting of paddy is ancient practice of paddy cultivation in lower Bengal possibly due to complete inundation of the land during monsoon. Heuen Sang's (fifth cent) description of vast uncultivated land in Bengal (*'Aprahata birat'*) was not acceptable to historian Rakhaldash Bandyopadhya in 20th century. We feel that Heuen Sang must not have seen the vast inundated south Bengal during monsoon and if at all a look from far off place has not helped him to get the correct picture or he visited in Rabi season. It was only a successful agriculture (huge wealth) could develop during Gupta rule large number (Karnasubarna-10) of *'Sangharam'* (Buddhist prayer hall), temples (50 in Karnasubarna) *'Stupa'*, *'Chaitya'*, opened ponds (Queen of King Aditya Sen) etc., places visited by Heuen Sang are *'Champa'* (Angadesh), *Paundrabardhan* (*'Gaur'*), *'Samatat'* (present Bangladesh), *Karnasubarna* (Rarh), and *Tamralipti* (*Sukshma*). The prosperity of these areas were all from wealth generation through agricultural production. Not many evidences or records are available that directly speaks about agriculture of those days in Bengal. Hence the picture of the villages, its people and the society as described, is being used as indirect evidence of progress of agriculture. Many gold coins of '*Skandagupta*' (Seventh and Eighth Cent AD) are obtained in Mahammadpur (*Jashohar*), Dacca and Kotalipara (*Faridpur*), Bagura, Bhatpara, Savar, Katagaunge and other areas of Bengal prove the prosperity. In fact literature on this period published and consulted by present author provided very little informations on agriculture excepting the records of extensive activities about land-transfer. Much informations on land donation and presentation, sale and purchase of land etc. is there, since one '*Pustapal*' (record keeper) used to do this job for the Emperor. Most of the donation and sale of land has been done by State/ King although villagers also did it for development of places for religious purposes. Persons skilled in cultivation were invited and given settlement to improve agriculture. Such people also accepted these offers since they learnt that lower Gangetic Plains was most fertile among the lands in the country. Moreover skill of; Bengalis in running water transport system also helped marketing of agricultural commodities. That the prosperity of Bengalis was due its success in agriculture is proved indirectly.

Human habitations in villages grew, as per '*Arthashastra*', from before Fourth Cent. AD. In Bengal, habitation with 200 villages was called '*Kharbat*', with 400 villages called '*Dronemukh*' and with 800 villages called '*Sthaniyo*'. However 'areawise' they were not equal (Bhaskar Chattopadhyay, 2003). Names of many villages are there in the '*Lekhamala*' of Bengal and in the peoples' life of Bengal villages are extremely important all the time. Village life is continuing to remain agriculture-dependent from ancient times till today and the village-economy was also centering round agriculture. *Kautilya* noted sugarcane cultivation and production of '*Gur*' or country sugar in Bengal. Kalidasa (Fifth Cent) in his poetry – '*Raghubangsa*' has mentioned that wives of farmers used to guard '*Shalidhan*', sitting under the shade of sugarcane (Atul Sur, 1986). Cultivation spread over large areas and many '*Brahmins*' from outside Bengal were given settlement to live in this land. These people being used to marry many women, increased population of the land very fast consequently increasing food demand. In his book '*Bangla-o-*

Bangalir Bibartan' Atul Sur discussed the '*Anushasan's* (orders) of fourth and fifth century the farmer groups were being named like '*Kshetrakaran*', '*Karshakaran*', '*Krishikaran*' etc. according to the type of agricultural job they were doing and they earned much importance (equal with businessmen) in village life. During this period in villages demand for cultivable land increased. The '*Mahasthan*' inscript on stone in *Bogura* (Third to Second Cent) described '*Dhan*' as one of the main wealth of Bengal. Most of the '*lekhamala*' were about donation and sale of land which were termed '*Pattoli*', possibly the ancestor of '*patta*' now in use. That the cultivable land were costlier than housing land in Bengal of that period also proved importance of agriculture. Depending on quality of land cost of one '*kulyabap*' land was *one to four* '*Dinar*'. However most land transfers were for religious purposes. The measure of land in Bengal in those days were like this – 8 '*musti*' = 1 '*kunchi*' = 1 '*pushkali*', 4 '*pushkal*' = 1 '*aari*'; 4 '*aari*' = 1 '*drone*', 8 '*drone*' = 1 '*Kulyabap*' or '*patak*' (Niharranjan Roy, 1993).

Classification of land on different basis was in the beginning. Up, medium and low land terms were used to determine the crop to be grown and method of cultivation. Depending upon the up, medium and low land water accumulation or drainage on the land and depth of accumulated water were determined. Finally ownership of the land starts with '*Raja*' (King) at the top (entire land) followed by number of '*Jamidars*' (landlords) ruling over portions and then large number of cultivators ('*Chaasi*' or '*Krishak*') with still smaller portions. Besides the nature and characteristics of the soil of the land, and the purposes of use also leads to another classification of land.

Copper-plaque inscriptions obtained in Faridpur (Bangladesh) during the last Stage of Gupta rule under '*Dharmaditya Gopalchandra* and '*Samachardev*' were later determined to be land-purchase documents for donating the land to '*Bramhans*' (Rakhaldas Bandyopadhyay, 1914). Side by side people of '*Gour-Banga*' were inclined to earn independence as revealed from stone-inscriptions obtained '*Haraha*' village. People of '*Banga*' by that time developed a very strong Navy and established a kind of rule in coastal area. On the other hand during

Bainyagupta's rule this was destroyed by "*Huns*" (Gunaighar Copper plaque order). Agriculture in these days also continued undisturbed. After '*Samachardev*', in Seventh Cent. AD, '*Sashanka*' ceased the power to rule '*Bengal*' as independent state, although '*Bainyagupta's*' rule continued for some more days in some areas of Bengal (North West of *Cumilla*). Bhaskar Chattopadhyay 2003 claims that in Sixth Cent. two independent nations were – ***'Bango'*** and ***'Gaur'***. '*Shashanka*' became ruler of 'Bengal' since 606 AD having '*Karna-subarna*', Murshidabad as capital of his state. '*Karnasubarna*' was on the south of *Baharampur* at '*Rangamati*' and North and West of Bengal was under his rule. '*Gaur*', '*Utkal*', '*Magadh*' and '*Kangod*' were within his kingdom and Emperor '*Harshabardhan*' could not conquer his kingdom till 641 AD when he died. During this long period of *Shashanka's* rule farmers of Bengal were fully engaged in agricultural production. They cultivated different varieties of rice and sugarcane and achieved great success in production. Heuen Sang in his travelogue (637-638 AD) described Bengal in *Shashanka's* time. *Shashanka* was a heir of *Guptas* but he being a 'Shaiba' did not like '*Bouddhas*' but Heuen Sang's allegation that he hated and oppressed Bouddha's was baseless and not correct as per Rakhaldas Bandyopadhyay's opinion. It seems that besides water transport, bullock-cart was developed by then in Bengal and bullock-carts were built using local resources like bamboo, wood and iron. Bullock-cart in those days had, 15 parts namely '*Ulo*', '*Dhuro*', '*Rodkhib*', '*Ninge*', '*Haal*', '*Jool*', '*Mode*', '*Ola*', '*Lappa*', '*Fad*', '*Chaal*', '*Prute*', '*Chatra*', '*Handi*', and a pair of bullocks.

6.2 *'Krshi Parashar* (Fifth cent. or earlier)

One classic poetical works written in Sanskrit, appearing to be the first Indian work on agriculture. The verses are creation of one sage of fifth century or of an earlier period describing different stages and aspects of cultivation. This was translated by one learned botanist and one Sanskritist namely Girija Prasanna Mazumdar and Suresh Chandra Banerjee on behalf of Asiatic Society, Calcutta (Bibliotheca India, Work No. 285 and Issue No. 1590; 1960). It contains besides translated English text, the original Sanskrit text and one valuable explanation of the text by the translators.

Jogesh Chandra Roy, 1925 (*Viswakosh*') told that '*Krsi Parasara*' is created in fifth century A.D. Translators felt that '*Krsi Parasara*' was written in between Second to Sixth Cent. Asiatic Society publication is 88 page booklet. This valuable document has created many controversies in regard to identity of the sage '*Parasara*', agriculture of which part of India is represented in this text, who is sage '*Parasara*' and he belongs to which part of the country etc.

First of all the original text described primarily rice agriculture, and very early literature of Bengal (Mahasthan, Bagura, now Bangladesh) written in '*Maurya Bramhi*' script (Second Cent. BC) describes distribution of 'paddy' (neither wheat nor jowar) suggesting paddy cultivation was continuing in Bengal from very early days.

Before going into further details we place herewith one biased explanation of '*Krsi Parasara*' (by Balkundi, 1998) claiming without any reasoning and evidence to be a description of agriculture of Sialkote, Pakistan, a place blessed with only 650-700 mm annual rainfall and no report of wild rice or any related species in its nature. The place suggested is an established wheat growing area. *Parasar* has described transplanted rice cultivation which possibly was not at all possible in such a low-rainfall area. Now let us examine what Sureshchandra and Girijaprasanna have understood. They expressed that *Parasar* must have talked about agriculture of a high rainfall area and the area is most likely to be Bengal. We feel that *Assam* is also a high rainfall area. But the translators raised more powerful logic in favour of Bengal. The verses of '*Krsi Parasara*' offered to have been composed during Second to Seventh Cent. AD. In this connection one is reminded that '*Smriti*' group of verses were composed in eighth Cent. In fact there were number of '*Parasar*'s in those days and '*Parashar Smriti*' (different book) contains 'agriculture' in only one part. Secondly '*Smriti*' has shown that '*agriculture*' is linked with '*cast*' which is not at all found in '*Krsi Parasara*'. Thirdly the method of marking of 'bullock' is different in '*Smriti*' and '*Krsi Parasara*'.

Next question is to which place *'Parasar'* belongs. It is noted that in *'Krsi Parasara'* only bullocks were used in plowing. In west of India plowing is done using Buffaloe and Horse. Thus *'Krsi Parasara'* relates to Bengali agriculture as claimed by Jogesh Ch. Roy, 1825 and Girija Prasanna. Now coming to equipments used in agriculture of those days *'Krsi Parasara'* describes use of *'Madika'* or *'Moi'* (ladder) in land preparation. *'Madika'* is a very old Bengali word, not found in *'Sanskrit'*. *Parasaras'* use of this word clearly suggests that he must have lived in this land life long to know this exclusive Bengali practice of using ladder in land-levelling and use of this Bengali word. *'Kartanam'* (harvesting) is a Sanskrit word but *'Kartan'* is widely used in Bengali. Among the main verses one is *'Bristi Mul Krishi Sarba'* meaning "agriculture is done mainly using rains". There in the book no irrigation method has been mentioned. On the other hand in western India, for reasons of scanty rains, some irrigation method was developed (as mentioned in 'Rk. Veda' and 'Arthasastra'. *'Krsi Parasara'* says – *'Annam hi Dhanya Samojatam'* meaning "Food means paddy" (wheat has not been mentioned). Many more indications have revealed through the work of Girijaprasanna and Sureshchandra. And the most important is the paddy cultivation that *'Parasar'* discussed is transplanted rice that is the method of rice cultivation in Bengal for long period.

'Krsi Parasara' (KP) mentions that rice that is a gift from 'paddy' seeds is a 'goodwill' and "blessing" of paddy plant to human being. Rice is the power of life. Without cultivation one can not have rice; hence one has to go for agriculture leaving behind every other thing. KP points to the relation of weather with agriculture. Rain comes from cloud. Cloud has four categories namely *'Anabarta'*, *'Samabarta'*, *'Pushkar'* and *'Drone'*. How much rain may come from each one and what is their influence on agriculture has been described. Besides that 'movement of ants' or 'calls of frogs' may indicate 'rainfall' has been stated. Fertility of soil has been related with time of plowing e.g. plowing in *'Hemanta'* (autumn) is best, *'Magh'* (Jan-Feb) is next best, *'Falgun'* (Feb-Mar) next and *'Chaitra'* (March-April) worst. Seeds has to be collected and cleaned to make them free from seeds of

grasses and weeds to sow in '*Baisakh-Jaistha*' (April-May) and never in '*Ashad-Sravan*' (July-August). Before sowing plowed land has to be levelled with 'ladder'. In case of transplanting, seedlings are to be placed at prescribed spacing which however shall change in case of late transplanting. Requirement of standing water and depth of transplanting has been discussed. The cultivation (transplanted rice) process has been discussed in detail using many Bengali words that strongly suggests that he belonged to '*Gour-Banga*' (Bengal). Examples in addition to '*madika*' (ladder) – '*Haal*' (plow), '*Iish*', '*Joal*' (parts of plow), '*Pasika*', '*Saula*', '*Sthami*', '*Pakkani*', '*Adakolla*' etc. '*Fola*' (share), '*Bida*' (harrow), '*Rajju*' (rope) etc. has been mentioned with their measurements and construction. Fixing of an iron sheet ('*Falika*') on the share for deep ploughing has also been mentioned. Toothed harrow (*Biddhak*) and determining auspicious moment for plowing has also been stated. These come to sowing seeds (Aus') on 21st May, seedling for seed-bed making for transplanted rice-21st April, sowing of sugarcane or pulses on 20th February and mustard seed sowing on 23rd October. Fixing reed (*Nal ropan*') in paddy field to attract birds to devour insect pests has been mentioned. '*Medhi ropan*' ('Bamboo fixing') was done to tie the bullocks that will rotate around it to trample rice panicles (laid surrounding '*Medhi*') to thresh seeds. Grains were then dried in sun for storing in store ('*Gola*'). The entire process is the exact one that has been going on in Bengal till the other day. Some stages or events in this cultivation process has been tried to illogically relate with some events like-'touch of widow' with seed quality, 'turtle in paddy field with death of farmer's wife' or 'licking nose by the bullock with very high production' etc. also. At the beginning the verses complimented the author and agriculture and main theme is its confidence in human capabilities and the positive role of paddy towards humans. The verses no doubt described paddy based agriculture of the east India.

Carl Soyar (1889-1975) US scientist of Geography has emphasised *Hoyabin Hean* culture of Thailand and claimed that oldest agriculture had the beginning in South East Asia in 4000 BC. Heuen Sang (637-638 BC) described this area of India to be flat plain of loam soil that is fertile and any kind of grains could be grown there. Earlier in fifth Cent. BC *Kalidas* in his '*Raghubangsa*' called this transplanting method of paddy as '*Utkhat Pratiropita Kalmaha*'. All these establish this unique method of paddy cultivation is being practiced in Bengal from ancient times since stagnation of water on land during monsoon is a natural phenomenon and primitive ancestors of Bengalis had no option but to develop such a technology applicable only in case of paddy.

'*Parasar*' however discussed cultivation of other crops like pulses, sesamum, barley, wheat, mustard, sugarcane, mainly grown in *Rabi* season. Verse no. 226 tells about betelvine which was again an old day crop in Bengal and '*Boroj*' (the thatched shade for growing betelvine) is an '*austric*' word, the primitive language of Bengalis. Comparing the situations existing in Bengal and Sialkote one would find average 1200 mm (minimum) and 600 mm rainfall respectively. The flowing river of KP is '*Ganga*'. The famines mentioned in KP is due to '*drought*' was possible in an area where no irrigation system existed that is Bengal. This however was possible in either of east or west India excepting that agriculture in West of India is used to growing drought tolearnt crops all along. In eastern India failure on paddy was synonymous with famine since there was no other irrigation system. KP has emphasised use of cowdung. Regarding irrigation rain water harvest in ponds for use in winter was suggested. No other irrigation system that existed in western India has been mentioned in KP. The suggestion for raising small mud bank ('*ail*') as suggested in KP is in the tradition of Bengal agriculture. Recommendation of '*ail*' making for low and very low lands also matches with the monsoon inundated situation in Bengal. The pests mentioned like '*Gundhibug*' snail ('*Sankhi*', '*Shamuk*'), white head ('*Pandurmundi*') are all problems of humid and wet atmosphere that exist in Bengal. Another – '*Dhuli*' (powdery mildew) must be a problem of mustard or wheat. '*Shringari*' may be a problem (rust) of wheat or any other crop-disease of low temperature and humidity season. Celebration called "*Pushyatra*" has been suggested both before and after harvest. Whether this is the origin of '*Nabanna*' festival, still a tradition in Bengal, is not known. KP contains use of milk, cowdung, cow-urine and oilcake after oil extraction in '*Ghani*' (pressing machine). These all are present in Bengal (Mazumdar and Suresh Ch. Banerjee, 1960).

6.3 Maxims ('*Bachan*'), Proverbs ('*Prabad*') and Agriculture of Bengal (9th to 12th century)

A great lady known as '*Khana*' (*Kshana*) may not be present in history but very much in the traditional or familiar report. The unique maxims composed in her name are mostly about agriculture and its relation with atmosphere. Many efforts for joining this '*Khana*' with *Ujjayini* or 'Sri Lanka have to fail since '*Khana*' is alive amongs the people of rural Bengal so much so that they remember and recite most of the sayings in her name concerning any issue of agriculture or atmosphere. The maxims interestingly, are composed in '*Bengali*'.

One '*Khana-Mihirer Dhibi*' at Berachampa, North 24-Parganas on excavation yielded '*Buddha*' idol, '*Kunda*' (fire place), temple made of bricks, different coins and costly ornaments (Debal Debbarma, 2010). Nowhere else such memories and articles of olden days in the name of '*Khana*' has been obtained. '*Khana*' was knowledgeable in mathematics, calculations particularly astronomical calculations. She composed her 'maxims' and 'sayings' mostly on agriculture, crops, and productivity. She had deep understanding and unlimited knowledge of geophysiography, climate, rains etc. and their changes and variations. She had deep understanding even about human nature and relations.

Khana-Mihirer Dhibi' is located in a place called '*Chandraketugarh*' that is linked with '*Gamgaridae Civilization*'. One gold coin, other coins of different kinds having sun, mountain, ox, horse, elephant, tree, lotus, ship etc. inscribed on them inspires one to think about '*Khana*' and '*Mihir*'. Many earthen plaques of conjugal figures were also unearthed. On the basis of all these Debbarma, 2010 offered an explanation. Possibly for some days '*Khana*' and '*Mihir*' went to *Ujjayini* and spent some days or months there. Thereafter they came back and continued to live in *'Chandraketugarh'* (Berachamp) in 24 Parganas. This famous astrologist lady has left behind very little proof or evidences than the 'peoples' says. But correlating agriculture with weather, time and season, her 'maxims' have stabilised in the minds of Bengali villagers. History of Bengal agriculture can not ignore her maxims (*'bachans'*). About 1000-1200 years back these *'bachans'* have suggested many important correlations that are of immense value to those farmers who seek guidance and inspiration from these *'maxims'* and *'sayings'* (1-4 line verses). Debbarma, 2010 claimed that *'Khanar Bachan'*s are remembered by people of Bengal (Paschim Banga and Bangladesh), Assam, Bihar, Odissa and Nepal and quoted often and their collection has produced books like *"Naari Grantha Prabartan", 'Khanar Bachan' "Kingbadontir Khana"* etc. She was aware of the characters of the crops.

Some such *'bachans'* as given below help us to understand ancient Bengal agriculture. *"Beng Dake Ghano Ghano, Shighra Bristi Hobe Jeno", "Khate Khatay Laver Ghanti", "Tar Ardhek kate chati", "Ghore Bose Puche Baat, Tar Ghore Ha Bhat", "Baishakher Prathom Jole, Aasu Dhan Dugun Fole"; "Shrabaner Puro Bhadrer Bhora, Roar Modhye Jato para"; "Baisakhe Bona, Ashade Roa, Jaygattoy Na Dhan Thoa"; "Thakte Balod Na Kore Chaas, Tar Dukhha Baromas"; "Aus Dhaner Chas, Lage Tin Maas"; "Ki Koro Shashur Lekha Jokha, Meghei Thake Joler Rekha;" "Kodale Kudule Megher Ga, Modhye Modhye Dichhe Gha"; "Chaasike Bolo Bandhte Aal, Aaj Na Borse, Borsabe Kal"; "Chaitre Kampe Tharothoro, Baisakhete Jhare Pathar"; "Jaisthate Tara Fote, Tobei Janbe Barsa Bote"; "Sholochase Mulo, Tar Adha Tulo, Tar Adha Dhan, Bina Chase Paan" "Chale Lau Uthone Jhal, Koro Bapu Chasar Chhaoal"; "Aame Dhan, Tentule Ban"; "Dur Shova Nikat Jol, Nikat Shova Rasatol", "Sone ore Chasir Beta, Matir Modhye Bele Jeta, Tatei Jodi Bumis Potol, Tobei Hobe Asha Safal"; "Taas Pasha Dure Thoy, Baisakh Jaisthe Halud Roy"; "Khona Bole Suna Suno, Sharater Seshe Mulo Buno"; "Mulor Bhuin tueo, Kusharer (Aakh) Bhuin Dhulo"; "Aghrane Jodi Na Bristi Pore, Gache Kanthal Nahi Dhore"; "Ekpurushe Roy Taal, Por Purushe Kore Pal, Tar Pore Je Sekhay, Tin Purushe*

Fol Pay"; "Kartiker Uno Jole Duno Dhan Khona Bole"; "Hat Bishek Kori Fank, Aam Kanthal Punte Rakh, Ghono Ghono Bose Na, Fol Tate Hobe Na". Such 'bachans' are very large in numbers. The 'bachans' tell about suitable season for a crop, extent of land preparation for each crop, benefits of timely operations, duration of crops and forecast of the climate.

In the middle age one important branch of Bengali literature was *"Lok Sahitya"* (Peoples' literature). Composed through recitation, the verses were stored in memory of people. 'Proverbs' covered agriculture and farmer's life although farmers have not received due importance. On the other hand some amount of sense of disrespect and pity have been expressed. For example – *"Chash Kore Khachhilo Abdul, Chilo Bhalo, / Chaukidari nie parane molo", "Ashay more Chasa," "Mone Mone Hase Chasa, KandheLangol Jat Babsa", "Nodir Dhare Chash, Balir opor Bas", "Dhan Dhon Boro Dhon Aar Dhon Gai / Sona-Rupa Kichu Kichu Aar Sab Chai"*. But among the proverbs and maxims *"Khonar Bachan"* received special admiration possibly for having many directions and guidance to farmers. She uttered – *"Jodi Borshe Magher Shesh, Dhanya Rajar Punya Desh", Baro put tero nati, tobe koro Boro Ksheti", "Samaye Na Dey Chaas, Tar Dukha Baromash," "Chale Lau, Uthane Jhal, Koro Baper Chasir Chaoal", "Der Hat Govir, Soa Hat Gai, Kola Puto Chasi Bhai", "Suno He Chasar Beta, Banshe Dio Dhaner Chita"* etc.

An important village festival after harvest was *'Nabanna'*, for which rhymes (*'chhora'*) have been composed – *"Koko ko Amago bari Shuvo Nabanna, Shuvo Nabanna Kaba Kak Bali Laba, Pati Kaua Lathi Khay, Danr Kaua Kola Khay"*. In 18th century the torture spree of *'Bargis'* inspired composing rhymes – *"Khoka Ghumalo para Juralo Bargi Elo Deshe, Bulbulite Dhan Kheyeche Khajna Debo Kise"*. Rhymes have covered rains and agriculture extensively. *"Aay Bristi Jhempe, Dhan Debo Mepe, Dhane Holo Poka, Jamai Shala Boka"*. Peoples' literature produced *'Dhnadha'* (puzzles) for example about pineapple – *"Bon Theke Berulo Tie, Sonar Mukut Mathay Die"*, about chilli – *"Ektukhani Gachhe Lal Peyada Nache"*, about Betel – *"Fol Nei Mul Nei Patay Bhora"*, about dehusking of paddy – *"Jotai Dibish

Totoi Khabek, Aakash Dike Han Fank Robek". Similarly peoples' song also contained message for agriculture as in harvest-song – "*Hare-o-Aamar Katisal, Bochor Bochor Thakis Bohal, Bhnui Hamader Mata Pita, Bhumi Hamader Nati Chaoyal, Sat Purusher Jamin Hamar, Tin Purusher Haal*" etc. (Tapas Basu, 1995).

6.4 Agriculture in vow ('*Broto*'), festival ('*Parob*') and fete ("utsav")

Vows that are described in religious books of Bengal and practiced by women has described some aspects of village life and agriculture. Abanindranath Thakur, 1945 in his booklet – '*Banglar Broto*' has discussed '*Kumari Broto*' and other vows concerning life of village girls and women to achieve success in different steps of village life. Genuine women's vows are actually not religious in nature. Literally the '*bengali*' word means – fulfillment of one's desire. However, some rituals and worships are performed along with in some cases. To mention some of them – in the month of '*Magh*' on the 11th day of the 'bright fortnight' '*Bhimpuja*' in Medinipur was meant for 'better plowing (*sukarshan*'), in '*Jaistha*' '*Rahim Puja*' in Puruliya, in '*Paush sankranti*' '*Rahadani*' in Bankura, in '*Ashad*' *Baghrai* and in '*Ashwin*' '*Dhan Daka*' – all aimed at crop production, crop protection and maximum productivity. Another popular peoples' festival was '*Gajan*' in which songs composed worshipping Lord '*Shiva*' and goodess '*Parvati*' and sang publicly. "*Dhan Laro Dhan Laro Gauri aulaiya matharkesh, Jol Chaile Na Deo Jol, Eiba Kemon Desh*?. People in groups use to walk in streets singing imagining '*Shiva*' and '*Gauri*' as farmer and farmer's wife. '*Gambhira*' is an ancient festival-song of Maldah that also centers round '*Shiva*' and '*Parvati*' as symbols of farmer and his wife, sang in a gathering of villagers. "*Tumi Hoye Chaasi Kashibasi Keno Kashiswar, Karmakshetra E Bramhanda Kshetra Tobo Hara*' or "*Mon Atma Dui Balode Bendhe, Karmajoal Chapie Kandhe*" etc. All these presented farmer and his wife, land, tilling etc. Even when 'dove-song' is sung ("*Baromasya*") the content is agriculture. "*Jaistha Mase Mistidol Ashar Barisha Kaal, Sha-Mase Jabe Naritar Bhabite Chintite, Agone Katibe Dhan Push*

Maase Ponnimate Chan, Magh mase Jabe Naritar Shahare Bondare, Fagunmasete Tegun Jwala, Chaitramase Mon, Baisakho Masete Jabe Purushta Bideshe". When farmer is busy in different jobs for his agriculture and marketing his wife sings this in painful loneliness. This is the picture of rural society in middle ages.

Another practice of floor and wall paintings with white coloured suspension of ground (pasted with water) rice grains ("*Aalpona*") is undertaken in most of such village festivals tells about agriculture and agro-produces of Bengal.

Family members abroad on business or on sea-journey build up tension in the women folk in their family. Praying for safe return and security of such family members the family goes for '*Bhaduli*' festival in which they paint '*aalpana*' containing '*Bhaduli*' figure, '*Jorachatro*', pair of boat for journey, and rivers on all side, sea, spiny bushes, ferocious animals that are dangers to the journey. Farmer's wife prays to goddess '*Bhaduli*' like – "*Nodi Nodi Kothay Jao. Bap Bhaier Barta Dao*" etc. '*Bosudhara Brato*" vow is - "*Astobasu Astatara Tomra Hole Sakshi, Aatdike Aatfot Aamra Rakhi".* Another important '*Brato*' is *Lakshmi* (Goddess of wealth) *brato*. In the 'full moon' ('*Purnima*') of *Aswin*, autumn crop harvest initiates this vow. From the early morning after taking bath, women folk paint '*aalpona*' with figures of lotus, leafy creepers in the room. The painting mainly show the foot of goodess '*Lakshmi*', the owl and rice panicle. On a wooden platform (*'chouki'),* the pair of feet of gooddess '*Laksmi*' and her crown are painted. The painted platform is placed in the room storing paddy and rice harvested. Pieces of *banana* pseudostem bracts are kept full of different grains. One play-boat made of wood is also kept after filling up with paddy, sesamum, mung, lentil, peas etc. Sometimes dolls are made of rice paste ('*pituli*') in the name of '*Lakshmi*', '*Narayan*' and '*Kuber*' in three different colours. In an earthen flat pot ('*Sora*') containing halved coconut seed, teeth of pig etc. Ladies of farmer's family make this vow. (Paramananda Pramanik, 2011) praying for protection, good production of land and prosperity of the family. In farming families '*pituli*' is coloured green, red and black by mixing with crushed leaves, brick powder, and charcoal powder for all these decorations. They used to worship goddess *'Lakshmi'* every Thursday and Thursday is often called *'Lakshmibar'*. *'Aalpona'* paintings included figures of owl, plow, sickle, *'Kunke'* (measuring volume of grains) and used turmeric and vermillion (*sindur*). Acually *'aalpona'*, worship, festival, vow all meant desire for prevailing peace and prosperity in village life.

In the mornings of *'Paush'* (December-January) womenfolk of farmers family go for *'Toshla'* or *'Tunshtushli'* festival. They used brinjal leaves, cowdung, 'Dubgrass' and vermillion having husks and bran (paddy grain) dusted on them. Now they place mustard, dolichos bean, and radish-flower and recite *"Tunshtushli Tumike, Tomar Puja Kore Je, Dhone Dhane Baronta, Sukhe Thake Aadi Anto"*. On *'Paush-Sankranti'* day women complete their 'vow' before sunrise and lit *'Pradip'* (candle) on earthen tray (*'Sora'*) and float it on river water. It is to be noted that in these fets 'cowdung' is the symbol of building soil fertility and different crops represented themselves wishing prosperity of agriculture. Another widely followed 'vow' festival is *'Senjuti' 'aalpona'* (paintings) included drawings of houses, moon, sun, arecanut trees, kitchen, cowshed, etc. In the prayer song like – *"Sanj pujan, Snejuti, Shologhare Sholobrati, Tar Ek Ghore Aami Brati, Brati Hoye Maglam Bor, Dhone Putre Puruk Baap Mar Ghar"* – all out prosperity is the desire. Young girls did *'Punyipukur'* brato opening a small 'pond' in the premises, pasting mud on its banks, planting a branch of *'bael'* (*Aegle*) at its centre and filling it with water. Girl put a garland on the *'bael'* branch and flowers around and prayed – *"Punyipukur Pushpa mala, Ke Pujere Dupur Bela ? Aami Sati Lilaboti, Bhaier bone Putraboti"* etc. In the prayer made in *'Baisakh'* (April-May) wishes that water in ponds and plants do not dry up for drought. In *'Gokul brato'* girls collected grasses, made balls out of them and cows are fed with pieces of ripe banana in a season when cows normally do not get enough grasses and leaves in open places. All these prayers are for welfare of farmers and their security. All these prayers are a part of life of farmers' family in Bengal since very olden days.

It appears that by this time from different cross-mentions Bengal's fruit culture started using fruits like *'jam'* (Rose apple), *'Jamrul'* (star-apple), *'sankhalu'* (*Pachyrhizas*), *'Kharmuj* and some others became common. Fruits like *'peyara'* (guava), *'anaros'* (pineapple), *tarmuj* (watermelon) and *'futi'* (muskmelon) came later.

At this point of time one would wonder if pulses were not eaten by Bengalis ? May be it was a very minor crop group, productivity being very low compared to paddy. In fact pulse cultivation was insignificant in east-south Asian and Pacific countries and islands along with Bengal. References are there to indicate that among rich people of Barishal and Faridpur there was a custom of tasting pulse preparation after taking all vegetarian and non-vegetarian items. Possibly cultivation and consumption of pulses was contribution of Aryans during middle ages.

6.4 Spices and Bengali cuisine

'Naisadhacharita' and *I. Tsing*'s writings (seventh cent) described Bengali foods served in a marriage festival that includes rice with various kinds of leafy vegetables, fish, and meat. *'Nalita'* (Jute) *pata* among leafy vegetables and *'Maurala'* among fishes are particularly mentioned. Among meat were preparations of deer, goat and birds, non-meat dishes looking like meat were mostly spicy and aromatic. Variety of sweetmeat like coconut based *'Pitha'*, *'Khir'*, *'Doi'* (Yogurt), *'Payas'* were served in many course dinner. Water was camphorated and at the end betel leaves folded with ingredients were served. On such occasions huge quantity of different foods were arranged by rich people and much of these was even wasted sometimes (*Nishaddachcrita*). In fact *'Paneer'* (cheese) making culture came in Bengal in Sixth century from Portuguese traders. In spite of the fact that killing of animals was considered improper in Buddhist, Jain and Hindu culture also, Hindus of Bengal justified fish and meat categories of food. In fact upper class Indians except those in the eastern region disliked this Bengali culture.

Later *'Brihaddharmapurana'* allows scaled fishes that are white (not black) and do not live in *'Paank'* (silt) like Rohita

(*'Rui'*), Shaphari (*Punti*), Sakula (*'Sol'*) etc. were permitted to be food for *'Brahmins'*.

White meat (particularly of Deer) eating in Bengal was possibly introduced by hunting groups called *'Shabor'*, *'Pulinda'* and others. Fishes were most liked by *Protoaustraloids* to most other groups (*'Kauma'*s) who lived in the often flooded land full of rivers, water bodies and ponds besides the roaring sea in the coast. Little later carp fishes on the one hand and goat-meat on the other were admired by all Bengalis-upper and lower caste people. In fact this region of Asia including China, Japan, Burma (now Mayanmar), like countries and islands of South East Asia, it is well known, were fond of fishes and rice. It is only from sixth and fifth Cent. BC killing of animals for food was declared unethical by *'Bramhanya religion'* and Aryan Brahmins started dealing this culture as low virtually meeting them with insulting behaviour. 'Bhatta Bhabadeva' justified this culture quoting sage *'Manu'*, *'Jagnyabalka'* and *'Vyas'* and claimed that fish eating was banned only in specific days and *'Tilhis'*. Eating fish and meat have been in the Bengali culture from ancient prehistoric times. *'Jimutbahan'* has discussed the quality of oils from fishes including *Ilish* (*Hilsa*) fish oil. *'Srinath Acarya'*, the *'smritikar'* of Bengal also strongly supported fish-eating culture. Only fishes looking like snake (*'Baan machh'*) or fishes without *'scales'* were not consumed by all classes of Bengalis. But talking about Bengali culture one can not just skip those Bengalis that are in distress and living in difficult areas and used to eat such fishes, snails, rats etc. They actually justify mixed culture of Bengal – a sustainable method now considered pride of this land.

7

Agriculture During Pal-Dynasty (750-1200 AD)

7.0 Administration and agriculture

During seventh and eighth Century Gupta dynasty slowly degenerated resulting in breakage of the empire into smaller areas. Enemies from outside also created lot of problems for the administration so much so that the empire became full of indiscipline and anarchism. Countrymen felt insecured, and their production efforts declined. Naturally villagers were often disturbed and their cultivation and crop growth was hampered. In those days small land owners often picked up quarrel and fights among themselves. Learned '*Bengalis*' felt that they have to get rid of this. They selected son of one '*Bishnu*', a skilled fighter named '*Gopaldev*' and was made King of '*Bengal*' to rule the state. According to Nagendranath Basu, *Gopaldev* or his son *Dharmapaldev* were not born in '*Gour*' but they lived in '*Bengal*' being heirs of '*Rajbhat*' family of Bengal. This information is obtained from '*Khalimpur*' declaration in copper plaque. Rakhaldas has quoted following as statement of Tibetan lama – *Taranath*. "During those days '*Khastriya*', '*Bramhan*' and '*Baishya*' themselves became king of their own lands like '*Odisya*', '*Bango*' and five other eastern Indian states. But there was nothing for the whole country.

During *Gopaldev's* reign there was peace in "*Gour–Magadh*" and people could freely work as required without much hindrance. Land distribution continued. Thereafter during '*Dharmapal's* rule (831 AD) battles in different areas was going on to expand Kingdom area. Ponds were excavated and Temples were built. As evident from '*Bongiyo Lekhamala*', Damodarpur order in copper shield (Gupta period), '*Khalimpur Lekha*' of '*Dharmapal*', '*Bangarh Lekha*' of *1st Mahipal*, '*Naihati Lekha*' of *Ballal Sen*, '*Gobindapur Order* in copper plaque' of *Laan Sen* and many others proved the importance of production in crop field (*Bhaskar* Chattopadhyay, 2003). Arab geography researcher (10th cent) Ibn-Khurd-Doba has written about production of '*Aguru* wood' and '*Kasturika*' or *Maskdana* (*Hibiscus*). King Mahipal (1070-71) was killed by '*Kaibarta*' king *Dibyok* and during his tenure "*Sadukti Karnamrita*' – a book of poet '*Papik*' described paddy fields in monsoon, heaps of harvested paddy in '*Hemanta*', sugarcane field, sugarcane crushing machine etc. giving the scenario of Bengal agriculture. '*Purkom*' or '*Pundras*' were expert in sugarcane cultivation. This may be one reason for calling sugarcane as '*Pura*'. In fact there was one sugarcane variety named '*Puri*' in Bengal. A common process of transformation of villages through success in agricultural production, trade based on agricultural produces and some villages grew into trade-centers, where population increased and increased amenities like schools, religious centres, sometimes administrative headquarters, river-port etc. converted the place into a town. Examples are '*Sidwal*' (Birbhum), '*Bhursut*' (Howrah). *Asrafpur* (Dhaka), *Chatigram* (Chattogram), *Tamralipta* (Medinipur), *Mahashangar* (Bogura), *Singhapur* (Hooghly), *Pushkaran* (Bankura), *Karnasubarna* (Murshidabad), *Tribeni* (Hooghly) etc. Mango, Jackfruit, Arecanut, Coconut etc. were grown during Pal rule and even 'Bamboo' groves were quite common.

Historians emphasised the point that during five hundred years of Pal rule and 150 years of Sen rule there have been not a single famine or food crisis. It definitely establishes success of Bengal agriculture during this long period. It is to be noted that in Vedic period (1600 BC to fifth century AD), the records of hunger and famine (Sukumari Bhattacharyya, 1998) are incidents of north and north-west India and not Bengal. No such records for Bengal has been obtained from ancient '*Lekhamala*' (third-second BC) as revealed in '*Mahasthan*' of Bogura (Niharranjan Roy, 1949) and others later.

Export of agricultural produces and import of other valuables continued over a long period of time in Bengal. All these speak in favour of existence of prosperity of agriculture and village industries of Bengal in those days. The geographical position of Bengal on fertile *Ganga alluvium* full of rivers, rivulets and water bodies justifies such claims. In '*Shabarpad*' of *charshageeti* blooming of cotton flowers have been described. Spinning of threads from 'lint's (*Shani 'pad*), making and selling of '*weaving machine*' (Tant) by '*Domnis*' ('*Kandapad*') and activities of weaving trainers described in '*Tantripad*' give a complete picture of cotton cultivation, spinning threads and weaving them into cloth. The same Bengali volume of '*Charshapad*', '*Shabaripad*' describes use of '*Chanchali*' or '*Chenchari*' (*split bamboo*) to build four walls of a house. Poet '*Shuvanka*' in 11th century described spinning of thread from cotton by ladies. Bhaskar Chattopadhyay, 2003 has stated "In Pal era '*Gaurbango*' had enough resources produced and from agriculture, forest and minerals. Among the agricultural produces were paddy, sugarcane, cotton, coconut, arecanut, betelvine etc. The cotton was used to spin threads ('*Suta kata*') and weave clothes. These were major and established activities in Bengal.

7.2 Basic method of food preparation

Rice was produced by dehusking paddy in '*Dhenki*' (country device). Again for longer storage of rice grains the unique method of treatment of rice by short-term boiling in vapour (*Par boiling*'), then drying again and milling that has a good pest repellant character. This parboiled rice, called '*alochaal*' or '*Siddhachaal*', that are not allowed in rituals, pujas etc. where '*Aatap chaal*' was a must. This technology of parboiling is a product exclusively of Bengal and non-Bengali Indians do not prefer or at all include '*siddha chaal*' or '*Aalochal*' in their 'food' or festivals. Paddy grains are soaked in water overnight and then stipped to boil them in earthen or metal containers under fire upto a level when half boiled rice inside the paddy grain swells to push open (temporarily) the hulls. Thereafter such grains are dried in sun. Such par boiled grains are milled to rice grains that are glossy to look and durable without pest or fungal attack for a longer period of storage. Primary processing of paddy or rice grains into three indigenous 'snack's of Bengal namely '*Khoi*' (sand-heated puffed paddy), '*chira*' (boiled rice pressed in '*Dhenki*') and '*Muri*' (sand-fried rice) are again very perfect consumable products of rice/ paddy that is unique and original of '*Bengal*'. This fantastic innovation following very simple methods, particularly the use of '*sand*' in frying paddy / rice grains successful in longer preservation of the food articles. Preparation of molasses ('*Gur*') from sugarcane juice and use of '*Gur*' in preparation of so many food preparations were common. Similarly using cooked rice and '*Gur*' for preparation of '*wine*' was also an ancient practice in Bengal.

Having prosperity, '*Gaur-Bango*' was engaged in domestic trade with other areas in India. Bhaskar Chattopadhyay, 2003 claims that inspite of the hindrances of non-availability of currencies and entry of Arab businessmen in Indian Ocean, *Tamralipti* port was established for trade and business. But in the administration the powerful '*Sreshthi*' and '*Kuliks*' also could not continue as ruling power. With the arrival of new '*Bhumadhyikari's* like, '*Mahamandalik*', '*Mandalik*', '*Mohamohottar*', '*Kutumbik*' etc. a new pattern of '*Feudal*' society started developing taking over the control of farmers ('*Karshak*'). Side by side development in science and knowledge gave shape to '*Ayurveda*' as also agriculture. Some of the experts in health and medicine sector were – '*Madhab*', '*Chakrapanidatta*', '*Bongosen*' and in crop-health sector was '*Sureswar*'. Progress in paintings, sculptures and architecure as also in education proves Bengali society to be a healthy, prosperous group. The taxes collected were '*Bhag*' (land tax for grains), '*Bhog*' (for fruits, flowers and fuel woods), '*Hiranya*' (in 'taka's for any special crop), '*Kor*' (property tax once a year) and '*Uporikor*' (for people living for short duration) etc. Land was measured as '*Kshetrap*' and '*Promatri*.

Till Gupta period there existed an 'all India' look in the socio-economic and cultural life in the country. Later it started expressing and spreading multi-lingual and multicultural characters. It is in the 'Pal era'. *'Gour Banga'* started to bloom and flourish its socio-economic and cultural uniqueness. During this period some characteristics in agriculture and food habits in Bengal also started to show off. Excepting the class of people dependant on the 'King', class of *'Bramhan's* dealing with education, knowledge, and religion, chiefs of *'Bouddh'* and *'Jain'* religions and different classes and strata among landlords (*'Bhumyadhikari'*) starting from *'Mahottora'*, *'Mohamahottaro'* *'Kutumba'* (small landlord), *'Kshetrakar* (*Krishok*, small land owner or share cropper) and *'Shramik-Sevak* (landless, deprived of state social rights). This lowest class were *'Antaj'*, *'Mlechha'* and *'Aadibasi'* 'Koum' having different low professions. They have been excluded from *'Lipi'* but mentioned in *'Samasamojik'*. Washermen (*'Rajak'*) and barbar (*'Napit'*) also worked as farm labour. There were other lower caste people like *'Mech'*, *'Andhra'*, *'Chandal'*, *'Pulinda'*, *'Sabar'* etc. in the society. *'Charshaapad'* described *'Dom'*, *'Domni'* (service provider in 'burning ghat'), *'Shabor-Shabori'* (hunters in jungles) and *'Kapalik'* (ascetic worshipper of goddess *'Kali'*). These people used to live in thatched houses away from habitation of people. It also mentioned *'Tantubay'* (weavers). Niharranjan tells that there were many *'brahmans'* in Bengal in those days, cultivating *'Veda'* and *'Vedanta'*. From eighth to twelfth century many vedic brahmanas from different areas of Bengal came to Bengal and settled. Many *'Brahmans'* migrated to different areas (sixth to seventh cent) and were titled according to the village they settled. These *'Gangi'* (*'Gaon'*=village) obtained titles like *'Bandyo'*, *'Chatto'*, *'Bhatta'* post fixed with *'Upadhyay'*. The couplets composed in *'Sandhya'* language by *'Bouddhas'* meditating in caves or jungles led to creation of oldest shape of Bengali language – the volume – *"Charshacharsho Binischay'*. At this stage it is to be remembered that from sixth to eleventh cent. *'Bango-Samatal'* area on the east bank of river *'Bhagirathi'* was ruled by *'Chandra family'* and *'Barman family'* in sequence and during these periods except one or two mentions of land transfer cases, no mention of agriculture is there possibly due to the fact that *'Pal rulers'* could not rule this land.

7.2 'Vriksha Ayurveda' and Surapal (Twelfth century)

'Vriksha Ayurveda' was a book on crop protection *'Sureswar'* or *'Surapal'* being the author. The book has discussed treatment of crop diseases based on the *'Ayurvedic philosophy'* of *'Tridosh'* (three basic weaknesses). Author has tried to analyse the symptoms of crop diseases under three classes namely – *'Baat'* (air), *'Pitta'* (gall-bladder and bile) and 'cough' or *'Kash'*. Under the class *'Baat'* are included sickly, bent stem, galls on stem and leaf; leaf and flower drop under hard, dry conditions, yellowing of leaves and fruits due to toxicity from soil or obstruction to root growth within soil creating galls or injury on roots or due to attack of alkaline soil, insects and nematodes or viruses. Secondly leaf-fall after yellowing, rotting of flower and fruits and irrigation with acidic or saline water were all related to *'Pitta'* (bile). This also was the cause of blighting of flowers and rotting of fruits due to invasion of fungi and bacteria. Delay in fruit bearing, immature fruits with bad taste and secretion of oily liquid from non-injured tissues resulting from excess irrigation/water are related to *'cough'* (*'kash'*). All these observations do not rely on logic, reasonings or proofs but the details of plant ailments noted established very close, meticulous study of plants in disease. Evidently failure to identify the correct cause of these disorders of plants, has denied correct treatment and crop health management.

This author and the place of composing of these couplets is neither known yet.

7.3 Development of Bengali food habit

Paddy was grown over very large area in Bengal. Next major crop to follow was sugarcane. Bengali food was thus mainly rice cooked into *'Bhat'* boiling in water. *'Bhaat'* was taken twice or thrice a day with curries and even only with salt (*'Noon bhaat'*) by poorer people. The starchy fluid (*'Fen'*) coming out of cooked rice also made a good food for poor people. Bengali housewives used to have some quantity of extra *'bhaat'* in *'Hanri'* ('burnt earthen pot') dipped in water to be used hours after. Even hot *'bhaat'* with *'fen'* called in Bengali as *'Fenabhaat'* is a favourite food. Sugarcane is another crop, sweet-juice crushed out from it, boiled dry to produce *'Gur'* (country sugar) to get a very common food item of Bengal as 'fresh' and in cooking. This '*Gur*' was used in preparation of a 'sweet-meat' ('*Mistanya*') called '*Batasa*'. '*Batasa*' has been very common sweet-meat for household use, worships, and social festivities. Preparing a thick syrup with the '*Gur*' and small aliquots (frothing drop) are poured on a dry '*Pati*' ('*Madurkathi*' and '*Sitalpati*') to dry up producing a hollow, light 'sweet-meat' storable for long.

Wheat and Barley, brought to Bengal possibly by Aryans and formed another two food grains. But to occupy the second position as food-grain in Bengal wheat never succeeded. During the end of British rule however Bengal did neither produce wheat nor there existed any supply of wheat from other states even during alarming food deficit in Bengal. Europeans like Ptolemy, Periplus and others have kept on record some informations about food-habit in Bengal.

Much later records like '*Ramcharit*' by Sandhyakar Nandi reported extensive mustard cultivation in Bengal that possibly supported use of mustard oil in cooking. Many vegetables like brinjal, sweet gourd, bottle gourd etc. were also grown. Besides many fruits e.g. mango, jackfruit, blackberry (*Jaam*), banana, amla, pomegranate, date palm, parkoti etc. also found place as food.

Most amazing was growing of spices like cardamom, clove, bay leaf, '*darchini*', chilli, onion, garlic, tamarind, ginger, etc. in the land and their use in food preparation (Atul Sur, 1986). Romans in those days admired the flavour and excellence of these spices of Bengal. Both Ptolemy and Periplus described spices of Bengal to be excellent and the taste of foods prepared with such spices were very good.

Bengalis developed a habit of chewing betel leaves with some selected spices like pieces of arecanut, clove, cardamom, etc. and paste of catechu ('*Khaer*) and lime after taking meals. This was a longtime practice among middle and old age ladies.

8

Agriculture During Sen Period (1095-1260 AD)

8.0 Sen rule was established in Bengal with the initiatives of '*Bir Sen*', '*Samanta Sen*' and others. According to Dinesh Chandra Sarkar, 1942 origin of Sen dynasty was out of mixing of '*Bramhin*' and '*Khastriya*'. Actually '*Samanta Sen*' was a '*Samanta*' of third '*Bigrahapal*' (1043-70AD) in Pal era. *Bijay Sen* (1095-1158 AD), the grandson of *Samanta sen* established one independent kingdom and became King of entire '*Rarh*'. He established capital at '*Bijaypur*' ('*Dhyee*', '*Pawandut Kabya*'), near '*Tribeni*', Hooghly on the west bank of '*Ganga*'. The other opinion was that '*Bijaypur*' is actually '*Nabadwip*' of present time, that according to '*Minhauddin*' is Nadia. Next rulers of this kingdom were *Ballal Sen* (1159-1179 AD) and *Lakshman Sen* (1179-1206 AD) in sequence. Capital of *Lakshman Sen* was '*Lakhmanabati*' or '*Gour*'. Another capital was *Bikrampur* (Rakhaldas Bandyopadhyay, 1914).

Kings of Sen dynasty used to donate land or even a village to priests as honorarium (*Dakshina*). Evidences of such land donation by *Lakshman Sen* from *Bikrampur–Joyskandhabar* at *Baghratati* and *Borendri* '*Poundrabardhan bhukti*' at *West Khatika* of *Barddhaman bhukti*, and at *Uttarrarha* of

Kankagrambhukti. *Madolna Minhajuddin* came from Delhi to *Gour* and wrote *'Tabkat-E-Nasiri'* – a book in two years (1260-61 AD) and praised *Lakshman Sen* for his rule (Bhaskar Chattopadhyay 2003). The socio-economic condition during Sen period was same as in Pal period. This period also experienced that village economy i.e. agro-based life and economy was the main determinant of the progress of the society. During that period the growth and spread of industry and trade was in decline. The main resource was agricultural production.

The desire of the Sen rule was occupying and spreading over larger land area to increase agricultural area and agricultural production. They tried to spread their kingdom in all directions like east, west, north and south to include larger agricultural land and ultimately increase production. All these caused huge tax-collection, that was used in welfare of people and to fulfill administrative and army needs. This provided funds also for lavish life of the rulers. Hence it is agriculture that laid the foundation of economic and state policies. *Idilpur order ('Sashan')* in copper plaque has described how plain land was advantageous for paddy cultivation. Even in festivals and occasions like worships (*'Jaag-Jagya'*, *'Puja'*) priests were given many villages or land as their 'fees' (*Dakshina*) that must have imposed great influence in different ways on agriculture. Side by side *Ballal Sen's* orders for running the society based on caste and reasonable rules etc. also improved *Gobindapur* copper-plaque order (*'Tamrasashan'*) of *Lakshman Sen* showed agriculture presentation of land in *Barddhaman Bhukti* and *'Betor'*. Howrah to some Byasdev Sharma (R.D. Bandyopadhyay, 1914).

It is important to note that *'Betor'* was an ancient river-port-market (*'Ganjo'*), where ships on river *'Bhagirathi'*, in case failed to reach *'Saptagram'* (river port in Hooghly district), unloaded all commodities. So both land donation and river transport dependent trade continued unhindered. Another aspect as stated by Ramesh Ch. Dutta 1874 in his "The Peasantry of Bengal", is the agricultural tax that was 1/6th of crop produce paid to the King in kinds. Collection was done by chosen persons for smaller areas. These people were very powerful and run a kind of

'*Jamindari*' (landlordism). In fact victorious Muslim rulers used to follow the same procedure. The end of Sen rule was instituted by *Md Bakhtiar Khalji* during 1202-12-3 A.D.

8.1 Agriculture in the published literatures of the time

"*Charshapad*" were composed during 1000-1200 A.D. Number of poets of different times during this period composed them. They give very deep and close pictures of Bengal and Bengali life. They do contain agriculture and not the farmers of Bengal (Sukumar Sen, 1965). They describe cleaning of cotton ('*Tulodhona*'), spinning cotton into thread and weaving. From felling of trees for wood to erect bridges ('*Sanko*'), crossing river on a boat and hunting deer. Description of giving irrigation in the literature was – "*Pant Kedual Porasnu Mange Pithat Kachhi Bandhi / Gaon Dukhalen Sinchuhu Pani na Poi Sai sandhi*". This is irrigating with swing basket ('*Sneuti*'). An example of Bengali couplet on cleaning cotton ('*Tulo Dhona*') is "*Tulo Dhuni Dhuni Aansure Aansu / Aansu Dhuni Dhuni Nirabor senu*". *Dom, Bagdi* and *Bauri*s were low ('*Aantaj*') caste, neglected untouchable in the society. But they also participated and pushed agriculture ahead. "*Logorer Bahirer Dombi Tohari Kuria, / Chai choi Jai Sebramha Naria, / Olo Dombi Tao Som Koribe Mosanga. / Nidhen Kanha Kapali Joi Lang*". *Shibayan*' of poet '*Rameswar*' ('Farmers Verse' according to Tapas Basu) describes that farm woman '*Gouri*' is advicing her husband '*Shib*' to make plow like "*Dekhbina Betana Bishaiya Bole Kali / Gach kati Goraib Langal Joyali / Khote Kore, Ghore Tare Pataibo Shal*' / *Shul Bhanji Saj Sajja Koraibo Kaal*". This is a reflection of pre-Aryan concept of agriculture in Bengal. Thereafter in thirteenth century (Pal Era), '*Ramcharit*' of *Sandhakar Nandi* describes about huge income from arecanut and coconut. Description of typical Bengali villages full of ponds, rivers, canals, bund, high and low tide in rivers, boats, pitchers, pistia, water chestnut, alga, fishermen, fishes and tools used for fishing have found place in the verses. But '*Vidyapati*', the royal poet have never mentioned village life and agriculture in his verses. The '*Mangalkabyas*' of that enriched Bengali literature composed over seventeenth to eighteenth century by large number of poets apparently appears to have neglected villages and agriculture.

But on analysis of '*Manasapuja*' part Ashutosh Bhattacharya, 1952 has stated that '*Ghot*' (*pitcher*) or '*Dhon*' (wealth) represent 'grain store' (*sashya bhandar*"). He has correctly said that the capital invested by '*Chand sadagor*' in his business and trade came from successful agriculture of the land. '*Dwija Bangsidash*' in his verse has described the large garden of '*Chandsadagar*' full of fruit trees and flowers that were planted by farm-labour. In the '*Dhanapati upakhyan*' of '*Chandimangal*' – verses were – "*Rara Majhe Saptogram Oti Onupam / chila Dui Sadhu Tahe Korila Bisram / Kinya Bachya Nana Dhon Naye Chilo Bhora / Baho Baho Bolyaghaho Naye Hoilo Twara*'. The '*Kabya*' contains exchange trade also e.g. '*Bodlashe Nanadhon Aanyachi Singhale / Ke Dilo Je Hoy Taha Shuna Kutuhole / Kuranga Bodole Turonga Pabo Narikel Bodole Samkha / Biranga Bodole Labonga Dibe Sut Bodole Tanko*" meaning a trade tour through river packing the boat with produces, Verses tell of '*Saptodinga*' and '*Madhyadinga*' and the boat-transport was preferred for being cheap. *Mukundaram's* '*Chandimongal*' states about land survey and measurements, like – "*Mape Mape Kone Dia Dora / Ponerokattay Kura / Nani Mane Projar Gohari*", '*Gomasta*' of landlord is - "*Sarkar Hoilo Kal / Khil Bhuri Likhe Lal / Bini Ubgare Khay Dhuti*". Description of dishonest and oppressor '*Khajnadarii*' (tax collector) is like – "*Potedar Hoilo Jom / Taka Aaraianikom / Pai Lovya Khay Din Proti*". '*Annadamangal*' of '*Bharatchandra*' tells about '*Kamar*' (blacksmith), '*Kumor*' (potter), '*Tanti*' (weaver) and '*Charmakar*' (shoe maker, tanner) that makes the village scene complete. Poet-singer '*Ramprasad*' composed songs for Hindu goddess – '*Kali*' or '*Tara*' that were full of prayers as also complains for sufferings of the farmers. "*Ke Bole tomake Tara Dindayamoyee / Kare Dile Dhonjon Ma, Hoy, Hosti, Rothi Jayi, / Aar Karo Bhagye Mojur Khata Shak – Anno Mele Koi. / Keha Thake Attalikay, Aamar Ichha Tenni Roi*" or "Keha Saradine *Payna Khete, Keha Sukhe Khay Sada Chini / Keha Suye Tetalate. Palanke Moshari Tani*'. All these are expression of dissatisfaction against 'Company' and landlords, who are actual oppressor of the people. Akshay Kumar Dutta, 1850 has written in '*Tatwabodhini*' journal – 'He who is protector is the destructor also. This proverb possibly targeted the landlords. Villagers feel uncomfortable even for a day when landlord is in power and position because they feel afraid of highhanded action of the landlords. Bankim Chandra has published details of these in his essays titled *'Bongodesher Krishak'*, *Desher Shribriddhi'* etc. or in the novel – *'Sitaram'*. To quote his writings like – "Bengali farmer produces very little through farming to fulfill cultivation cost, feed of cattles and debt or interest repayment to *'Mahajan'* (money lender) who otherwise confiscates the entire produce. Thus farmer's family life may go smooth or does not. These are farmers in middle ages. Rabindranath in a poetry *"Ebar Firao More"* has written (1874) like – *"Boro dukhha Boro Byatha – Sammukhete Koster Sangsar / Boroi Doridra, Shunya, Boro Kshudra, Boddho Andhakar / Anno Chai, Pran Chai, Aalo Chai, Chai Mukta Bayu / Chai Bol, Chai Sasthya Aanando Ujjal Poromayu / Sahos Bistrita Bakhapot"*. Elsewhere be stated that hapless *'Ryot'* has to be saved from 'others' control and 'own' control and made well educated, healthy and strong. He himself being a landlord could exclaim – *"Jamir Satwa Nayata Jamidarer Noy, Se Chaasir"*. He also suggested *"Palli Punargathan"* as the way out. He demonstrated this work as a model at *'Silaidaha'*, *'Patisor'* (now in Bangladesh) and *'Surul'* (Birbhum). He repeated time and again that agriculture has to progress following scientific methods. Earlier poet *'Krittibas'* in his *'Mahakabya' 'Ramayan'* has presented *'Ram'* and *'Sita'* as Bengali husband and wife and description of *'Bhagirath'* bringing down river *'Ganga'* is related to agriculture. Birth or arrival of *'Sita'* from plowed land indicated relation of agriculture with Bengali life. *"Chasbhumi Hoite Ei Konyar Janam / Tobo Kanya Bote Ei Koroha Palan"*. He has discussed drought in the kingdom as also fruit growing as expressed by *Hanuman*. *"Dilen Darimba Pakko Bidaria Sondhi. / Narikel Fol Dilo Sahastek Bandhi"* etc. *'Mahabharat* of *Kashiram* as in 17th century has not described Bengali life and society to that extent. However in *'Bonaparba'* of the epic he has described farmers in poor health and failure of rains. *"Durbol Aamar Putre Juri Langolete / Hinshakti Rugno Boro Na Pare Cholite / Mariche Krishak Boro Puchhamul More"* etc. But the kingdom of *'Judhisthir'* as described by *Kashiram* showed Bengal full of blooming crops and greens. Much later the narration of village situation by '*Saratchandra*' in his books is a degrading village and society. "*Onekeri Ek Fonta Jami Jayga nei*". The prosperity was lost due to debt against high rate of interest on loan against land, mortgage by '*Mahajon*'. In the story entitled '*Mohesh*', *Gofur Mian* lost his living hut, land and Bullocks and left for working in a '*Jutemill*'. '*Nildarpan*' of *Dinabandhu Mitra* speaks about a rich farmer who claimed – "*Aamar Mulapar Ganti, Aamar Ponero Gola Dhan, Aamar Kurikhana Langol, Kuari Jon Maindor ....*". *Tarasankar Bandyopadhyay* later successfully presented the changing village society as also the complexity of humans. '*Panchagram*' showed how *Aniruddha Kamar* and *Girish Chhutor* participated in the societal problem settlement sitting with dignity. The sitting ('*Majlish*') experienced rejection of the system of labour payment with paddy, or school teaching by a '*Sadgope-caste*' youth or silent participation of high caste Dwaraka Choudhury in the sitting excellently presented the changes in society-structure. Side by side forced unlawful harvest of standing crop or use of insulting words by one *Chhiru*, becoming wealthy recent times simultaneously presented collapse of one societal structure and growth of another. Another symbolic indication was there in the utterances – 'the land of plowmen passed into the hands of the gentlemen of the society'. Coming to Bibhutybhusan Bandyopadhya – we find '*Harihor*' of '*Pather Panchali*' who could not save his family from distress by writing 'ledger' of a shop, taking up the job of a priest or even leaving his village home to reach Benaras for fortune building. In subsequent chapters also we will pass through all these phases.

8.2 Food culture in Bengal

Interestingly Vedic Aryans also absorbed some of the rites and cultures of the pre-Aryans of Bengal. Ancient Bengalis used to take their food sitting on a mattress ('*Maadur*' made by weaving split and sun dried flower-stalk of a wetland plant (*Tagetes*) or wooden sit ('*Pinre*') specially made. The food habits of villagers was very plain and simple – fuming cooked rice on banana leaf sprinkled with '*Ghe*', fried '*Nalita*' leaves and fish preparation and the end course being milk. However along with one or two small pieces of ginger (hot chillies in East Bengal) and a pinch of salt was also there. But in case of rich and city dwellers there were so many items of food. A couple of words "*Chaushatti Banjan*" (64 courses of preparations) was well known about Bengali food.

Festivals and food

In Bengal many festivals, worships of different idols, celebration of occasions and different steps of life are recognised and remembered through different cultural rites and function – all having some relation with cooking, display of food preparations and finally consumption. Many of these are very ancient practices. Starting from a woman at advanced stage of pregnancy ("*Sadhbhokshan*", child birth, '*Aat Karai*', '*Mukhebhat*', '*Pakadekha*' (Bride selection), *Marriage* and so on and finishing with '*Sradhya*' after ones death. In the front of religious events '*Durgapuja*' begin with '*Nabapatrika*' – worship and ending with '*Visarjan*'. Similar events happen with so many worships. They say Bengalis have 33 crores of gods and goddesses. Over and above there were equal number of household religious festivals like '*Nabanna*', '*Lakshmipuja*', '*Sabebarat*', '*Paushparban*', '*Iid*', '*Holy*', '*Charak*', '*Ghentupuja*', '*Monosapuja*', '*Gajon*', '*Rathjatra*' etc.

All these are inclusive of different kinds of food preparation ('*Prasad*') and their distribution.

8.3 Fasting and food

People's lifestyle included many fasting occasions like '*Bhim Ekadash*' on 11th day of bright fortnight of '*Magha*', '*Shibaratri*' on 14th day of dark fortnight of '*Falguna*', '*Durgastami*' on eighth day of bright fortnight of '*Aswina*', etc. Women do not take fishes on the day '*Aranyshasti*' ('*Jamaishasti*') on every Tuesday in a week considering the day as '*Joymangalbar*' and all '*Hindus*' take vegetarian food on '*Sri Panchami*' or '*Saraswati Puja*'. Again on the day called '*Dashahara*' women take only 'fruits' as food while on the last day of '*Bhadra*' ('*Sankranti*') they do not take hot freshly prepared food. The day is called "*Arandhan*" (no cooking) and food prepared previous day ('*Basi*') is consumed.

Now abolished, the custom of banning some specific food on some specific day or month was followed rigidly. For instance '*Lau*' (bottle gourd) is forbidden in the month of '*Jaistha*' and '*Mula*' (raddish) is forbidden in '*Magha*'. Daywise '*Kumro*' (sweet gourd), small brinjal ('*Begun*'), '*parwal*' (pointed gourd), '*mula*' (radish), '*Bael*' (wood apple), '*Neem*' (Azadirachta), '*taal*' (palmyra palm), '*narikel' (coconut), 'Lau*' (bottlegorud), '*Kalmi shak*' (Ipomea leaves), '*Sim*' (dolichos bean), '*Puin shaak*' (Basel leaves) and '*Maash kalai*' (Kalai bean) are forbidden respectively on 1st, 2nd, 3rd, 4th, 5th, 6th, 7th, 8th, 9th, 10th, 11th, 12th and 13th day of a month. (Atul Sur, 1986). Interestingly these customs were practiced from so ancient times that it could not include potato and cauliflower-cabbage since they were for the first time brought from abroad in Bengal only 300 years back.

8.4 Foods in worships in Bengali homes

In any puja or worship occasion the idol is offered in number of trays soaked rice, banana, '*batasa*', '*sandesh*', in one uncut fruits of the season, like mango, or guava or banana, or '*bael*', or coconut with cotton, '*paite*', vermillion in another etc. called '*Barandala*'. One smaller plate carries rice powder made into dough, given a cone shape and decorated with pieces of dough given different colour of mostly plant leaves and flowers is called '*Sri*' (locally '*chhiri*'), '*Muri*', '*Khoi*', '*Nadu*', '*Chira*', are in a separate bowl. Even in some occasions cooked food like '*payas*', '*khichuri*', fried potato, brinjal etc. are offered.

In the Bengali households '*Lakshmipuja*' used to take place frequently. '*Lakshmipuja*' in the months of '*Pausha*', '*Chaitra*' and '*Bhadra*' required '*Purohit*' (proffessional worshipper) and this continued in Bengal villages till the beginning of twentieth century. People used to call this '*puja*' as '*Khandapuja*' – dictionary meaning of the word '*Khondo*' is 'crops' (*Fasaladi*). '*Lakshmipuja*' was common among primitives too (Atul Sur, 1986). This is evident from the '*Bahan*' (carrier) i.e. '*Pencha*' (owl) and "*Lakshmi's Jhampi*" (Bag) contains articles like paddy, '*Kodi*' (small white shell of a snail), '*Aaltapata*' (paper dipped in lac insect's red pigment), vermilion, '*Kajallata*' (case with black eyeliner) all suggesting the primitive origin of goddess '*Lakshmi*' (Goddess of wealth). Usually women used to worship '*Lakshmi*' every Thursday and called the date as '*Lakshmibaar*'. All these occasions were accompanied by '*Naibedya*' of different produces (mostly different categories of food like fruits rice etc.) and "*Bhog*" cooked food like '*Khichuri*' by boiling '*Atop chaal*' (rice) and '*Daal*' (pulse) with spices which finally after the '*Puja*' is over, consumed by family members and neighbours with respect. All these required offerings like different agricultural produces and food. Another such '*puja*' common in a Bengali house is "*Sashthipuja*" performed once in each month (Bengali calendar) like '*Chandani sashthi*' in '*Baishakh*', '*Arassyasashthi*' in '*Jaistha*', '*Kardamisashthi*' in '*Ashar*', '*Notonsashthi*' in '*Shravana*', '*Chaprasasthi*' in '*Bhadra*', '*Durgasashthi*' in '*Aswin*', '*Naarisasthi*' in '*Kartik*', '*Mulasashthi*' in '*Aghran*', '*Guhasashthi*' in '*Pousha*', '*Sitalashasthi*' in '*Magh*', '*Goshasthi*' in '*Falgun*', and '*Ashoksashthi* in '*Chaitra*'. Besides '*Jamaisashthi*', '*Bhaiphonta*' and '*Itupuja*' were also very popular occasions. In all these occasions the offerings include different fruits, flowers and variety of cooked foods.

This entire process and culture practised in '*Bengali*' society presents fantastic list of cooked food, fruits and other foods along with different categories of milk-based sweet-meats. Raw sugar (*Gur*) was also a component of offer in '*Pujas*' and that made from '*Poundrak*' variety of sugarcane was preferred. Some people believe that the name '*Gaur*' originated from this '*Gur*'. '*Panini* said "*Gurasya ayng desha Goura*".

Bengalis are fond of 'fish preparations' since long time and it was not rejected even during spread of '*Bauddha*' religion and '*Buddhist*' Bengalis also did not stop taking cooked fishes. It is to be remembered that Bengalis consumed cooked, spiced fish and not uncooked ones like many others.

9

Muslim and Post-Muslim Period in Bengal (1204-1553 AD)

9.1 Muslims in Bengal

As described by Kamrun Nahar (net) Bengal had only Hindus including Buddhists and Animists living in this land till 1200 AD. Ruling power was in the hands of '*brahmans*' e.g. 'Sen's. 'Turk' Bakhtiyar Khilji defeated Lakshman Sen (1204) to create a rule favouring Muslims to live in this land. Since then number of Muslims in this land started increasing. Muslims of foreign origin are recognizsable by their titles like 'Shah', 'Sayyid Khan', 'Sultan' etc. that are foreign. Descendants of 'Sufi'-saints had titles like 'Pir' and 'Faqir'. Racial origin of Bengali Muslims are of Sultanic period. In fact two groups of Muslims are in Bengal namely (i) immigrants from different Muslim countries and (ii) local converts. During Sultanic period (1200-1576) uncountable number of Muslim outcomers rushed to this Greenland mostly from Arabs, Persia, Turkey, Abisinia and Afghanistan. Generally such people were conquerors, preachers and traders. People came during the time of Bakhtiar Khilji and Ilyas from Iran, Habshis from Abisinia, Husain Shah from Arabs and Afghans later to settle mainly around 'Sonargaon', 'Satgaon' and 'Lakshanawati'. The 'wazirs' or ministers, 'amirs' or nobles and soldiers of the 'rulers' generally settled. 'Preachers' came during Bakhtiar's time like 'Baysid

Bustami' at 'Chitaganj' (874 AD), 'Sultan Md Mahiswar' (1047 AD) in Mahasthan, Bogura, Sultan Rumi in Maymansing (1053 AD) and 'Baba Adam' in Bikrampur (1158 AD). 'Traders' also started coming in Bakhtiar's time in 'Chitaganj'. Convert's are mostly both upper and lower class of 'Buddhists' and 'Animists' among 'Hindus'. 'Animists' are actually tribals like 'Koch', 'Mech' and 'Tharu'.

9.2 Agriculture in midst of religious unrests and battle

Mahommad-e-Bakhtiar in 1208 defeated Sen rulers in '*Gour*' and '*Rarh*' to occupy and rule. From the time of Bakhtiar (1204) to 1282, 20 rulers ruled over Bengal with non-stop fighting and battles for power. During this period one can not think that agriculture of the land continued and progressed smoothly. Ramesh Chandra opined that nature of infighting and rule of these '*Pathan*' rulers appeared comparable with the European lords fighting each other for power and occupation. Later (1282-1301) during 'Sultanate' in Bengal (ruled from Delhi) it was the rule of *Balbon* families and only informations about battles and fights are available (Rakhaldas Bandyopadhyay, 1914, Atul Sur, 1986).

Thereafter Bengal's independent Sultan rule was started through Fakruddin Mubarak Shah (1338-1349) followed by Danujmardan Deb (1415), Mahendradev (1418), Mahmud Shah (1435-1487), Sultan Sahajada and others (1487-1493) and Husen Shah (1493-1538)'s rule. In 1538 Mughol rule reached, Bengal and in 1576 Emperor Akbar made Bengal a separate '*Suba*'.

During Muslim rule many of the rulers were busy with religious fanaticism destroying temples and religious places and religion-transformation of people neglecting development of society and agriculture. In 1350 Ibn Batuta, during Fakruddin Mubarak Shah's time came from Egypt and visited '*Saptagram*' (Hooghly) also. From his travelogue one can gather some information about agriculture during that period. Prices of food articles or cloth were quite cheap in Bengal during those days. Side by side the main crops in Muslim period Bengal included rice, sugarcane, sesamum, cotton, and animals reared included cow, poultry and sheep. It is also to be noted that processing different agricultural produces, in addition to the ancient process of rice from paddy (hulling), oil from sesamum seeds (mechanical pressing in 'Ghani'), sugar from sugarcane juice (boiling and cleaning sugarcane juice), cloths (spinning cotton into thread and weaving (*Tant*) into cloth) and others. It means agriculture in Bengal was competent to produce and meet all requirements in daily life. But the producer farmers did never receive their dues for creating all these through their hard labour and skill. One can not ignore the fact that the practice of selling young boys and girls expressed the otherwise unhealthy condition of the society. The prevailing law of the country permitted Emperor only to collect tax but in reality rulers used to impose all out dominance on the '*Ryots*' who were compelled to depend on the pity shown to them by the rulers to become all in all for the '*ryots*'.

Sikandar Shah, the ruler of independent Bengal built the famous and majestic *Adina Masjid* in Maldah. In 1357 AD he conquered Kamrup, then known as '*Chaulistan*'. Afterwards during Saifuddin Homja Shah's rule Emperor of China sent Yung-Lo-Cheng as his representative ('*Dut*') (1405 AD) whose bilingual translator '*MaHuan*' translated in English by George Philips, whose report contained information about agriculture of Bengal in those days along with others (Rakhaldash Bandyopadhyay, 1914). According to MaHuan, this land was '*Bangla*' and its currency was '*Tong-ka*'. The atmosphere was like the warm days of China. She has listed many crops like paddy, wheat, barley, mustard, sugarcane etc. Among the fruits banana, jackfruit, mango, pomegranate, etc. were there. The land also produced coconut, Palmyrapalm and Date palm ('*Kajang*') and people used to ferment rice, coconut, and sap from Palmyra palm and Date palm into 'wine' or alcoholic drink. Details of woven cotton cloth their, at least six different qualities – all having length and breadth equal to 19 'hands' and two hands (18 inches) were there. Report shows the progress of rearing of silk insects and also production of silk-cloth in Bengal. It also stated the physicians, business persons, astrologists, painters and learned people used to live and act in the land. Export of different produces were mostly made through water-transport comprising of ships. Export items included pearls and gems too. Possibly at the beginning of this era a form of administration like '*Jamidari system*' took roots (Ramesh Chandra Dutta, 1874). Usually top of the administration never interfered in the activities of subordinates. As a result, being afraid of torture, farmers became 'daily hand to mouth community' having no courage to resist. They lived the life of 'slaves' depending on mercy of the '*lord*'. For a short period (1409-1442) '*Hindu rajas*' namely *Ganesh ('Kans')*, *Danujmardandeb* and *Mahendradev* ceased power and ruled but Nasiruddin Mahmud Shah (1442) to Jalaluddin Fateshah (1487) brought back Muslim rule. Thereafter for many reasons including incidents of torture of the subjects, killing of ruler by *Habshi* slave – all created anarchy in Bengal. Subsequently *Alauddin Hosen Shah*, becoming ruler of Bengal (1493-1519) could control the situation to some extent particularly giving low cast people protection to live with dignity. Side by side he extended his kingdom to *Assam* and *Tripura* that enlarged agricultural land and offered security to poorer section of people. All these made possible creation of some unique literature in Bengali namely '*Mansamangal*' by *Bijoy Gupta* in 1484 AD. During this period land distribution and digging of wells took place although well-digging had primary purpose of supplying drinking water. Highly educated *Biswambar*' or '*Chaitanyadev*' (1485-1533) of Nadia (Nabadwip) left teaching job and led large no. of poor disciples in chanting religious prayers while moving on roads in long human rows. Thereafter '*Sher Sah*' won the power at Delhi (1532-1553) and ruled India. During this period agriculture in Bengal did not change much. The long tradition of cultivation of variety of crops continued and fruit garden development continued in Muslim period also.

The '*pattoulis*' of this era (12th and 13th) mentioned the quantity of produces of lands and income from them. Repeated mentions were made about '*Kshetrakar*' (farmers), '*Kshetrakaran*', '*Karshakan*', '*Krishakan*' etc. The ship-dependent (river) trade from '*Saptagram*' (Hooghly) both domestic and international dealt with agricultural produces. In fact both Muslim and Hindu rulers established some kind of feudal rule in Bengal. Ruler or king used to keep one or two areas under their direct rule, leaving rest of the kingdom under control or rule of feudal landlords. The relation between the ruler and the farmers ('*ryots*') was full power in one hand and 'slave' like life for others. However few kind-hearted landlords had the farmers in their area relatively happy. In the context of agro-economy of the land very poor, farming community could see no future in the provisions for them and lost any interest in farming leading failure of agriculture to generate resources for development. Sukumar Sen, 1965 concluded that at the end of 14th century Bengal severed all control and rule of Delhi to become free. Independent Bengal again gained back its identity and atmosphere so that people could again apply their own intellect and progress in their own way.

9.3 Enrichment of Bengali food culture

Kamrun Nahar (net) feels that before 1200 AD Bengal was habitated by Hindus including '*Buddhists*' and '*Animists*' when ruling power was in the hands of Brahman Sens. After defeat of Lakshman Sen in the hands of Bakhtiyar Khilji Muslims became interested in this land. The opinion like Muslims in Bengal are only converts – is not acceptable. Some of the Muslims came from foreign lands bearing titles like Shah, Khan, Saiyad etc. settled here. Descendnts of 'Sufi saints' have titles like Pir, faqir etc. Thus racial origin of Bengal Muslims is in 'Sultanate period' and two kinds of Muslims comprise Muslim Bengalis namely (i) immigrants from different Muslim countries and local converts.

These people while living in this land mixed their traditional culture of food with local preparation methods using local food resources. During Sultanate period (1200-1576) large number of Muslim outcomers rushed to this greenland mostly from Arabs, Persians, Turks, Abysinians and Afgans. They were either conquerors or preachers or traders. All these people settled mostly around '*Sonargaon*', '*Satgaon*', '*Lakshanawati*'. Wazirs or ministers, amirs or nobles and soldiers of Sultans mostly settled.

These people obviously of different strata of Muslim culture carried with them different food culture that slowly passed into the existing Bengali food culture.

Hindu Bengali families by then developed in their own way vegetarian and non-vegetarian cuisines. Having social provisions for only vegetarian foods for widows and on many occasions for 'Brahmans' too. Hindu Bengali housewives simultaneously developed variety of fish preparations. In fact being surrounded by water bodies and rivers various species of fishes and other aquatic animals were available and 'Bengalis' developed taste for different fish preparations. While widow ladies developed excellent and exclusive veg preparations like '*Shukto*', '*Chachhari*', '*Chenchki*', '*Jhol*', '*Jhal*', '*Dalna*', '*Siddha*' or '*Bhate*', '*Bora*', '*Bori*' that are beyond anybody's imagination. And the kitchen for fish-takers had excellent non-veg preparations like – '*iilish jhal*', '*mourala jhal*', '*Chingri kalia*', '*Punti bhaja*', '*Chital-muthi*', '*Chenchra*', '*Tel-koi*' and so many others. Poorer communities developed '*Loittar makha*', '*Googlir jhol*', '*Kankrar jhal*', and so many preparations of '*Bele*', '*Gule*', '*Lata*', '*Tengra*', '*Parse*', '*Nadash*', '*Kucho chingri*', '*Katla*', '*Rui*', '*Aar*' etc. Preparation of '*dry fishes*' or '*nona fishes*' was for meeting off-season requirement. Bengali market thus had a very important section of fishes in both towns or villages in addition to the door to door sale by fishermen. Historian Rakhaldas examined relative position of Indian currency (Tong ka) and Egypt's currency ('*Rtl*'). India's one '*Rs*' was equivalent to 20 R*tl* of Egypt and 1 *Dinar* (silver coin) fetched rice of 25 Rtl cost.

Ibn Batuta 1350 in his writings recorded prices of different food articles which on conversion to price level of 1980s by historian Atul Sur, 1986 showed prices for '*1 mound* rice is 12 paisa, for 1 maund '*Ghee*' is 145 paisa, for 1 maund sugar is 145 paisa, for 1 maund '*Tiloil*' is 73 paisa, for 15 yard fine cloth is 200 paisa, for 1 milch-cow is 300 paisa, for 12 healthy poultry and for 1 sheep 25 paisa only. On the whole expenditure of a family of husband, wife and a servant on food purchase over a period of one year was only Rs.7.0 (Atul Sur, 1986).

9.4 Food in festivals of Bengal

Bengal is often called 'land of festivals' ('*baro mashe tero parban*') some examples of which are given. '*Arandhan*' (no cooking) and '*Poush Parban*' are two majors in villages. On the day previous to '*Arandhan*' varieties of innovative food items are cooked to offer invited relatives and neighbours on '*Arandhan*' day. The other famous food festival was '*Poush Parban*' when Bengali housewives show their skill and ingenuity in preparing "sweets" – mainly '*Pitha's* (rice cake) found nowhere except in Bengal. The innumerable varieties of pitha, roskora, bhajapuli, rosbora, patisapta, pulipitha, siddhapitha, saruchakli, aaskepitha, nontapitha, served with 'payash' or 'nolen gur' are excellent and unique with their taste, flavour and consistency. No food festival in the world can reach this excellence in terms of varieties, contents deliciousness, and aroma. In terms of peoples' participation, being arranged in crores of rural and some urban houses of Bengal it is also the largest one the housewives leading the occasion. Like any other food festival it does not follow any illumination, grandeur and much ado but done in a soothing homely atmosphere following the basic principle and procedure of the '*parban*'. Bengali women take scented rice grains, grinds them into powder using home-grinder ('*Shil-Nora*'), take milk of their '*Kalogai*' ('*Shyamali*') and prepare '*Khir*' ('*Khoa*') by boiling, coconut scrapped ('*Kora*') in a scrapper ('*Kurni*'), '*Khnejur Gur*' (Date palm sap boiled to thick consistency) as raw materials and with extraordinary skill and intelligence they adopt different procedures like 'steaming', boiling, frying, baking as they require over the whole day. In the evening usually they are ready to serve different 'pithas' like '*aske pitha*', '*siddha pitha*'. '*bhaja pitha*', '*saru ckhakli*', '*patisapta*', '*roser pitha*', '*rosbora*', '*pulipitha*', '*hontapitha*' along with '*payas*', '*nolen gur*' etc. and the festival is celebrated in all the families – rich or poor in their own way. On the occasions of marriage or '*paite*' (sacred thread) one uncommon fried '*nadu*' is prepared in many families mixing rice powder, sesamum seeds and '*gur*', made into balls and deep fried in mustard oil called '*Ananda Nadu*'.

10

Bengal Agriculture in Mughal Period (1556-1707 AD)

During the period of Emperor Humayun (1553) '*Gour Bango*' became a part of Mughal empire but in reality Afghan dominance ruled Bengal till in 1586 Emperor Akbar and one of his army chief Khan Jahan defeated and killed King Dayud (Atul Sur, 1986). Thereafter different initiatives were taken to control the powerful '*Jamidars*' by stopping collection of all kinds of 'taxes' and only lawful tax to be collected was declared and publicized. All these relief came from the learned surveyor of the country – '*Todarmal*' at Delhi and locally Murshidkuli Khan, Nawab of Bengal. In 1580 Bengal was brought completely under Mughol rule and *Todarmol* established direct (*Khas*) relation with '*Ryots*' abolishing all 'middle men' in between and a system of depositing 'tax' directly to the treasury of the Emperor (Ramesh Ch. Dutta) through '*Subadars and* '*Kanungos*' who started spelling out the amount of tax for a 'Ryot'. This system prevailed all over the empire. In 1701 Murshidkuli Khan transferred *Jaygirdars* to Orissa, placed '*Jamidars*' directly under '*Subedars*' and withdrew their tax-collection authority. This increased *Subedar's* collected tax. He got all land areas surveyed again, identified fallow, uncultivated land and reclaimed them to bring under cultivation. He directed tax-collectors to offer advances to poor farmers so that they can purchase bullocks with the arrangement of repaying advances through their produces. *'Jamidars'* were also granted *'Nankar'* (monthly grant). Newer taxes imposed were 'forest-tax' and 'water tax'. He used to complete tax collection by *'Chaitra'* and send to the Emperor at Delhi in gold and silver to the extent of 'Tong-ka' 1 crore 30 lakh to 1 crore 50 lakh. The whole thing was carried by buffalo-cart having 300 animal riding and 500 general forces as guards. His responsibility was to send these to Patna where responsibility was transferred to another *'Subedar'*. Alongwith different animals, Rhino skin to be used as *'Dhal'*, *'Mat'* from *'Srihatta'*, Muslin of Dacca, Silk of *Kashimbazar* and tusk of elephant (ivory) as offerings to the Emperor. But unfortunately from the last part of rule of Nawab Alibardi and Nawab Sirajddoula the *Jamidars* gained back their power and authority.

10.1 Land use order and tax system

Owner of land was King or *Badsah* in Mughol period. The tax or *'Khajna'* was considered to be fee for the service of protecting subjects and providing justice to the people. The second opinion was that owner of land is the cultivator. That the cultivator had permanent and successive right on the land was largely accepted by people (Irfan Habib, 1985). The tax system during Mughol rule was widely accepted as supported by *Abul Fazal.* Two administrative orders during the period of rule of *Akbar* and *Jahangir* worth mentioning. In *'Jamin-E-RiAaya'* staffs of royal administration were advised that they must not convert cultivators' land forcibly to their own land (*'Khud Kasta'*). Rights of cultivators were permanent (*'Maurushi'*). During that time there was huge land and small number of cultivators.

Naturally rulers used to encourage cultivation in different ways. The resource-poor people in villages like small farmers (*'Rej Riya'*) were granted *'Tokabi loan'* for helping them to purchase seeds and animals. Landless agricultural labour (*'Kshet majur'*) were usually pennyless people in villages. Some of the jobs like leather use and leather-article making or scavenging works in villages was never done by upper caste villagers. But along with *'Kshetmajurs'* cobeers participated in harvesting, carrying harvested crops etc. Dehulling paddy was done by still lower caste people in the villages called '*Dhanuk*'s. However, majority of the villagers were farmers in those days.

Besides crop production farmers used to conduct many more works jointly (Habib). Usually heads of the families discussed the works that will be performed jointly and how. Habib feels that this was actually the '*Gram Samaj*' but not exactly '*Panchayet*'. They built up a '*common fund*' from the donations of the farmers. If required against this common fund as security they took 'loans' to take up any work, like overcoming any natural calamity, raising borders of channels, buying seeds. This common fund was used to make payments to Government staff, refunding loans taken, payment of allowances to '*Modol*' and '*Patoari*', fee ('*Dasturi*') for '*Kanungo*' and '*Amin*' and entertainment for '*Chowdhuri*'s. All thse expenses were considered as "*Kharaj-e-Deha*" or expenses in village-life. Again these expenses need not necessarily exist in all the villages. Later this practice also changed. Some of the well-to-do farmers became rich and villagers slowly divided into economic classes. Society thus had '*Mokaddam*', ('*Modol*'), '*Kolanttaran*' (rich people), '*Mutagolliban*' ('influentials') etc.

Government employees included accountants ('*Patoari*'), '*Modol*' (from among farmers) and others, later being important in village-society and responsible to collect tax from villagers. For this service 2.5 per cent of his taxable land was made tax-free or he could take 2.5 per cent of the tax collected by him. But in all these exchanges the poor farmer had to pay some 'commission' or '*dasturi*'. '*Modol*' used to distribute fallow land among villagers interested in farming. They established new village also. During '*Mughol*' period, the *Samanta Chief* of a village was called '*Jamindar*' or '*Dhumi*'. '*Mughols*' actually maintained some areas under their direct control and rest under '*tax-collector's* ('*Karad-Pradhan*') control. Bengal and four more provinces like Bihar, Odissa, Berar and '*Khandesh*' were under tax-collector's control. In some occasions in place of words '*Jamindar*' and '*Jamindari*', '*Talluk*' and '*Tallukdari*' have been used. In Bengal '*Jamindars*' had to pay a fixed amount land tax every year. Emperor used to remove a '*Jamindar*' for any mistake like non-payment of tax or involvement in activities against the State or such other acts. Evidences of such punishments from Jahangir to Aurangjeb's time are there. But in Bengal larger area was covered by small estates (*'Mohal'*) having smaller number of *'Jamidars'*.

Irfan Habib, 1985 opined that farmers' life was just to fulfil the needs required for living. The quantity produced extra over that required by one farming family was usually taken by the State as land tax in kinds others being helpless. As a result farmer could not have extra income to be used for his family. As per Abul Fazal *'Sher Saha'* followed a policy of taking one-third of the average of produce determined on the basis of weather, soil fertility and the minimum standard of living. But possibly during *Mughol rule* tax collection was not done regularly. The informations gathered from *'Ain'*, *'Majhar-e-Sahajahani'*, *'Khafikhan'*, *'Khulastus Siak'* etc. by historians suggest that tax collection depended on time, state, and area and varied between half to 1/3rd or th of tax determined. During that time share cropping did not exist in Bengal and survey for measurement of land was also skipped often. The tax that *Jamidars* imposed on farmers was not steady and increased whimsically. Sometimes tax calculation was based upon number of yokes of the farm family. *'Nasak'* was a method that depended on average of last ten years' tax and the paper records of the area. Abul Fazal stated that Bengal farmers are regular in tax payment i.e. *'Kheraji'*. They used to pay tax in *'Taka'* or *'Mohor'* in installments for eight months. Tax collection in Bengal was done indirectly through *Jamidars*. During the last part of Aurangjeb's rule Deputy Chief of Province (*'Nayeb-Najim'*) was employed. Murshid Kuli Khan, the *'Subadar'* made a comprehensive reform of the tax-system and surveyed all lands (cultivated and fallow) of the village. The tax determined through *'Nasak'* system remained unchanged for long time. In addition to land, animal folk and fruit gardens were also taxed. *'Jahangir'* however excused tax on fruit orchards. For two instances namely 'famine' and 'development work of agriculture' – tax relief was allowed. But development of agriculture in those days meant increasing cultivated area and emphasis on cultivation of commercial crops (Emperor Akbar's period). For repair of 'well' tax was reduced. Besides the farmers having no money, seeds or bullocks and in distress were granted '*Takabi*' loan, with assurance of long-term recovery. Royal staff were asked to organise works like digging wells and erecting bunds. Excavation of large canals and smaller channels during '*Sahajahan's* rule improved irrigation facilities. But the use of agricultural implements was in primitive stage. There was no iron-blade on the 'share' of the yoke since iron was very rarely available. As a result only soft land was plowable with wooden share. Fishes were composted into manure and used. In some areas or pockets as many as three crops were grown in the year on the same land following a planned rotation of crops. Besides rains dug-wells, ponds, and canals were used for meeting the irrigation requirement of the crops. Southern plains had large number of rivers and canals, often dried up and refilled during rains and floods, to be used for irrigation.

Paddy was the main crop in Bengal, adjoining areas and states. But by then wheat was also cultivated in Bengal. But Barley was not common and good ("*Ain*"). Cotton was also a major crop particularly in Dhaka and Maymansingh (now in Bangladesh) the quality of cotton was excellent. Sugarcane grown in vast area was a major crop. The quantity of sugar produced in Bengal and its quality was notable. The main fibre crop of Bengal was jute but areawise flax was number one fibre-crop of Bengal. Indigo was common in Agra, Aligarh (north India) area but not in Bengal possibly since Infan Habib described "Dhayana-Doab-Neoat", "Sarkhej" and "Sehayan" as indigo cultivated land. Opium and '*Bhang*' were also cultivated, but area of such crops declined during Mughol period and '*Aurangjeb*' ordered compelete banning of cultivation of these crops. Among the spices '*Morich*' (chilli) was most important for it being produced in large quantities. But this did not include staff (large) chilli and red chilli. Betel was cultivated for long time. To meet the demands in cities vegetables were cultivated extensively. Cultivators doing this were called '*Mali*' (gardner). Cultivation of potatoes and sweet potatoes was started during this period. Mango and coconut were already in cultivation and Portuguese people brought pineapple from America in 16th century (Habib). Similarly cashewnut and papaya also reached Bengal but have not spread all over the country so quickly. Guava has come to this land later. Earlier making of grafts of plants was forbidden in the country. This ban was lifted during *Sahajahan*'s time. This unreasonable prejudice opposing spread of cultivation of mango and mandarine orange was removed by the Emperor's order and boosted horticulture development. Dutches came to *Chuchura* in business interest and their activities there for 200 years taught Bengalis to develop fewer garden in front of living house. During this period rearing of silk insects and producing silk was quite big industry and 'Kashim bazar' was the main export centre. 'Lac' production was also in an advanced stage. Use of cattles and other draft animals (goats and pigs) started earlier than 17th century. There were pastures and grazing lands even in the intensively cultivated areas of Bengal. According to *Abul Fazal* four bullocks per each plow and two cows and one buffalo were allowed tax-free. Production of huge quantity of butter in Bengal helped develop the food habit of taking steaming rice and butter with a pinch of salt. Since there was no dearth of fuel wood, most of the cowdung was possibly used as manure for crops etc.

Farm women used to convert paddy to rice in a 'striker' ('*Dhenki*') (*Dhenkighastet*), found in the house of almost each farm family. Stone grinder (*Janta*) was used to grind wheat, rice and pulses to be used in different food preparation, only for home-consumption. A different class of family called '*Teli*' or '*kolu*' who had another kind of wooden grinder of oilseeds to extract and produce oil, oil-cake being a by-product. This was used as animal feed as also manure for crops. Sugarcane after peeling was placed between two wooden roller, rolled manually to extract juice, and the juice was boiled in a metal shallow-pan to produce '*Gur*' (indigenous sugar). Use of '*Gur*' in food preparation and food taking was extensive in Bengal. For preparation of indigo blocks leaves and succulant branches of indigo plant was retted in water in a stable container ('*Choubachha*') to extract blue pigment. This was the beginning of indigo preparation.

Marketing : Both water and land transport were in vogue for transport of agricultural produces. Land transport was primarily effected through large armed contractor groups called '*Banjara*' who carried on the back of the bulls food grains, sugar, butter, salt etc. to any destination. They used to move with family, halt in tents on way and cook their food. Since the grazing land required for their bulls were scarce in dry summer, this form of transport did not operate in summer. In fact river transport was cheaper. Using 300-500 ton ships ('*Bojra*'), this transport system was through rivers '*Ganga*' and '*Jamuna*'. In larger city ports. State used to charge 2.5 per cent tax which Aurangjeb made 5 per cent for Hindus only. However during recession and distress this tax collection was withheld. There was system of 'loan', granted for such purposes. Commodities in Bengal were usually cheaper and food items were produced surplus for such marketing programme. For example, during 1650-1659 and in 1983 sugar price was within Rs 4-5 per maund (Habib). Wax, black pepper, rice, butter, oil and wheat were available at half the price in other places in Hooghly and other areas of Bengal. Rice and silk were sent from Bengal to Patna, Gujarat, Agra, Delhi, Lahore, Ahmedabad, Dhaka and other places. The demand was mainly from 120 large and 3,200 small cities in the country during Akbar's rule, some of them being in Bengal. Monopoly and large scale ('*paikari*') business was there even though they were not permitted. But 'indigo-business' in large scale was approved (in 1633) and sponsored too. Although the permit was for three years, it was abandoned in Bengal after two years for massive movement against the owners or marketers of 'indigo'. Poor farmers wore only a small piece of cloth (*Longuta*'). Generally men used a small '*Dhuti*' and women only a '*saari*'. Huts for dwelling were small and made of mud with straw-roofing on bamboo structure.

10.2 Farmers' life and food

Paddy was the main crop and as a result rice was the staple food of Bengalis. Bengalis used to take some cooked vegetables alongwith. Fish preparations were 'must' in Bengali cuisine. '*Ghee*' (burnt butter) production in Bengal was common to all houses and they consumed '*Bhat*' (cooked rice) with '*ghee*'. '*Gur*' was used to make the last sweet dish often with milk or curd (*Doi*). Salt in those days was difficult to procure and poorer people used the 'ash' (contained some salt) from burning the pseudostem of banana plant. Use of black pepper or chilli was not widespread but use of cumin, coriander and ginger was common.

Bengalis were fond of fruits and besides common fruits they liked many wild fruits too. '*Tari*' or '*Tody*' was a common drink and smoking tobacco was widespread, possibly to overcome the ill effect of humid climate. But the poors were in great distress and starvation was common among them (Comment from a Dutch tourist during Jahangir's rule).

Usually burnt earthen utensils were used for cooking and storage of different articles. Just before the beginning of *Mughol* period there was a famine in the country (1554-55 and 1555-1556) mainly in North West India. Gujarat faced series of famines while Bengal and Bihar did not. During the rule of Akbar, Jahangir, Shajahan and Aurangazeb food crises, famine and massive human deaths occurred, Bengal remaining unaffected (Habib). Again heavy rains during 1644-45 and 1848 destroyed sugarcane standing in the field but there is no record on any incident of food crisis in Bengal. Mughol emperors opened 'Langarkhana's in large cities '*Langarkhanas*' (free cooked food distribution centre) were not in villager and villagers received no such help and many died due to no food intake. However root-cause of any such sad incident resulted from failure of crop production. Such affected villagers usually did not flee to cities to get food but they started eating non-food plants etc. and often could not survive. During 1741 to 1751 large number of horse-mount dacoits ('*Borgi*') came to Bengal from Maharashtra, forcibly collected '*Choutha*' (tax), tortured villagers that terrified farm-families and were later controlled by Alibordi Khan.

10.3 Mughol food and other culture in Bengal

Mughols ruled Bengal for more than 150 years from 1556 to 1707 and influenced Bengali cuisines too. It is said that Bengali cuisine perhaps is the only one in Indian continent that still holds its authenticity over 100 years though this region was once ruled by Mughals or later by Britishers. Much earlier Tipu Sultan was exiled from Mysore. For 500 years Muslim rule in Bengal centered in Dhaka, Murshid Kuli Jafar Khan, first Nawab of Bengal under Mughols (1717) and he shifted his capital from Dhaka to Murshidabad. Dhaka evolved a vibrant cuisine under influence of Mughalai cuisine characterised by rich sauces and generous use of meat especially beef. This food tradition continued in courts of Nawabs of Bengal or puppet rulers from 1757 till 1880. Courts, manners, and even maintaining cuisine by the puppet rulers depended on doles from English rulers. Another key influence came later from Wazid Ali Shah, the last Nawab of Awadh exiled to Metiaburz, Calcutta in 1856. Nawab brought with him hundreds of '*Bewarchis*; (cooks) '*Khansamas*' (stewards) and '*masalchis*' (spice-mixers) who were skilled to use Jafran or saffron and mace. On his death, these specialists dissipated into population, started restaurants and food courts all over Bengal propagating a distinctly *Awadhi* legacy and preference of mutton to beef spread. Along with liberal use of '*attar*' or aromatics (rose or kewra) creeped in culture of rich people. Calcutta became refuge for such Nawabs and imbibed their food culture. Influences of Christianity came to Bengal hundred years after it reached western India. Bengal's culinary habit was little influenced. But influence of western immigrants like Baghdadi Jews was evident in establishment of Jewish bakeries in Calcutta.

Influence on food was top-down and more gradual resulting in development of unique cuisine and this happened at all levels of society and some such preparations are '*Biriyani*', '*Korma*', and '*Bhuna*'. Wide range of cooking and special way of marinating meats found place. In Bangladesh, it has become staple food and specialities all over Bengal include '*chap*' (ribs slow cooked on '*tawa*'), '*rezala*' (meat in thin 'yugort' and cardamom gravy) and the famous 'kathi roll' (kebabs in a wrap). Influence include extensive use of 'ghee'. Mughol influence was most distinct in preparations involving mutton. Even chicken and other meats were prevalent. Influence was on 'desserts' through increased use of milk, cream, sugar, cardamom and saffron.

10.4 Food culture from abroad

Different people like Dutchs, Portuguese, French from Europe and Chinese came to India – Bengal for different purposes and lived for long periods around Calcutta. Such people being in Bengal exuded their culture and habits including food culture that was imbibed by Bengalis around.

A. *Portuguese food culture in Bengal*

Portugese started coming to Calcutta since 1530 to purchase birds and leopards. They built a port in Hugli in 1580 (permitted by Emperor Akbar) for smooth trade and business through '*Satgaon's* Chittaganj, in the land. These trading posts dealt with spices and cloth particularly the famous 'muslin' cloth of Dhaka. The main trade passage through river Saraswati, which however started drying up. In those days Portuguese people were making sweet-meats and pickles from mango, orange, lemon and ginger (1670). Some of them who settled in and around Calcutta were commonly consuming boiled potatoes, tomatoes and cucumber. They prepared dishes of Mackerel fish and very often used coriander leaves with lime juice. By that time the new outlet to sea was 'Tolly's Nala' and 'Adiganga' through which ships came to Garden Reach. During 1670 there were 20,000 Portuguese in Bengal and they were behind building of a cathedral (Armenian-Brabourn Road) with figures of Madona and child. On the western bank of river Ganga 'Betor' in Howrah was also prosperous being a business post. On the east bank four 'Basak' and one 'Seth' families that settled first had '*Gobinda*' – the family-deity of both the families and the village town was Gobindapur. Some of Portuguese surnames found in Calcutta are Cruz, Dias, Pereira, Fernandes, Gonzalves, Rodrigues, DaSilva, Correa etc. Possible '*Ginger restaurant*' in Russel St is a Portuguese contribution. They used to boil '*Gur*' or sugar in water, poured thick sugary liquid '*Chhanch*' (mould) to prepare sweets in the shape of a church ('*Moth*)/ temple in Christmas and became popular in 'Holi' (Dol) festival in Bengal.

B. *Food culture of Dutch in Bengal*

(a) Dutch businessmen came to India in 1605 and continued upto 1825. They reached Bengal in 17th century (1653) and tried to settle at Chinsurah ('*Chunchura*') on the eastern bank of river

'*Ganga*' in Hooghly district. Before English people came and ousted them from Chinsurah in 1884 very little of their culture, particularly food culture was imbibed by local people. The Dutch were fond of bread and herring (eaten raw). Potato started occupying greater space in Bengali cuisine, although unlike the happening in Nederland (replacing wheat, potato became staple in 1800), potatoes could not knock out rice from its staple position. But with time potatoes introduced gained popularity in Bengal during 18th century oysters and shrimps, were in the food list of Dutch and different kinds of shrimps were already in the Bengali food list, preparations being spicy. Dried sausages like '*Gromingen*' or smoked sausage like '*Rookworst*', favourite of Dutchs could not make entry in Bengali food habit. Not much of cooking and spice use was in the Dutch food culture. As a result Bengalis accepted some of their foods after modifying them using oil and spices in addition to lots of boiling, frying in oil etc. Beverages like beer could not make any headway in Bengali life excepting the '*Advocate*' a rich creamy liquor made with eggs, sugar and brandy, that crept in some rich Bengali families with modification. Dutchs were fond of cheese produced from Goat milk. Goats of different breed (black Bengal) were already in the Bengali families but goat milk was favoured for weak, suffering persons as well as babies. Both cow milk and meat were consumed by Dutchs while Bengalis' favourite was cow milk and meat from Black Bengal he goat ('*Pantha*') was long and only cherished meat in a Bengali family. Inspite of goat remaining an important animal in Bengal, the Dutch culture of cheese production from goat milk is not found in Bengal. Many of the winter vegetables like cabbages, cauliflower, beet, carrot, spinch etc. started entering Bengal through Europeans although they are often called as English vegetables. Bengalis were not much used to fruits like apple, pears, cherries and plums as Dutchs liked. Overcoming their habit of taking juicy fruits like mango, jackfruit, '*Bael*', '*Kalojam*', these fruits of Europeans tastes dry and not much available.

C. Food culture of French in Bengal

(b) In the same Hooghly district on the east bank of river 'Ganga' is another town '*Chandannagar*', known initially as

'*Farasdanga*'. In 1673 some French people established a French colony and obtained permission from Ibrahim Khan, Nawab of Bengal to establish a trading port there. This led to settlement of many French business family who finally obtained permission of Emperor Aurangjeb, Delhi for establishing a permanent French settlement. In 1730, Joseph Francois Duplaix came to Chandannagar as Governor of the city. By then 2000 brick houses were erected and French were busy in maritime trade. Chandannagar became for sometime the main centre of European commerce in Bengal. In Europe, France-Britain war started and British in India conquered Chandannagar and the city came under British rule. In 1763 it was restored to French rule to be liberated after India became independent in 1947, Chandannagar also became independent in 1947. French had a colony at Pondicherry also and both the places were led by a Governor General post placed at Pondicherry and French rule continued till it was liberated and merged with Indian Union in West Bengal (1950). This town since 1990 turned into a town – as a Calcutta suburb or little more. Regarding French food culture and its any impression or influence on Bengali food culture, there developed only a few Bengali restaurant in Chandannagar to serve French food and bakery products and some foods with French influence. However the '*Steak kabab*', '*Shapherd's pie*' or *Duck-a-b'-orange* etc. are true to French culture at Brown Sahib's, Delhi than at Chandannagar restaurant. But some traces of roasted duck in orange juice and preparations with minced meat, potatoes, flour and egg continued to be available in restaurant of Chandannagar. But the influence possibly had no direct entry in Bengali household.

The period from 1759-1954 was the period of French activity in India through French East India Company.

D. Chinese culture and food in Calcutta

Chinese arrived in Calcutta later in British period. Some Chinese possibly came much earlier to Calcutta as nomad persons with business purposes, as peripatetic monks or scholars and curious travelers but the first Chinese settler in Calcutta was young Atchew in 1780 when Warren Hastings was the ruler. He tried to set up one sugar mill but due to paucity of fund and inadequate skilled labour he could not succeed, but his Chinese associates and workmen settled in Calcutta. Originally they settled in a village *Achhipur* in south of Calcutta possibly in 18th century, later moving to the city and settled in Tangra. Some sailors from Chinese ship deserted from their service. Being close to this state new faces arrived from China in every decade and Chinese community in or around Calcutta linked its cultural link with their motherland China's ethnic integrity, cultural characteristics and social paradigm in the field of their business here. During revolution also some people migrated to Calcutta making a 20,000 strong Chinese population here. The settlers include Hakkas of tannery and shoe business, Cantonese of carpentry or restaurant business, Hupey's specialised in dentistry, and Sanghai group in laundry business together making a little China in Calcutta i.e. China town.

Food culture as expressed in food market of China town providing delicious cuisine made by Chinese cook and appreciated by citizens of Calcutta. By 19th century Chinese are established as industrious, skilled, and clean people. As a part of their culture they created traditional temples, dragon architecture and festoons in Chinese. But their real skill was in generating the excellent aroma of the food dishes, their varieties and nutritious quality. Their settlements in Central Calcutta (China town), east Calcutta (Tangra) and few others are peaceful and decent. Besides leather industry they have ventured in carpentry, dentistry, hair dressing, pharmacentric job, restaurant and food making. They publish two Chinese dailies (from Calcutta). They celebrate festivals with gaity during Chinese New Year in February and prepare their favourite food like rice pudding, whole pig (*'sanchu'*) and others along with ceremonial red candles, jass sticks etc. and other accompaniment of festivities. It is clear that Chinese food culture though difficult to be repeated but its impression on Bengali culture is felt. Among the beverages tea has been most popular in both Chinese and Bengalis growing independent of each other over a long period of time.

One of the major ingredient of foods is *'Gur'* or sugar. Sugar was prepared first in China suggesting that since it initially came from China during Mughol rule it was named '*Chini*' (sugar) in Bengali. However preparation and use of '*Gur*' (country sugar) and growing sugarcane was in Bengal from ancient times. The dominance of sweetness (*misti*) and spicy heat ('*Jhal*') are two major characters of Bengali food. Chinese-origin people of Kolkata form a substantial and successful community with a distinct identity. With this came Chinese food now in almost all street corners in Kolkata, thanks to the taste and quick cooking procedure and no similarity with original Chinese receipe other than the use of soy sauce. Mostly Cantonese tradesmen and sailors are those who first settled. Monosodium glutamate (taste maker) came with sweet corn, much later and got infused into what is widely popular as "*Kolkata Chinese*" or Indian Chinese. Mashrooms not used here. Greater use of pork is one character. Chinese opened restaurants for Bengalis, spiced up bland Cantonese sauces with slice of chillis and hot sauces, creating unique dishes e.g. *Chicken sweet corn soup, Chilli chicken* and *Manchurian* (names given by them).

Unique *secretic* cousine are known in India and Bangladesh as '*Chinese Food*', Bengali migrants carrying this abroad like USA and UK.

Indian Chinese food was given a second boost when large number of *Tibetans* migrated to India following 14th Dalai Lama's flight. *Tibetans* brought their own delicacies to add to this genre e.g. very popular *Momo* (a kind of dumpling) or *thukpa* (hearty noodle soup). Tibetans and some Nepalis entered kitchen as 'Chinese cooks' in innumerable eateries all over. '*Chopsucy*' became another favourite making Chinese chopsucy very popular. East Bengal, now Bangladesh hosts a large number of Chinese restaurants called '*Chinese Khaowa*'. With greater usage of chilli, soysauce, lemon, peanut and Bengal spices these restaurants evolved from Cantonese roots. Similarly many restaurants in Chattogram (Bangladesh) has Mayanmarese influence.

11

Bengal Agriculture During English Rule (1757-1946 AD)

11.1 Bengali villages in Nineteenth Century

Mughol rule over whole Indian sub-continent turned weak during 17th century. Regional forces gathered strength and utilising the weakness of the ruler in Delhi, many of them revolted and were successful in ceasing power to rule their region or state. Side by side the foreigners who came to India in disguise of business and trade activities also got involved. In such conspiracious activities English were in front line. In the last decade of 17th century (1690-1698) English traders joined hands to form East India Company with its headquarters at Kolkata. They started purchasing *'Jamidaris'*. During that period Murshidkuli Khan, Alibardi Khan and Sirajudoulla (1717-1757) were provincial rulers of Bengal (Atul Sur, 1986). Thereafter utilising the family feuds of the Nawabs, lust for power of Chief of army, treachery of some influentials, *Robert Clive,* the chief of the company arranged to kill *Nawab Sirajoudoulla* and made *Mirzaafar* the proxy-ruler in 1757 to cease power. In the field of agriculture through stabilising personal property right on land etc. *'landlordism'* or *'feudalism'* was established. The foundation of agriculture-dependant India was strongly rooted in land

(Uliyanovski, R. 1985; Beng. Prabir Basu). The defacto English rulers of India started to exploit India in different ways since 1757. As an example, the tax collected from Bengal in 1748 and 1757 was Rs 14,245.0 and Rs 14,704.0 only but that became Rs 28,181.0 in 1777 under English rule. English rulers collected a sum upto Rs 4 crore. Gradually India came under direct administration of English rulers that was made settled through appointment of Warren Hastings as Governor General in 1773. Tax collection from farmers continued vigorously that generated extreme discontent among farmers. Farmers' revolts of different composition and forms namely '*Chuar*', '*Sandip*', '*Sannasi*' etc. came in a row one after other. From '*food crisis*' in different corners of the state ultimately it led to famine as was '*Chhiattarer Mannantar*' of Bengal during 1769-70. Revolt spread to Tripura, Kharui, Chakma etc. In the midst of all these there was indisciplined administration and torture on the farmers that are pathetically poor. One third of Bengal's population died in the famine, but collection of tax continued and even increased with time. Revenue collection accumulated Rs 1.5 cr. in 1768 and Rs 1.57 cr. in 1771. Increase of land tax continuing for generations made heirs of landlords penniless. The land tax system never reached a steady state in any of '*Eksaali*', '*Panchsaali*' or '*Doshsaali*' system. After EI company was closed down British Government sent Lord Canning, Lord Lawrence and Lord Ripon in order as Governor General of India. Judiciary was so long under the control of landlords. Now English rulers ceased that power and started running judiciary themselves and established a relatively impartial judiciary that earned confidence of people and even in the contest between landlord and 'Ryot' also found a justified decision. Very specific orders were issued regarding the amount of tax to be collected from '*Ryot*' and if excess is collected, that has to be returned with penalty. Taking productivity in the current year as the base, the tax for next year be collected.

Following these developments when Lord Cornwallis, the next Governor General one enactment during his rules, promulgated in 1793 that gave landlords permanent settlement of the land that was under their respective control. As a result the system of tax-collection through '*Kanungos*, as was introduced by Hastings was then abolished. Ramesh Ch. Dutta's comments on this issue was an assessment of the effects of such measures helped to understand the situation at that time. He said that this enactment and follow up action created upheavel of a kind that has never occurred anywhere in the world. This actually allowed the landlords to go into any kind of contract with the farmers according to their sweet-will and exploitation reached peak. Farmers virtually lost their right to cultivate the land or grow crops as per their need. This Act however stated that people of all communities, caste and creed shall have right to cultivate and grow crops and the measures to be taken to prevent torture of farmers. Eighty years after implementation of permanent settlement act, Ramesh Chandra reviewed the position of Bengal farmers and found that lakhs of farmers had to bear with torture by landlords and suffered inhuman conditions. In 1859, Lord Canning made some amendments so that the farmers whose previous generations were owner of the land concerned will enjoy tax-free ownership of the land and those who are controlling the land and cultivating, shall enjoy less tax burden. Those who are cultivating for less than 12 years shall continue to be under landlords. Landlords used to deposit 9/10th of the collected tax to English rulers. Landlords were authorised to sale the land or evict one farmer from the land to settle another in his place. In addition landlords used to occupy and use forest land lying unused. Landlords however engaged '*Nayeb*' and '*Gomosta*' to do on their behalf all these jobs. Akshay Kumar Dutta in his '*Tattabodhini Patrika*' published all these affairs and called such landlords as – "*Rakshak I Vakshak*". Many Bengali literature in their stories, fictions, narrations expressed all these incidents and practices e.g. '*Jogajog*' of Rabindranath, '*Dena Paona*' of Saratchandra, and '*Krishna Kanter Will*' of Bankimchandra. Characters like Nikhilesh in '*Ghore Baire*' or Dwaraka Chowdhury in '*Gana Debata*' has spoken out. British rulers in 1828 issued a 'decree' to bring under their control all unused pastures, grazing land as state property. Landlords followed the Government to occupy all uncultivated land in their area. This act led to all investment (this capital earned in unfair manner) was used in '*Mahajani*' business (releasing as loan to earn interest) and this class of money-lenders became powerful friends of British rulers. '*Mahajan*' used to occupy land of farmers who failed to repay loans but he never invested in agriculture. As a result agricultural production in Bengal was also unsatisfactory. Moreover many of the irrigation projects became non-functional during British rule. Decline in agriculture production resulted in food shortage and famine leading to death of six crore people. Even after a long time rule (British) only 16 per cent of land was irrigated with water from rivers, tanks and dugwells leaving rest 84 per cent area rainfed. Farmers having no options put their land mortgaged or crops (paddy, jute) surrendered to money-lenders at ususl 10-37.5 per cent rate of interest and sometimes even 300 per cent interest particularly in east and north Bengal.

Ramesh Chandra Dutta, 1874 has given details of villages and agriculture in Bengal. Low huts in shade covered villages are reached through walk-way under the thick leaves of green trees passing by the side of bamboo grove and the "*ails*" of paddy fields. A ryot has one small piece of land as only asset. He plows the land number of times, does weeding in field and when the crop matures he spends nights in the field to protect the crops. During sowing and harvesting he is in field for the whole day, wife carrying food to field. In the early morning he consumes '*panta bhat*' (rice cooked previous night and stored under water), proceeds to crop field and works hard (untiringly) to hard noon. His mother or wife or daughter carries food to field that he eats and then take short rest on the '*gamchha*' (piece of cloth) laid under shade. He again works upto dusk and reaches home in the evening tired. He gets a part wash and consumes fuming rice (*bhat*) with a mixed curry of different leaves etc. Those days Hindus and Muslims in villages lived in separate settlements called '*Hindupara*' and '*Muslimpara*'. '*Malopara*' i.e. settlement of fishermen ('*Jele*') and 'boatmen' ('*Majhi*') used to live beside. They spent their days in fishing etc. and helped people to cross rivers on boat. Fishermen in groups start fishing early in the morning. They used to pay water-tax to *Jamidars* (landlords). On one side of the village lived '*Domes*' (deadbody manager) '*Muchi*' (cobblers) and '*Hari*' (cleaner). They rear bore, weave and sale those things. The landlord's staff namely '*Gomosta*'. *Paik-Peyada* (forces) played role in this system. '*Mahajan*' (money lender) offered loan (for all needs) to villagers and *entire* produce (paddy) of farmer is stored in '*Mahajan*'s store ('*Gola*') and '*Mahajan*' offers the quantity of paddy required for their food ('*Khoraki dhan*') as loan, pays daily wages to farm-labour, loans for marriages etc. Almost everyone in the village is under his control which he gets back after harvest. '*Patoars*' were also dignified people in the villages. Blacksmiths, and carpenters also played very important role in villages. '*Choukidar*' (security personnel) acted as guard of the village and protected the village whole night following traditional method of giving loud calls ('*Hank*') and walking with a *lathi* in hand round the village. Finally farm labours of the village conducts all operations for cultivation on other's land against which received their only money for running the family. They transplant rice, harvest crop and after all steps they store the produce in farmer's store ('*Gola*'), even go out of village or state to harvest crop, earn wage and use that money for feeding family members since 'money-lender' does not offer loan to them. Hut of the '*Ryot*' is twin huts on a upland, the riches have two more huts. Alongwith this they have one cowshed, with a '*Dhenki*' (grinding device) on one side. Beddings in the hut are mat and wooden cot in affluent house. In the kitchen some utensils of brass-made and '*Kolai*' (enamel) articles. Poorer families had burnt earthen utensils. One plow, one country-cap ('*Toka*'), '*Kolke*' (smoking device) etc. In one earthen container, the valuables are kept in a cloth-packing ('*Puntuli*'). *Ryot's* wife, as her dress use a '*saari*' (a long, cloth with designs and colours on it) cover herself winding around with on end-part on her head (*Ghomta*) with long hairs. She is the home manager cooking and serving food, cleaning utensils, de-husking paddy grains, sweeping their rooms and courtyard, carrying drinking water from ponds, caring her children as also domestic animals in the house. In time of need she goes out for transplanting rice or carrying harvested paddy on her head etc. Farmer wears a short piece of cloth (white) reaching only his knee from waist, carrying another piece of cloth ('*Gamchha*') on his shoulder if however he can afford. He uses a country hat ('*Toka*') during monsoon and summer to protect his head from rains and sun rays. Affluent farmers had plow, yoke, bullock, cow etc. while poor for all these depended on others.

11.2 Farmers' uprisings in 19th century

Bengal farmers had extreme patience during the long Muslim rule followed by 100 years of British period without challenging the misrule. They were so tolerant and hard-working that their hard and sorry life did not lodge any protest or movement. Even there was fighting on religious ground but they never revolted. All this patience burst into Indigo-revolution of Bengal (mainly in Nadia and Pabna districts) in 1854.

The farmers' movement in '*Pabna*' (now Bangladesh) raised a call for stopping tax-payment. During those days the cloth industry in England developed a strong demand for 'Indigo' (blue pigment) and some rogue English tried forcibly on Indian farmers to grow and process Indigo in place of food crops. After harvest of aerial parts of Indigo plants they forced the farmers to chop and ret them in cement vat ('*Choubachha*') and finally get blue pieces (blocs) to be sent to England. British Government on the other hand made provision in Sec. 10 of concerned law of 1859 and criminal law that '*ryots*' have some rights to speak against landlords (Ramesh Chandra). Ramesh Chandra has called this awareness of farmers to protest against landlords or English '*Nilkar*'s as '*Naba-Jagaran*' (new uprising). In Muslim period some of issues received judgement through '*Kaji*' (Judge) deciding on the strength of '*Shariyat*' and there were '*Panchayet* system of judgement managed by some dignified personalities of the village. Judiciary built by British rulers were often under influence of '*white*' people. There were other influences even from the landlords. In 1800 AD, Biswanath Sardar (farmers' Robin Hood) organised farmers against '*Nil Kuthiyal*' Samuel Fredi and English influence compelled the judiciary to 'hang' Biswanath. Dinabandhu Mitra composed a drama "*Nil darpan*", English translation of which shaken the civilised world and British Government was compelled to launch "*Nil Enquiry Commission*". Nisarat Ali or '*Titumeer*' was leading farmers' struggle against *Jamidar-Mahajan's* of Barasat and built '*Bansher Kella*' (bamboo fort) in the battle. He died and 800 farmers were put behind the bar. In 1855 *'Sidho and Kanho'*, two brave young men of *'Bhagnadihi'* village of Saontal Pargana organised poor *saontal* farmers against British Government that spread all over eastern India and gave rise to a revolt. This was against the move of English rulers in combine with landlord and moneylender class to evict *'saontal's* from the land they cleared from jungle for growing crops. This movement spread like fire through Birbhum, Bankura, Medinipur, Bardhaman, Puruliya to Hazaribag, Bhagalpur, Singbhum and Munger of Bihar and Mayurbhanj of Odissa. *Saontals'* had only bamboo-stick and bow and arrow to fight against firearms of the British police *'Sidho'* was killed in the battle field and *'Kanho'* was hanged to death. English rulers then created district *'Saontal Parganas'* prohibiting *Jamidars* and *Mahajans* to live there, but they did not reduce their tax rate. In 1873, there was a farmers' movement in 'Pabna district' (now Bangladesh) which turned violent. In the same year farmers of *'Bagura'*, *'Dhaca'* and *'Bakhargaunge'* districts declared revolt against British rule. At this stage the farmers of Bengal realised that the English rule in collution with *Jamidars* and *'Mahajons'* unless removed, their condition is not going to improve. Slowly these farmers' movements were turning into struggle for partial or full independence (*'Angshik* and *Purna Swaraj'*). Battered, deprived and neglected farmers went to form *'Bangiyo Krishak Sava'* in 1937. Starting from 1938 farmers' struggle gradually turned into 'farmers' revolt' in Bengal in the last part of the year 1946.

11.3 Farmer's movement : *'Tebhaga'*

Under the leadership of *'Bongiyo Krishak Sava'*, farmers of *'Sundarban'* area mainly of South 24-Pargana's *'Kakdwip'*, *'Sonarpur'*, *'Bhangor'* and *'Canning'*, *'Te Bhjaga'* movement was the face of farmers' revolt. Farmers' main demand was *'three-fourth'* of the produce from the share cropped land should come to the *'Bargadar'* (share-cropper). Along with they demanded abolishing of *'Jamidari'* system and *'Bargadar'* has to be awarded *'Dakhalisatta'* (right on the land). This movement spread over 19 districts of Bengal from 1938 to 1946. The movement was particularly extensive in districts like Dinajpur, Rangpur, Jalpaiguri, Khulna, Jashore, 24-Parganas and Medinipur. The '*tanka*' movement started simultaneously in Mymansing by tribals (Asitava Dash, 1998). To examine the state of agriculture and farmers of Bengal from analysis of 1921 and 1931 census data, number of *ryot's* came down from 92 lakh to 60 lakh and number of share croppers and farm labour increased from 18 lakh to 27 lakh. The increase of non-agricultural job seekers was from 4.0 lakh to 6.5 lakh. This process of increase in landless people in Bengal is continuing and alarming. Census, 1951 showed that in 1946-47, 71 per cent of people are landless. This state was a great problem for village life and agriculture of Bengal that ultimately appeared as a negative development for State's economy.

In 1939 due to start of Second World War, England was under great pressure. In the midst of this situation 'Quit India' movement started in 1942. This movement was spread in villages against English rule by the Communist Party and its Farmers' organisation. In south of 24-Parganas oppression by landlords and moneylenders dragged villagers to slavery and started buying their agricultural lands. Hungry farmers were selling or mortgaging their land against a small sum and were themselves becoming share croppers or landless farm labour. That was a time when share croppers had to commit entire cultivation expenses along with his labour and receive only 50 per cent of the produce. And after all these farmer was not allowed to take his share unless he pays for '*Selami*', '*Khamar Chilani*', '*Koyali*', for festivals of Jamidar's house, marriage ceremony, '*hat tala*' (if he goes to '*hat*' for selling) and 'fine' (Mandal, K. 1999). Hence share croppers irrespective of their religious identity launched joint movement demanding '*three fourth*' ('*Tebhaga*') of produce as per recommendation of Floud Commission. Reversing the harvest practice they now brought the entire harvest to their own premises and asked '*jamidar*' to take one-fourth. In 1945, this led to clashes in Bajbaj, Falta, Diamond Harbour, Sagar, Kakdwip, Namkhana, Canning, Basanti, in south of 24-Parganas and many other areas in north of 24-Parganas and elsewhere under the leadership of Jatin Maity, Jagannath Maity, Gunadhar Maity, Hemanta Ghoshal, Jyotish Roy, Pravash Roy, and others. This movement continued from 1945-1952 when the incitment by the Jamidar of Budhakhali converted the movement violent. Farmers started fighting with stick, bows and arrows and later gun also to combat the armed squad of Jamidar ('Lethel, hired goons) and the Government police squad and farm women also had to participate with konch, bell etc. Vikram Sardar led tribals, burnt jamidar's house, tortured women and kill people that were undesirable. At Chandanpiri, Kakdwip no less than eight people sacrificed their life. Since this oppression and torture continued even after independence 86 people sacrificed their lives in addition to what happened in Kakdwip.

11.4 Award of some rights to farmers

Following the position during Mughol period Bengal had provisions for two kinds of cultivation and cultivators. '*Khudkasth*' or resident cultivators who had both cultivating land and land for residence. The second category i.e. '*Paikastha*' or non-resident cultivators who had only cultivating land in the village' his residence being out of the village. In 1885, Bengal Prajasatwa Act was passed that provided every cultivator has to repay loans or advances of a year within a period from 1st Baisakh to 31st Chaitra of the year. The word '*Rayatisatwa*' was emphasised and word '*Jamidari*' was replaced with words like 'estate' and '*Jami*' for use. In the system '*Upajamidar*' and '*Jamidar*' could collect upto 10 per cent tax from cultivators. Bengal Rent Act, 1859 provides cultivators right to land. If any cultivator cultivates land continuously for 12 years or more he gets '*Dakhalisatwa*' on the land. This Act was meant for keeping farmers' movements subdued. 'Prajasatwa Act' has offered '*ryots*' some facilities like, even after sale of the land the '*ryot*' shall continue to enjoy right on the land i.e. a kind of permanent '*ryot*'. Secondly, eviction of those who failed to deposit tax in time would require consent of court of law. However the Act has not provided any protection to '*Bargadars*'. This Act was amended thrice in 1928, 1938 and 1940 but nothing has been done for share-croppers. During Fazlul Haques time (1938) the Commission with Sir Francies Floud as Chairman constituted, submitted a report that has advised 'Jamidar's to consider '*Bargadars*' as citizens of the state and shall accept one third of the produce only as tax.

11.5 Cultivations in 19th Century

'*Agrarian Problems*' by A. Mukherjee published in 1928 showed that average size of the holdings of Bengal was 2.59 acre while average holding of permanent *Jamidars* was 425 acre and that of temporary *Jamidars* was 813 acre. Regarding the number of permanent Jamidars that was 92,506 and temporary Jamidars 3,886. Again the total picture of India's land holdings and their size groups was obtained in B.H. Baden-Powel, 1982. Small estates of 500 acres size were 85,500 in number, 500-20,000 acres were 10,000 in number, larger than 20,000 acres were 500 in number. In another estimate since 1875 number of landless cultivators is constantly increasing. From 80 lakh in 1875 to 3 cr 40 lakh in 1901, 5 crore in 1911, 3 cr. 70 lakh in 1921 (Uliyanovski, 1989, Transl). In regard to rural people in India it was 9.6 per cent in 1891, nine per cent in 1901, and 1911, and three per cent in 1921 as per 1931 census. The number of active agricultural worker was in between 61-73 per cent. From during this period Bengal was most thickly populated state in India having five crore (5,100,000) or more people in 82,227 square mile area.

According to Uliyanovski there was a many layered parasitic pyramidal tax-collection system comprising of '*Etmondar*', the tax-collector approved by the '*Jamidar*', '*Ijaradar*' or rich farmer taking land from Jamidar on lease, '*Abadkar*' (Mondal) or rich cultivator who used fallow land or forests taken from Jamidar and '*Patnidar*' who used to collect tax all over Bengal. K.B. Saha, 1930 in his "Economics of Rural Bengal" has claimed in Bengal large number of cultivators has become '*Ryots*' for gradual transfer of land from actual cultivators to moneylenders and other non-cultivator people. Moneylenders occupying lands of cultivators who failed to repay loan in time and then giving the said land in '*Barga*' agreement increasing number of '*Bargadar's*. According to Banking Enquiry Committee, which stated that in 1931 the total debt of Bengal cultivators to money lenders was Rs 100.00 crore and there was no steady rate of interest charged. During English rule there was no specific investment by Government in agriculture, particularly in irrigation development, although Provincial Government used to earn 75 per cent of its revenues from agriculture. A very low budget allocation was usually made for agriculture as evident from 1929-30 budget. As a result agriculture remained single crop per year business or in other words people had job for 3-4 months only per year. Royal Commission on Agriculture reported that there was no public health network and being situated in lower Gangetic plain, breeding of mosquito and spread of Malaria that confined male member of a family for two to three months failing to participate in cultivation work. Even then agriculture in Bengal occupied a major part in Indian agriculture.

Ramesh Chandra in his "*Banglar Krishak Samaj*" (1874) has described crop cultivation round the year in Bengal. The Bengali new year in '*Baisakh*' (April-May) makes the beginning of agriculture in this state. The land that has dried up and cracked open in winter to spring is plowed in this month. After long dry period the rice produced are bold grained and cheap. Paddy grains mature and harvested in '*Bhadra*' (August-September). '*Aman*' paddy transplanting takes place in monsoon in waterlogged low land and harvested in '*Aghran*'–'*Poush*'. '*Dadghani*', '*Balam*' etc. rices are fine, slender and costly. Cultivation of such rices requires loan from money lenders at a high rate of interest. In the month of '*Ashada*' on small plots near their 'huts' seedbed is made and the seedlings are taken up to be transplanted ('*Thnai Nara*') away in main field in '*Bhadra*'. For having standing water *aman* crop do not require weeding ('*Niren*'). But in '*Aswin*' large number of labour is required for harvesting that takes place last in India and within Bengal paddy harvest is last in the '*Sundarbans*'. '*Aman*' rice is harvested in '*Poush*' (Dec-Jan.). Different home-scale festives and worships takes place and different sweets ('*Pithe-Payas*') are prepared. Paddy becomes the medium of exchange ('*Len Den*'). '*Ryots*' take paddy on loan from '*Mahajon*' in April – September, a part which is used to take oil and salt from grocer ('*Mudi*') in exchange. Sometimes even clothings and utensils are also purchased in exchange of paddy. All these are repaid after first paddy (*Aus*) harvest in September. During this century other crops grown in Bengal were mustard, sesamum, linseed, chickpea, pigeonpea etc. and wheat and barley in winter after *Aus* harvest. Linseed oil was exported to Europe. Among vegetables chilli, peas etc. were grown in winter. After the first rain in '*Baisakh*' jute seeds were sown. In the end of August jute was harvested, bound in small bundles after few days, soaked in water in a pond or canal, retted and then fibres are pulled out, washed in clear water and dried. Jute fibres are sold to get some cash, although most of the produce was exported to Europe. Tobacco planting was done in early winter (September) and the leaves are harvested in January but land preparation required to be very good for tobacco. Cut leaves are dried under shade (cattle shade), cleaned, bound in bunches and sent to market through water transport and/or bullock-cart.

Date palm plants grown here and there produces sap ('*Khejur Ros*') in winter after becoming 30 years old. At the beginning of November professional sap collectors ('*Shiuli*') use a sharp sickle ('*kaste*') to scrap the upper surface at the neck ('*Gola*') of the plant and hangs earthen pot to collect the sap twice (Dawn and Dusk) a day. The sap is boiled and cast in earthen container ('*Nagri*') to get the '*Gur*' in cake form ('*Patali*'). This brown sugar has an excellent aroma commanding great demand in market. The liquid form is called '*Nolen Gur*'. Sugarcane is planted in March end and harvested at the end of January. After deep plowing oil cake and compost is mixed in soil before planting of setts. After harvest canes are peeled and pressed in mechanical press to extract syrup which is boiled to get hard cakes (*Chaak*) of brown sugar.

Indigo was planted in April and harvested in September. It is best cultivated on sandy soil in river banks. Plants are cut into pieces, put in water in cement tanks ('*Choubacchha*'), water is boiled out, and pasty precipitate is dried and cut into square blocks, packed and sent to Europe. Generally a group of Englishman ('*Nilkar*') used to invest in this cultivation through advances like seeds and money. But *Nilkar's* often forced farmers to cultivate '*Indigo*', and farmers revolted against one company like Bengal Indigo Company, Nadia. Both kinds of cotton – *Ceiba* and *Gossypium* were cultivated in Bengal those days. '*Shimul*' (*Ceiba*) trees were grown that produced cotton in the '*Chaitra*' month every year. The cotton is produced in '*Chaitra*', that were collected and used to make pillows, beds, etc. that are used in sleeping etc. Cotton seeds sown in '*Baishakh*' every year and cotton is obtained in '*Paush-Magh*'. Cotton was spun into thread by women ('*Katuni*') and sold to weavers. Subsequently development of cloth industry in Manchester created problem for Bengal cotton. In Bengal, also cotton mills were developed and Cloth Mills in England facing this problem pressurised British rule in India to impose tax on cotton products of India in 1898.

Evidently in 19th century agriculture was the only source of making wealth in India. Eighty-five per cent of Indians directly or indirectly depended on agriculture. In regard to taxation, British rulers more or less followed '*Muslim Badsahas*'. In 1764 the last Muslim king collected Rs 81.75 lakh as land tax. Thirty years after that English ruler collected Rs 2.68 crore. During English rule all these steps led to great setback of Bengal agriculture and agrobased industry particularly the cloth industry. Ramesh Chandra showed the tax rate in British India was much higher than that in Europe, America and Japan, and most of this collection was taken to England in the name of '*Home Charge*'. The pressure of land-tax on cultivators was so much that some officers of British Government after retirement like Chief Justice, Sir Richard Garth, Mr. Reynolds, and many other personalities submitted an application with some proposals. Proposals desired to keep the maximum limit of land tax by deducting cost of production from half of the actual production, secondly, the direct tax collected by Government should be less than one fifth of the produce. In fact, Famine Commissions of 1880 and 1900 recommended 31/100 and 20/100 part of produce respectively to be fixed as land tax. Thirdly, unless prices of produces goes up or the land has gained with irrigation facilities through excavation of channels, tax should not be increased. Besides land tax should not be made heavier with imposition of local cess. Incidentally 'cess' was 10 per cent over land tax in those days.

In 18th cent English rule, weaving was the main agro-based industry of Bengal. This industry was affected greatly and destroyed due to imposition of unjustified tax on it and starting mechanised 'weaving mill' in England. In fact in the years 1801,

1802 and 1803 Calcutta exported to England 600, 1,40,000 and 13,000 bell (*'Gant'*) of cloth while after 1826 export did not cross even 1000 bell and from 1855 India started importing annually cloth worth of Rs 7.5 crore from Europe. Later modern mechanised weaving industry has developed in Western India particularly in Gujarat and Maharashtra. Bengal's one time pride-weaving industry has not yet been rebuilt. In the mean time cotton cultivation of eastern India is abolished. The black-cotton soil in western India has started producing huge quantity of cotton to feed the industries in India.

Besides paddy, oil seeds were major crops in Bengal. Paddy was cultivated in all districts in *'Aus'*, *'Aman'* and *'Boro'* seasons on upland, medium land and lowlands. *'Aus'* paddy was grown sowing seeds while *'Aman'* and *'Boro'* paddies were grown transplanting seedlings produced on seedbeds-wet or dry. On an average productivity was 15 maunds per acre. During English rule oilseeds were grown over 40 lakh acre. Since no oil industry developed oilseeds exported annually was worth of Rs 12.0 crore. Oil required in the state was obtained from country-made crushing/pressing machine (*'Ghani'*) villagewise. Taller plant *'Tori'* mustard (*Brassica campestris dichotoma*), indigenous mustard (*Br. glauca*), and Rai (*B. juncea*) were usually cultivated. Linseed was also grown by sowing seeds in Aman paddy field before the later was harvested. Light soils were prepared for cultivation of sesamum and light sandy soil for *'Sarguja'* (*Niger*). Bengal had many more mustard in cultivation namely Kalimpong Rai, Black mustard, white mustard, *Trilocularis* etc. Pulse cultivation was less popular may be due to its low productivity (10 maund/acre). *'Maghi' Arhar, 'Chaitali Arhar, 'Kulthi'*, Lentil, *'Urd Kalai'*, *Maskalai*, Lathyrus (*Khesari*), Gram, Mung, Guar, Soybean, Cowpea, Peas etc. were cultivated in small plots in some areas only. Mixed cropping of linseed and gram as *'Paira'* crop in *Aman* paddy field was also there in Bengal. Among other crops grown in those days are jute, maize, wheat, sugarcane, marua, tobacco etc. N.G. Mukerji, 1901 in his "Hand Book of Indian Agriculture" mentioned some more crops like chilli, pointed gourd, brinjal, potato, papaya, onion, plantain, datepalm, banana, coconut, turmeric, ginger, flax, indigo, betelvine, rubber etc. Surprisingly this list also did not include ash gourd, bottle gourd, bhindi, bitter gourd, mango, jackfruit, sapota, hog palm, guava, orange, elephant apple (*'Chalta'*) etc. But inspite of the list possibly remaining incomplete the variety and diversity of crops in Bengal is noteworthy. Starting from its variety of soils in different regions, climatic variations and diversity in its population, Bengalis being a mixed population group with high skill and merit crops chosen also were diverse. Lac culture and silk insect rearing to produce silk has been mentioned but surprisingly fish culture has not been mentioned.

Mukerji, 1901claimed that the quality of rice and sugarcane produced in Barddhaman was comparable with these produces from any part of the world. During that period the cultivated areas of crops in Bengal were - Rice-2.11 Cr. acre, Jute-20.59 lakh acre, Mustard-7.69 lakh acre, Sugarcane-2.09 lakh acre, Sesamum-1.66 lakh acre, Wheat-1.25 lakh acre, Cotton 90,200 acre, Barley-82,600 acre, Linseed-12,400 acre, Jowar-4,500 acre and Bajra-2,400 acre. Transformation of Bengal agriculture with time has been its another characteristic. For instance in case of fibre crops cotton of earlier days slowly disappeared for reasons described earlier and jute occupied the position and continued. With in-road of synthetic fibre Bengal may not have this fibre crop for long. Similarly disappearance of direct sown *'Aus'* rice and extensive spread of transplanted *'Boro'* rice was however due to clear, sunlit weather of *'Boro'* season resulted in much higher productivity along with available water through spread of minor irrigation. Cropping intensity increased since farmers' holding size became smaller, and farmer required to produce more. All these ultimately increased farmer's family income and nutrition.

The land that is Hooghly district is a part of ancient land mass of Bengal. Author of a history of Hooghly district, Sudhir Mitra, 1952 has mentioned some relatively unknown crops like 'Kamranga' (*Averrhoa carambola*), 'Jamrul' (Eugenia malccensu), Tamarind, Hogpalm, *'Tepari'* (*Phaseolus latifolius*), *'Golapjam'*, Aegle, Castard apple, *'Nona'* (*Anona reticulata*), Mangosteen, *'Bilati Amra'* (*Spondias dulcis*), *'Anshfal'* (*Illicium verum*), Sweet potato, *'Basak'* (*Adhatoda vasica*), Ivygourd, Spinygourd, *Alocasia*

(Mankachu'), *'Senji'* (*Melilotus indica*), *'Kulekhara*, (*Hygrophila spinosa*), Drumstick, *'Bok'* (*Sesbania grandiflora*), *'Gandhal'* (*Poederia foetide*), *'Juin'* (*Jasminum auriculatum*), *'Kolmi'*, (*Ipomea reptam*), Clitoria, *'Shiuli'* (*Nyctanthes arbor-tristis*), Jasmin, Pandanus, *'Chameli'* (*Jesminum grandiflorum*), *'Malati'* (*Aganosma caryophyllata*), *'Rangaalu'* (*Ipomoea batatas*), Bamboo, Cane, *Tagetes*, *'Shitalpati'* (*Clynogyne dichotoma*), *Azadirachta*, *Acacia*, Sirish (*Albizia lebbek*), *Emblica*, *'Horitaki'* (*Terminalia chebulae*), *'Boyra'* (*Ternninalia bellerica*), *'Chirata'* (*Gentiana chirata*), *'Shatamuli* (*Asparagus*) *'Pudina'* (*Stephania*), *'Nishinda'* (*Vitex negundo*), *Nigela*, *'Madurkatti'* (*Cyperus tagetus*) etc.

11.6 Influence of personalities on Bengal agriculture

In nineteenth century Bengal had many personalities who were not only concerned with villages and agriculture of Bengal but also tried in different ways for their development. In their writings and activities they expressed their strong and continuous desire and efforts for improvement of agriculture and conditions of the farmers. Sir William Carey (1761-1834) came to Bengal and started a Farmers' School in Madanbati, Nadia and then in 1820 established Agri-Horticultural Society to create awareness in scientific agriculture and horticulture among farming community. Carey himself started in 1818 teaching Botany and agriculture at Srirampore College, Hooghly. But his main work was to introduce high yielding varieties of crops like cereals, cotton, sugarcane, tobacco, potato, different vegetables, fruits and ornamentals by importing them from abroad. Society also imported different domestic animals as also modern agricultural machineries to bring all out change in agriculture of the country particularly of Bengal. Branches of society were opened at Dinajpur, Baharampur, Jabbalpur, Nagpur and other places to improve economic conditions of farmers through agriculture development (Bose, 1998). Society used to arrange different exhibitions, fairs and published 'Transactions' and later 'Horticulture Journal'. At Calcutta Radha Kanta Deb (1783-1867) used to write articles on agriculture in *'Farsi'* also for publicity of agriculture. Jay Krishna Mukherjee of Uttarpara, Hooghly developed demonstration farms, introduction of new technology and crops and establishment of Peasant Boys' School to popularise scientific agriculture. Social reformer Raja Rammohan Roy of Radhanagar, Hooghly also thrust his influence to support farmers' right to tax-free agriculture (no tax on agricultural produces) and to oppose East India Company to enter agri-business. Bhuban Mohan Roy (1841-1941) of Howrah was a famous gardening specialist of the century who established a nursery in Chetla in 1875 and started offering plans and advices about garden-layout in houses and Bunglows of Viceroys, '*Raja*'s and other '*big-guns*' in the country. He regularly published 'Gardeners' Magazine and one valuable book – '*Hints of Gardening*' that became so popular in those days. Another event was the establishment of one paper production industry in 1855 in Srirampore, Hooghly. Thereafter the first college level teaching of agriculture was initiated in Shibpur at Central Engineering College by Nitya Gopal Mukerji (1860-1907) a graduate in agriculture from Royal Agricultural College, Cirencester, England. Both diploma and certificate courses were offered. In 1901 his book '*A Hand book of Indian Agriculture*' was published and that was first comprehensive book on modern agriculture in India. He also authored another book on 'Sericulture'. This college level agricultural education continued for seven to eight years at Shibpur and then shifted to Old Pusa, Bihar to become Imperial Agricultural Research Institute. Dwijendralal Roy (1863-1913) of Krishnanagar, Nadia, also graduated from Cirencester joined Government services in Bengal in land and related Department. He used to oppose different anti-ryot measures of the Government as a result of which he suffered in his service life. Side by side he wrote many drama, fiction, songs and poetry to become famous in the field of Bengali literature. The great poet of the east Rabindranath Thakur (1861-1941), was awarded Nobel Prize in literature for his poetries. But he was equally concerned about the villages, villagers and agriculture as is revealed from his writings and experimental programmes of village reconstruction work at *Shilaidaha* and *Patisar* (now in Bangladesh) and *Surul*, Sri Niketan, Birbhum. His thoughts in this regard are original and fundamental. Since 1890 he went to

Shilaidaha, *Patisar* and *Sajadpur* (now Bangladesh) and lived there and learnt the village situation and the farmers' problem. He strongly felt that farmers are to get freedom from others ('*Parer haat*') i.e who intervened and influenced and also from own hand ('*Nijer Haat*') misunderstanding, superstition, and social taboos and should learn to oppose oppression of '*Jamidars*'. He also felt that for rural rejuvenation there shall be schools for education, handicraft training etc. to make villagers capable. '*Palli Samaj*' (village society) has to be organised to clear jungles, build roads, excavate drains (or repair drains), excavate pond etc. Self-confidence and self-initiative needs to be aroused among villagers. Teachers, students and workers should join hands for village reconstruction work in such a way that the school may be considered as nerve-centre for the village. Afterwards coming to Birbhum he tried to organise "Shiksha Satra' (a school) in the same manner and in this case people like Kalimohan Ghosh, William Pearson, Rathindranath, Santosh Kumar, Elmhirst and others acted as volunteers for village reconstruction. Slowly in 1923 the activities led to establishment of Department of Rural Reconstruction at Sriniketan. After arranging land farm plan was drawn and pond excavation was completed. The water was used for irrigation and fish cultivation. Animal feed crops were cultivated, some part of which made into silage; cattle shed, shade for poultry were erected. Residence for teachers and workers and self-managed latrine was developed. Using agricultural implements multiple crops on the same field were grown. New crops and varieties were introduced, and production of compost and its use was started. Rathindranath Thakur (1888-1961) studied agriculture at Illinois, USA and returned in 1909 to join Rabindranath in *Shilaidaha* in his reconstruction work. He later joined *Sriniketan* (1922) programme and established soil testing laboratory, farm mechanisation, use of exotic seeds of maize, potato, preparation of organic manure from waste fishes, erection of Persian wheel as irrigation system from '*Jhakuran Pukur*' to establish a farm and grow jowar, jute, tomato, pineapple, papaya, banana, datepalm, guava, sweet orange and other citruses. He also developed a beautiful ornamental garden behind '*Udayan*' building and established a school for teaching agriculture. Sir Daniel Hamilton in 1903 started village reconstruction work at *'Gosaba'* in Sundarban. Following co-operative philosophy all out agriculture and village development work progressed under a trust named "Hamilton Trust" and one of the earliest efforts for development of agriculture on saline soil in the country. Rajeswar Das Gupta (1878-1926) studied agriculture in Civil Engineering College, Shibpur, Howrah and joined Department of Agriculure, Bengal as Agricultural Inspector, and later Principal Agricultural Superintendent and applied newer technologies, introduced new crops and varieties, and green manure crop (*'Dhaincha'*) in crop rotation. He developed one modern plow (Rajeswar plow), spread cultivation of potatoes in Bengal and selected *'Rangpur'* breed of cow for this area. He started publishing magazine – *"Krishikotha"* and wrote a book in three volumes – Krish Vigyan-1 (Science and Policies), Krishi Vigyan-2 (field, vegetable and fruit crops) and Krishi Vigyan-3 (Animal Husbandry) (Mukherjee, 1998).

Many other (published booklets on agriculture) came out. Moulabi Fakruddin Md. Choudhuri (studied variety of plants and published a book), Dwijadas Dutta (served Dept. of Agriculture), Satish Ch. Das Gupta (Bee keeping and books on cow rearing), Santosh Kumar Mazumdar and Kalimohan Ghosh (Village rejuvenation), JBS Haldane and P.C. Mahalanabis (studied statistical analysis of crops and their production), Jnyanendranath Mukherjee (soil studies, 'Calcutta School of Soils') and others left profound influence to shape agriculture of Bengal. In the course of events the dedication of Leonard Elmhirst at Sriniketan or Shibchandra Banerjee at Boral, south 24-Parganas can not be ignored. Shib Chandra's creation of 'Giant Spinach' or *'Poliflower'* (Broccoli and Cauliflower crossed) are events of modern time (1944), the agriculture to be discussed later.

11.7 Agricultural development through Government initiatives

Keeping parity with western countries Earl Mayo, the Governor of British India created Department of Agriculture in 1871 with headquarter at Dacca. Initially Octovious Hume alone controlled, Dept. of Revenue, Agriculture and Commerce. The Famine Commission, 1880 reports stated that from 1870 to 1878

52.5 lakh people died of starvation. Commission also proposed to establish Departments of Agriculture at both Centre and State levels and the proposals were implemented in 1881. At that time 'Bengal Province' meant the area covering Bengal, Bihar, Orissa, Assam and present Bangladesh. In the same year the first Director of Agriculture, Bengal was appointed and posted at Dacca. Thereafter Agricultural Chemist, Economic Botanist etc. were recruited one after the other. Side by side for extension of agricultural technologies to farmers an extension-structure was organised starting with recruitment of three Deputy Directors of Agriculture under Director to organise agricultural extension work in three circles of the state. In 1917, an expert from Indian Agriculture Service was placed to become Director. From this period initiative to establish one Agriculture Farm in each district was taken. These farms were used for production of quality seeds for distribution to farmers. In addition demonstration of modern methods and techniques or varieties were also made. Different projects of work on different crops were taken up. The Dept. of Veterinary and Animal Husbandry was also created with its headquarters at Calcutta.

In 1915, the staff-structure of Department of Agriculture was divided into three to four stages or tiers (Mondal, Sen Gupta and Trivedi, 1998). The stages were Bengal Provincial Agricultural Service, Sub-ordinate Agril Service-Class I, SAS-Class II and Lower Subordinate Agricultural Service. This structure was spread upto District, Union and Villages, that created very effective machinery to spread and extend scientific agriculture to the remote corners of the villages. But the weakness was absence of initiative to build and spread irrigation network (except DVC and Mayurakshi) that was so much necessary and resulting in failure to reach the required quantity of food grain production. The steps taken to build up structure and infrastructure of agricultural education, research and trainings were very late in Bengal – only in later part of modern time, this deficiency also played a negative role in overall agricultural development in Bengal. The efforts at Makhala and Shibpur was ephemeral and Dacca effort was ultimately limping for so much of political upheavals and turmoils. *Shibpur* programme was shifted to Old Pusa, Bihar and then to Delhi (IARI) leaving Bengal deserted.

11.8 State of affairs in different sectors of agriculture

(a) Crop seasons

Mukerji, 1901's Handbook described seasonwise different crop in Bengal of those days. In *January* seeds of '*Kuli Begun*' and '*Desi Peanj*' and *Ol (Amorphophallus)* seed-corns are sown to be harvested in August-September. Potato and winter vegetables are given last irrigation; cotton, kalai and peas are harvested, land preparation for sugarcane and sweet gourd is made, threshing of paddy and harvest of Arrawroot and cassava are started. In the month of February, the field operations are – mustard, mung, linseed and sugarcane are harvested. '*Gur*' making right in the field starts. Sowing of sugarcane setts and seeds of bittergourd, ridgedgourd, watermelon, sweet gourd, cucumber are sown. Planting of brinjal seedlings and land preparation for kharif crops is done. In the month of March, crops harvested are barley, oat, wheat, gram, lentil, lathyrus etc. Sugarcane is manured and irrigated. In April, sugarcane and sweet gourd group of vegetables are irrigated, seeds of '*Ol*' *and* '*Kham alu*' are put in soil, maize, jowar, jute, '*mechta*' seeds are sown. Longer life crops like banana, indigo, bamboo plants are manured with silt (*Pank*) from ponds and channels. *Aus* fields are also enriched with cowdung, silt, compost etc. Sale of cucurbit vegetables start. Farmers prepare for brinjal seed sowing. In the month of May, seeds of *Aus* paddy, maize, *Dhaincha*, pigeonpea, jute etc. are sown. Seedlings of brinjal and cotton are also planted. With rains earthing up in sugarcane, maize and jowar is done and the sugarcane crop is irrigated. Seeds of sweet gourd, cucumber etc. are sown. Chilli and Aman paddy seeds are sown on seedbed for raising seedlings. In *June Aman* seeds are sown on seed bed for getting seedlings. Seedlings of brinjal and cotton are planted. In the fields of *Aus* paddy, pigeonpea, jute and mesta interculture is done, earthing up is done in case of cotton and brinjal, unripe maize cobs are harvested and sold, and seeds of '*Bhadoi Kalai*', '*Kulthi*', '*Bhringi*', Sem, and cowpea seeds are sown. In the month of *July* Guineae grass is planted, *Aman* transplanting and early chilli planting takes place. Weeding takes place in fields of jute, pigeon pea, cotton, brinjal, turmeric and ginger. Staking of sugarcane goes on and if required drainage of rain water from fields of pigeon pea, cotton, sugarcane, jowar, jute, kharif pulses, *ol* and *kham aloo*. In August, *Aman* transplanting continues and pulses and *Kham Aloo* are harvested and taken to market. *Dhaincha*, jute, *mechta* are also harvested and retting and washing of jute is done. Seeds of early winter vegetables are sown. In the month of September, land preparation for some winter crops start. Maize, *Aus* paddy and *Bhadai* pulse are harvested. Sugarcane staking continues and seeds of cowpea, peas, palak, *Chukha Palang*, *Kanak Note*, Radish, cucumber, sweet gourd, early cauliflower, mustard, knolkhol, sesamum etc. are sown. Only cauliflower is sown in seed bed to grow seedlings. Stem pieces of pointed gourd and sweet potato are planted and land preparation for winter vegetables is completed. Seedlings of papaya and saplings of banana are planted. Sale of jute fibre and early winter vegetables start. In October, planting of winter vegetables is an important job. Starting from Artichoke in sandy soil to celery lettuce, *Olkopi*, Frenchbean, Pas, Radish, tomato, Carrot, Brussel's sprout, cauliflower, cabbage, knolkhol, sweetpotato, onion and wheat. Standing rain water is drained out and erection of shade for early cauliflower are done. Fields for sugarcane, brinjal and cotton are ploughed and made ready. Planting of *Aloe* bulbils is completed. For irrigation small basins around newly planted banana saplings are excavated. Land preparation is completed within this month to sow seeds of gram, linseed, sesamum, Lathyrus, Lentil, and mung. Harvesting of cotton also starts. Sowing of mustard and '*Kalai*' started earlier. In the month of November, soil at the base of newly planted cotton, brinjal and fruit plants are worked with '*Nirani*' to make loose. Seeds of barley, oat and pulses are sown, followed by sowing of wheat, winter vegetables and potato. Others like radish, cotton, muskmelon, water melon, sweet gourd, coriander, onion etc. are sown or planted. Crops sown or planted earlier are intercultured, potato and cauliflower are irrigated, *Aman* paddy is harvested, sugarcane field is hand-hoed and irrigated and sweet potato and taro are harvested. Then in December, important operations are harvest of *Aman* paddy sale of winter vegetable, giving irrigation to potato and cauliflower, working of land at the base of fruit plants and harvesting cotton, chilli, *Kham Aloo*, Ginger, Turmeric, groundnut, radish, etc. Another crop *Amorphophallus* (*ol*) is usually planted at this time and harvested in August-September. Early sugarcane, *Kalai*, and mustard is harvested. When irrigation was there '*Champa Note*' was sown. Sale of pointed gourd and brinjal started.

It appears that even in those days the entire description as stated above, show a general similarity in the cropping patterns as we see now. Generally the seasons have moved little backward with the passing of more than one hundred years. The unique culture of overlapping of crops, the possibility of the same crop twice a year and such other characteristics of Bengal's agriculture establishes its strength. This unusual and amasing flexibility of Bengal's agriculture from very early days to date due to some reasons which we have identified following till now.

1. Geographical location locating the land between a very tall hill range in the north and vast waterbody of the Bay of Bengal at its south being located in sub-tropical position.

2. Being located in the basin of one of the greatest rivers – '*Ganga*' as also in lower gangetic plains its deep loam soil over a vast area of the state.

3. All these have created an excellent agro-climate that is unique for agriculture with vast range of crops and combinations. Availability of round the day sunlight, moderate temperature that encourage growth of organisms to the maximum enhancing prospect of agriculture.

4. Agroclimates of hill zone in Darjeeling, high rainfall Terai zone in north Bengal, lateritic acidic soil with semihumid atmosphere in western districts and coastal saline districts present different agroclimates making diverse agricultural possible.

5. Bengal has been a land of people of mixed tribes or class with continuous addition of newer people and all this resulted in a truly mixed strain, which learned and wise people think

that this has caused increased expression of skill and merit of Bengali people. From the nutrition point of view that from *'fish'* the extraordinary nutrition input might be the reason. This however is a development over thousands of years of development of Bengalis.

(b) *Use of manure in agriculture*

Cowdung, auto-composted refuse and waste, silt from ponds, deposits of drains etc. become manure for crops long back. The sweepings of cowshed, deposited in a convenient place turned into good quality manure with time and subsequently used as manure. The daily sweepings of the courtyard (*Uthon*) containing droppings of goat and poultry (duck), kitchen refuse, floral refuses of worships room (*Thakur Ghar*) or fish cutting refuses together make a good quality manure used on different crops. From very early days cart-load of such manures were the only nutrition-source for crops. Longer time-gap between pouring such manures here and there in the field and plowing in to mix them with field soil, more is the loss of nutrients due to solar oxidation and rainfall washings.

After netting search of a pond the 'liked-fishes' are taken for consumption leaving behind quantity of mollusks, non-consumable fauna that is also composted and used. This phase of manure-use was prevalent in ancient Bengal which was followed by use of dead bodies of larger animals that was otherwise left to weathering. Similarly plant-body wastes, crop harvest wastes etc. was also dumped in fallow fields and allowed to rot in weather i.e. wetting in rains and warming and oxidation in sun. The changes taking place under weather possibly peeped the idea of composting.

It is in the British period Bengal slowly received the idea of manure making that started already in western countries for instance grinding of the bones of dead animals by some means. While bone dust preparation might have started this way, use of oilcakes started much earlier. Excepting few, oilcakes were good feed for cows. Some of these feeds went to composting site as cow-shed sweeps and its impact on growth of plants was realised.

NG Mukerji, 1901 has mentioned that HH Mann, the Indian tea specialist for the first time sowed *'Dhaincha'* seeds in Tea gardens to enhance N-nutrition in tea-plantation. In Bally of Howrah district and Uttarpara of Hooghly district in pulse cultivation and growing mango and coconut without any manure application created problems for the crops. In this connection he has discussed use of phosphatic manures in cultivation. Incidentally there was a '*Bone mill*' ('Harkol') in Uttarpara in the 4th to 5th decades of last century. This mill prepared bone dust mainly for cleaning of sugar and some use as manure was possible.

Nityagopal listed bone dust, cowdung-cake's ash, and oilcake as source of phosphate and as N-fertiliser, the crusts on rocks and stones (salt petre, potassium nitrate) was available. Animal blood, flesh, hairs, hoofs etc. are also good source of nitrogen. Salt petre was applied @ two maund per acre. Oil cakes contained phosphorus, nitrogen, potash and calcium. All kinds of 'ashes' contained five to ten per cent potash. Wastes from animals, rotten leaves, silt from ponds, silt from '*indigo*' retting tanks also contain nutrients. Shells of snails and stones contain calcium that is good for pulses particularly in acidic soil. Some crops like cabbage, asparagus, coconut etc. require salt. Chalt-salt being a good source it makes the fibre of cotton and jute stronger and prevents excessive leaf formation. Those days in isolated place far off from the village where dead animal bodies of the village is dropped along with faeces of humans in trenches to ferment and rot so that a good compost is produced and the place is called '*Bhagar*'. Starting similar dumping in another field the entire mass of ready compost is excavated and applied in crop field.

Another practice was to collect urine of animals, diluted 10 times and applied to field before plowing. *Dhaincha* was used as green manure to get the aerial nitrogen fixed in their root nodules by *Rhizobium* group of bacteria to enrich soil. But culturing of such bacteria to be used as biofertiliser was uncommon. Production of phosphate fertiliser in a factory at Rishra, Hooghly was there.

(c) Use of agricultural implements and machineries

In ancient Bengal it all started through using stone pieces to till land. Thereafter slow and steady transformation led to a stage which we get beside other references discussed earlier, the situation in British period in 19th century (NG Mukerji, 1901). However sharp weapon, metallic weapon, stick-plow, iron-share on wooden plow etc. use stages of development has been crossed long back. Use of '*Khurpi*', '*Nirani*', '*Bida*', ladder etc. were also started long back. Each of these implements undergone improvement with time. In the matter of irrigation some devices like '*siuni*', (swing basket) '*nauka*' (boat) were sufficient in Bengal only a short-height lift is enough since water level in ponds, canals, rivers etc. are generally close to the field surface. Persian-wheel type lift is not required. '*Kodal*', (spade), '*Kaste*' (scythe/sickle) etc. are common.

In 19th century or earlier, bullock-drawn plow was being used, the plows in Bengal were lighter and could open furrows of 3-5 inch depth and 2 inch depth in Jalpaiguri or Rangpur but plows of Noakhali were heavy. *Shibpur* plow was partly mould-board. First plowing used to cover one third of an acre per day (eight hrs.) and second and third plowing covered half acre. Bengal bullocks were unable to drag plow of more than 100 pound weight. The plow in Bengal was simple in structure, light and cheap but the wood was quite hard and suitable for two bullocks. The plowman was very skilled controlling and managing by tails the pair of bullocks, successfully. *Archie Hills* tried steam plow at *Patkabari*, Murshidabad and found that unsuitable. Farmers used hand-drawn or bullock-drawn harrow for interculture and weeding. Harvesting was done with sickle ('*Kaste*'). Threshing was done either by guiding the bullocks to trample harvested paddy plants or by striking bunch of plants (panicles) on a '*Bera*' (frame made of bamboo splits). Cleaning was done by blowing on a split-bamboo-woven structure ("*Kulo*") by women with excellent skill. Thereafter paddy grains were steam-boiled (par-boiling) on large shallow metallic containers and dried in sun before de-hulling in "*Dhenki*' or primitive huller.

(d) Cultivation of fodder crop

Grazing fields (*Gocharan Bhumi*) decreased fast in 19th century. Those still there are not well-maintained keeping grasses green. Besides grasing on grassland animals were fed with leaves of mango, jackfruit, *Albizia, Ficus, Acacia, Drumstick, Ceiba, Aegle* etc. During drought leaves of Datepalm are chopped to feed domestic animals. Some crops were cultivated as fodders e.g. *Bhringi (Phaseolus aconitifolius), 'Kalai'* (Mukerji, 1901). Free-grasing cows were fond of grasing spiny *Amaranthus*, and dropped flowers of *'Mahua'* and others. Regarding free-grasing Bengal's goats are very efficient and aggressive. Animal keepers used to feed animals by collecting *Ceiba, Delonix* etc. flowers, or seeds of cotton and different leaves and twigs. Broken rice (*'boiled khud'*), husks of foodgrains, straw-chopped in special toothed cutter (*'Khor Kata Bonti'*) mixed with molasses, salt etc. The thick starch solution from cooked rice was also fed. Besides after harvesting for days together the main crops like cowpea, *Dolichos*, pea creeper, etc. were also fed. The 'left out' of ripe jackfruit (skin and *bhuturi*), peels of mango and its stone were also in the feed-list.

(e) Pests of crops

After the 1880 food-crisis in Bengal, a commission was constituted with John Augustus Voelker of Royal Agricultural Society as Chairman. As per commission's recommendation one Agricultural Chemist was appointed followed by appointment of Imperial Entomologist in 1903. Before this and before constitution of Department of Agriculture in Bengal, one Director of Agriculture and three Assistants were recruited and sent to Royal Agriculture College, Cirencester for training. After completion of that study NG Mukerji joined Civil Engineering College, Shibpur, created Shibpur Farm and started giving lessons in agriculture to students. His lessons contained discussion on crop pests that became one chapter in his book "*Handbook of Indian Agriculture*". Following publication (1874) of a leaflet on sericulture in Bengali in 1919 he published a monograph – "*Handbook of Sericulture*". Practically he was first to publish on insects and pests. For prevention of stemborers he suggested use of HCN gas and fumigation burning *Mahua* cake. To prevent scale insects he adviced spraying of resin-solution and painting of 'lime sulfur' on stem and branches. He recommended sufficient irrigation to prevent termite, cutworm and grasshopper infestation. For soft bodied pests use of kerosene emulsion was suggested. For others burning of dry branches of plants or hanging a lantern with kerosene water kept below was proposed (light-trap).

In winter vegetable crop fields he has advised to grow coriander like umbelliferus spices odour of which repels pests. For sugarcane borers his advice is to sow *Arhar* and *Sem* flowers of which will attract borers keeping sugarcane free. He has talked about Indian Moyna (*'Salikh'*) that picks up and eats pests. Thereafter the works of M. Lefroy and B. Fletcher worked extensively on insect pests and Indian pest studies became widespread. In 1914, Destructive Insect Pest Act, was passed to prevent entry of exotic pests in the country. The next major step was establishment of Agriculture College at Dacca in 1939 where Entomology naturally had an important position. The works of Dr Samarendranath Moulik in Calcutta University included coleoptera pests much earlier. Subsequently in 1921, Dr Durgadas Mukherjee studied many different insect pests and Entomological Society of India was established. Since 1944, in the Zoology Dept. of CU, entomology became a special paper. Prof P. Sen of this department was placed in a special position in World Health Organisation who later in 1964-69 became Prof of Entomoogy, in Faculty of Agriculture under Kalyani University. Prof D.K. Choudhury in KU was Colembola specialist, Dr S.K. Das Gupta of CU was aphid specialist and D.N. Roy Choudhury – taxonomist and biodiversity specialist Dr A.K. Ghosh became Director, ZSI, Calcutta. Pests of jute and tea were studied in depth by Dr. G.M. Das and Dr. N. Dutta. Dr. S.N. Banerjee was State Entomologist, West Bengal later becoming Chief Advisor, Dept. of Plant Protection and Qurantine, New Delhi. Silk insect culture was studied by S.N. Das and K.C. Sengupta. Besides the studies at Calcutta and Kalyani Universities insect pests were studied in greater details at Bidhan Chandra Krishi Viswavidyalaya where studies of agriculture entomology was made over wide spread area and taught in undergraduate, postgraduate levels and doctoral researches were conducted.

(f) Disease problems of crops

NG Mukerji's *Handbook*, 1901 has little mention about fungal diseases and fungicides. This however has not mentioned any specific disease name but has suggested preparation of Bordeaux mixture and Lime sulfur mixtures for spraying to control diseases. On the other side upto 1905 E.J. Butler, Mycologist under Dept. of Agriculture, Govt. of West Bengal made extensive studies and recording of plant diseases in Bengal which made a foundation of plant pathology in India. Butler's famous book on plant diseases and publication of number of leaflets on different diseases in Bengali language were great contributions upto 1926. During that period in the Dept. of Botany of Calcutta University, Dr S.N. Banerjee was studying mycology while in RG Kar Medical College S.R. Bose was studying fungi and their products. After Independence establishment of SARI, Tollygaung under Dept. of Agriculture in 1948 and the first Mycologist appointed was Dr Sudhanshu Bhusan Chattopadhyay after coming back from Imperial College, London University with Ph.D. degree. He started research and demonstration on plant protection. At Kalimpong S.P. Roy Choudhuri and at Barrackpore Tarashankar Ghosh conducted researches respectively on large cardamom and jute to find out protection measures. Taresh Ch. Roy studied and conducted researches on betelvine diseases. At Agriculture College located at Tollygaung, Kalyani and Mohanpur under Calcutta, Kalyani, Bidhan Chandra Universities offered lessons on plant diseases to B.Sc. Agri., M.Sc., Agri and Doctoral students on disease problems of paddy, wheat, jute, pulses, oilseeds, vegetables, fruits, flowers, spices etc. and their management.

11.9 Husbandry of different animals

In case of rearing domestic animals also Bengal showed diverse animals – small to large in their husbandry at home-scale generally. Large animal farms were not there even upto British rule.

(a) Cattle rearing

Farm families in Bengal used to rear cattles along with crop cultivation. In ancient Bengal many quality milk producing cows were common in such families in villages. Milk of a black cow ('*Kalo Goru*' or '*Shyamali*') was of excellent quality. In those days there were pastures in every village and cowboys (*Rakhal*) used to collect cows from houses of villagers and take them to the 'pasture' ('*Gocharan-bhumi*'), allow the cattle to graze and take them back to respective houses in the evening against some monthly payments. Village girls used to conduct festivity called "*Gokul*" to feed cows in dry season. It is to be noted that fresh milk was used in different festivals, worships as also in welcoming newly married housewife in a house. With all these glorious practices of providing cattles enough nutrition through rice husks, molasses, soaked '*moong*', were mixed with chopped straw became victim of negligence and milk production declined to a pathetic level. The situation from 18th to 19th century under British rule may be described briefly. Attempts to increase milk yield by introducing 'Bankipur Cross Breed' and subsequently 'Jersey'. Hissar breed was brought for drought work.

(b) Goat keeping

For long time 'Bengali's used to rear goat the breed of the land was '*Black Bengal*' that was appreciated world wide for its quality meat and skin. However, for 'inbreeding' over long period, the quality and size of the animal declined although its milk is more nutritious than that of cow. It was also a neglected animal having only 'grazing' as its source of nutrition. Mukerji, 1901 however has not mentioned 'Black Bengal' but one 'Aangura' breed.

(c) Sheep rearing

In South 24-Parganas particularly in Sundarbans people rear sheeps for historical days and the concerned breed '*Garole*' is unique being used to humid climate of the area (contrary to the concept of sheep generally like dry climate). Moreover, it gives larger number of kids at a time. People here however do not know use of its wool but consume its meat and milk. Mukerji, 1901 has not mentioned this animal.

(d) Rearing poultry

Rearing of chickens generally by Muslim and ducks by Hindus, all using indigenous breeds is common. Mukerji, 1901 mentioned 'Chattogram' as the breed of chickens with red, black etc. feathers and musk duck. These birds were trained to incubate eggs under their body to get 'chicks'. Small duck breed was 'Patihans' and larger one 'Rajhans'.

(e) Pig rearing

Usually in society lower caste people used to rear pigs, breeds being 'Ghungru' (large black) and 'Deshi' (small white with grey patches).

(f) Fish culture

Many Bengalis from ancient times used to catch fishes through different methods from ponds, rivers and other waterbodies. All these were natural produces and culture of fishes came much later. Different groups and types of fishes grew in water-bodies and spread to different areas through flooding and population declined during summer and drought. In those days a particular class of people (*'Jele'*) used to catch fish using nets and traps. Large fishes were hunted with spear and even bare hands. Fish marketing was a duty of women-folk (*'Jeleni'*) of fisherman family by visiting door to door, later in village 'haats' or markets (*bazar*). These families used to weave different nets (*'Khepla'*, *'San'*, *'Tana'*, *'Hat'* etc.) and treat the nets in gum from green *'Gab'* (Mangosteen) fruits. Using thin sticks made from bamboo they used to make 'traps' (*Ghuni'*) that are placed in drains in front of flowing water mainly during monsoon. Bengalis also used fishing sticks (*'Chhip'*) or 'wheel's for angling in a pond against priced tickets and very skilled Bengalis were known to use 'tridents' for large fishes by throwing it targeting the big fish. Persons rented out or leased out their pond to 'fisherman' on contract for one to three years against some payment and some quantity of fresh fish for owner's family consumption. Most of the ponds silted over long period having no reclamation programme, slowly became unfit for fish culture etc. Similarly large number of ponds and waterbodies were filled up limiting the scope of fish cultivation.

The sweet water fishes common in those days include – *'Punti'*, *'Mourala'*, *'bele'*, *'gule'*, *'tengra'*, *'chanda'*, *'kuchochingdi'*, *'nedosh'* *'kunche'*, *'leta'*, *'magur'*, *'singi'*, *'banmach'*, *'Koi'*, *'folui'*, *'rui'*, *'katla'*, *'mrigel'*, *'shole'*, *'shal'*, *'kalbos'*, *'Aad'*, *'chital'*, *'golda'* and brackishwater fishes were – *'parse'*, *'khoyra'*, *'bhangan'*, *'bhetki'*, *'pabda'*, *'bagda'*, *'topse'*, *'bhola'*, *bagda* etc. Few seafishes are *'lotta'*, *'fensa'*, *'ilish'*, *'mackerel'*, *'sankar'*. In addition crabs of different kinds, *'genri'*, *'gugli'*, etc. were also quite nutritious but consumed generally by low caste people and tribals.

Cultivation of all these depended exclusively on these '*Jele*' community and some traders. '*Jeles*' hardly cleaned ponds, used waste foods, cooked rice, oil cakes etc. as fish feed called '*char*'. They brought fingerlings and released in these ponds, and create turbulence in pond-water for faster growth of these fishes. This much was done for fish cultivation.

(g) Silk culture

Rearing silk insects for silk production is continuing since long. As per evidences available, silk culture started in 400-300 BC during '*Gangaridae*' time. But details of silk-rearing in Bengal is only available in NG Mukerji, 1901 and in one of his exclusive volume on '*Sericulture*' published in 1919. During those days silk cultivation was done (i) indoor and (ii) outdoor. The silk insect *Bombyx textor* was grown indoor feeding them mulberry leaves. However, cocoons of this species of *Bombyx* was not equally hard or tough like that of *B. mori*. Selection of another species *B. croesi* famous in the name '*nistari*' which lays eggs eight times in a year, gives yellow cocoon and the silk fibre was very thin and soft. Indigenous species *B. fortunatus* produced small insect and silk fibre was tough and bright-yellow. Another species *B. sinensis*, Chinese cocoon, produced small, white cocoons and was reared in Medinipur mainly. Among the silk insect grown outdoor was *Antheria militta* or '*tasar*' cocoon. Fibre of this silk is relatively thick and rough the larvae were fed by placing them on '*Arjun*' leaves (*Terminalia arjuna*) right on the plants in fields. Another species *A. assama* reared in North Bengal on '*Som*' (*Machilus*) and '*Soalo*' (*Tetranithera*) leaves outdoor, the fibres are called '*muga*' that are also not so fine. The larvae and cocoons of these outdoor grown species were quite large. Seasonwise three kinds of '*tasar*' were produced in Bengal. In winter small '*Naria*' cocoon was produced, in summer '*Dhuria*' cocoon was produced in June and '*Barshati*' cocoon in October. But among all these the main silk production was indoor with species of *Bombyx* and mulberry leaves. In the room eggs were allowed to transform into small larvae that are fed with young mulberry leaves on '*Dala*' (tray weaved with thin bamboo slices) which are cleaned and changed daily and when grown up they stop feeding and they are picked up and placed in '*Chandraki*' (tray with concentric channel configuration) where the insect starts covering own body with silk threads to get metamorphosed into 'pupa' or cocoon. Mature 'cocoons' are dipped in boiled water to kill the insect inside and the silk thread is reeled to get the silk fibre.

Another kind of silk was produced in Bengal called '*Endi*' or '*Eri*' where the insect was fed castor leaves. This silk was also long, tough and fine fibre. All these silks were weaved in country-weaving machine called '*tant*' by skilled persons called '*Tanti*' to get silk-cloth to be marketed and used by people.

(h) Bee keeping

Bee keeping was also practiced by Bengalis since ancient times. On the one hand the hives built on trees in forests by wild species (*Apis dorsata*) in Sylhet, Khasi hills area, orange orchards in Darjeeling in the north, in Murshidabad in Central Bengal and in Sundarbans in South Bengal were sliced to get thick honey by a group of expert villagers called '*Maoli*'. On the other hand special wooden boxes packed with frames to hold the hives to be built by reared bees (*Apis indica*, much later *A. melifera*) which is extracted in a improvised machine that uses centrifugal force. These boxes are placed in mango, litchi etc. orchards or in fields of crops like sesamum, mustard etc. (Eucalyptus forest is included in 20th century). In hard winter and summer when flower-honey are not produced the reared bees required to be fed sugar-water for their survival while in hard summer water needs to kept beside boxes. This beekeeping in boxes was already there in Bengal in 18th century or earlier.

(i) Lac culture

In western districts of Bengal '*Kusum*' (*Scleichera kujuga*), Flame of forsts (*Beautea frondosa*) and Zuzube (*Zizyphus jujube*) etc. grows naturally and lac insects grow on their branches to multiply and produce in the process '*lac*'. Local people for long time back collected lac-insect bearing sticks (branches) and tie them on younger branches of the trees in both the months of June and November.

June sticks were often washed away by following rains, hence November programme was more dependable and practiced. On selected young branches one ft long lac-sticks were tied upto ten ft. length of the branch. Generally growers used to prune branches in June so that new branches start growing and this make new branches to become ready for fixing lac-stick. The lac insect comes out of lac-shelter on lac stick and sucks the new branch and secretes lac to cover their own body in layers. The female lays eggs and covers them in same way. After completion of this covering the female produces a red liquid to feed young ones. Lac-sticks under this condition are collected. The insect coming out of eggs spread on the new branch. '*Kusmi-lac*' is best in quality followed by '*Falsa-lac*' while '*Jujube-lac*' is relatively of poor quality. Lac from '*Palash*' is red and poor in quality.

In primary processing the red deposits are scrapped with knife, ground, washed in clean water, rubbing on a '*Dhama*' (basket woven with '*Bet*') and red pigment dissolved in water produced '*Aalta*', a cosmetic item in use by Bengali women for over long period. The '*lac*' being totally free of red pigment appears golden in colour. This natural '*lac*' is a very costly commodity in country and foreign market. From eighties in the last century the SC and ST Dept. of the state started to distribute '*lac-stick*' and give them training.

11.10 Mushrooms : Collection and Cultivation

From ancient times different groups of people in Bengal used to consume naturally growing mushrooms after cooking. They were tribals, forest inhabitants and people living in vast paddy growing areas. Mushrooms were commonly called as '*Chhatu*' or '*Banger Chhata*' (toad stools). In the light, sandy or loam soil areas many of the mushrooms pushed out of soil (called '*Bhuinfore*'). Many of these were linked with the termite nests, deep inside such soil. Two such species were later identified as species of *Termitomyces* - one being white, medium large in size with a long thick stype coming out of soil while the other – white, very small in size and delicate, both edible. In the paddy-growing area a third kind ('*Poal chhatu*') – *Volvariella* sp. was in the list of diet of large number of Bengali farmers.

Nityagopal Mukerji, 1901 has shown the differences between 'poisonous' and 'edible' species simply by –testing a very small piece of the mushroom whether bitter (poisonous) or sweet (edible). He also suggested to crush the piece between two fingers to see the colour – white (edible) or green (poisonous). According to Mukerji, 1901, Great Eastern Hotel used to import mushroom 'spawn' (seed) from France, grew mushrooms on artificial medium and served mushrooms to their clients. But in those early days mushrooms growing in nature were collected and eaten. Later two more species of mushrooms namely *Pleurotus* (Oyster) and *Calocybe* (Milky mushroom) were located in Bengal and produced for consumption.

11.11 European food culture and Bengali foods

Christianity introduced in India (52 AD) by Thomas in Kerala and 2.3 per cent of population of India are now Christians. In Bengal William Carey came to India as a missionary and started spreading education from Srirampur, Hooghly. British rulers ruled India from 1757 to 1947 although their activity started in India much earlier (1613).

The mixed Indian and European ancestry is a contribution of mainly British but other Europeans came to India in British period on business and other purposes. Many of them were railwaymen, teachers, secretaries, nurses and singers besides preachers. But their numbers are vanishing fast after independence, many leaving for North America, England, and Australia during fifties and sixties of last century. In 1947, there were about five lakh Anglo-Indians that declined to 1.5 lakh by the beginning of next century.

At home Anglo-Indians take chicken, jalfrezi, with tomato and green chilli and few other dishes. Behind Boubazar Police Station, Central Calcutta '*Bow Barracks*' is a small settlement of Anglo-Indians. Other places in Bengal they live are Krishnanagar, Ranaghat (Nadia) and Bandel (Hooghly). Anglo-Indian cuisine is a result of intermingling and intermarriages between some European races and Indians and the taste buds of these people (community) have been influenced by both European and Indian (Bengali) foods resulting in development of an unopposed cuisine that is relished by many. They include thick

'Multigatawani soup' with small chunks of meat, rice and vegetables, stuffed crumbled crabs, duck recipes etc. At 'Tollygaunge Club' steak-cabab and shephard's pie (potatoes mixed with meat) attracted Anglo-Indians, may be remembering discovery of '*Pie*' in England (14th cent). Bakes like 'Banofees', 'Shepherd's pie', 'Roasts', 'Bacons' are British contribution while 'Vindaloo', 'Beveca', and 'Dodol' are from 'Portuguese' and 'French's in Calcutta. 'Dodol' – a sweet toffer like dish made from rice flour, coconut milk and jaggery (prolonged cooking) was brought by 'Goans'. Thus Kolkata has gained variety of Anglo-Indian foods developed in various parts of the country. European officials and their families in Assam, West Bengal (later Uttaranchal) and south India got their dishes cooked by European housewives and Indian cooks and the efforts in kitchens produced many new dishes like 'caramel custard', 'crepe suzette' and other deserts. Their chicken dishes are seasonal with garlic, ginger and pepper with spicy chilli sauce laddled with rice and meat on the side.

Anglo Indian or Rajcuisines are not pure British but something of French, Portuguese, Dutch and other European collective influences resulting in delicious and unique cuisines made with local ingredients adapted to French, Italian and Bengali cooking techniques characterised by use of creamy sauces, restricted use of spices and new technique like baking. English and Jewish bakers (Flurry's and Nahoum's) dominated the confectionary industry that migrated from British tables to everyday Bengali ones. All these resulted in unique creations e.g. '*petis*' (savory turnover from English 'pasty'). Another enduring contribution to Bengali cuisine is '*Pau-ruti*' or western styled bread. '*Raj*' era cuisine lives on especially in the variety of finger foods, popularised in '*Pucca clubs*' of Kolkata e.g. 'mutton chop', 'Kabiraji cutlet' or 'Fish orly' etc. British influence reached Bengali kitchens in other ways also. British families hired local cooks and through them discovered local foods that were toned down to suit the taste of '*memsahibs*' (British housewives). For example distinct influence on desserts were evident. For instance '*Ledikeni*', named after first Vicereine Lady Canning was a derivative of '*Pantua*' a famous Bengali sweet.

11.12 Processing , Storage and Bengal agriculture

(a) Processing and preservation of food items

Bengal agriculture since long produces variety of agricultural commodities. As a natural consequence preservation and processing of many of these also started much early and indigenous methods developed were unique in the sense that they were designed as per the facilities available. The wonderful method of 'parboiling' (vapour-boiling of paddy grains, drying and milling) of rice produced rice grains with longer storagability. These rices (*'Alochal'* or *'Siddhachal'* are still the main food item in Bengal. The rice produced without 'parboiling' i.e. *'Atap chal'* used in most other rice consuming states and in Bengal only in *'Pujas'* (worships).

Other processing procedures for rice was production of *'Khoi'* (popped rice) was by toasting paddy grains (*'Dhan'*) in heated sand using some selected varieties of paddy, toasting rice grains (*'chal'*) of some specific varieties in heated sand gives *'muri'*. *'Chira'* was prepared by bating boiled rice of selected varieties in *'Dhenki'*. All these were done by Bengali housewives in their kitchen or in separate shade. This processed rice 'trio' (*'Chira'*, *'Muri'*, *'Khoi'*) were ancient in origin and a matter of glorious heritage of Bengal agriculture and food culture.

Actually in those days people had only two energy-sources namely solar radiation and fire to be used in preservation and three commodities namely country sugar (*'Gur'*), oil (mustard) and table salt available for the purpose. In addition sour, edible organic acid sources like tamarind, lime etc. were used in processing and preservation of many fruits and vegetables. In another field grains of rice, pulses, and wheat etc. were ground with *'shil-nora'*, *'haman-dista'* and *'Jnata'* (all grinders) for use in preparation of different food products like *'sobeda'*, *'besan'*, etc. that are storable and used for preparation of different kinds of Bengali foods. Pulse grains are fried and ground to *'chhatu'* – a very popular food of many Indians. In addition through different procedures host of food commodities like – *'pnapor'*, *'chanachur*, *'bori'* etc. from pulses and *'pitha'* of different varieties, were produced. *'Nadu'* of different kinds using fried *'Chira'*, *'muri'*, *'khoi'*, *'groundnut'*, *'chickpea'* were very common in Bengali households. Sugar or '*Gur*' boiled in water to thick consistency to cast – '*michhri*', '*patali*', '*takti*', '*batasa*' etc. like food articles are a good way of preservation. Rice boiled to '*bhat*' is packed in earthen pots and incubated to produce drinks like '*haria*'. Many of the fruits like mango (green) are cut into pieces, dried in sun to get '*aamsi*', ground into powder to get '*aamchur*' or pickled with '*Gur*' or '*sugar*'. Pickles prepared with ber, mango, lime, '*chatta*', '*aamda*', tamarind, and some vegetables were very popular way of preservation. Using '*Gur*', '*bael*', mango, asparagus and others are preserved in the name of '*morabba*'.

Milk has been used to prepare and produce different kinds of food items after preparing butter, '*Ghee*', '*Chhana*', '*Khir*' ('*Khoa*') and sweet preparation slowly became a business of a class of people called '*moyra*' who later developed sweet-shops that are now innumerable in number all over Bengal. Milk-based sweets of Bengal that have been admired all over the country and abroad also are – '*sandesh*', '*rasogolla*', '*rabri*', '*sarpuria*', '*sarbhaja*', '*monohora*', *rasmalai*', '*payas*', '*pantua*' etc. However, sweet industry uses along with milk, rice powder, pulse powder, flour, etc. and sweets like '*sitabhog*', '*mihidana*', '*moya*', '*muger nadu*', '*goja*', '*jilipi*', etc. are produced Bengal produced huge quantity of fishes that are preserved by solar drying, salt treatment and oil frying for short duration.

Bengal had possibly its first 'ice producing shop' (*barof kol*') in '*Chnuchura*', Hooghly in 1775 bringing in another means of preservation of different perishables for different periods. '*Chalkumro*' and '*Lau*' pulp (mature) was used to prepare '*petha*' in sugar.

(b) Processing of non-food items

Spinning of cotton (*Ceiba* or '*Shimul*' initially and later cotton) was commercially started in Bengal first in the beginning of 18th century at Kishanlal Barman Rd., Bandhaghat, Howrah. However, homescale spinning started in Bengal much earlier. With decline in '*Shimul Tulo*' production its cost became prohibitive and was replaced by *Gossypium* cotton that was cheaper. Inspite of the fact that qualitywise, '*Shimul tulo*' was non-absorbent of water and better compared to *Gossypium* tulo that was absorbent this change occurred. At this stage only pillows were made of '*shimul tulo*' and '*lep*' (blanket) and '*toshok*' (bed) with '*Gossypium tulo*' to minimise expenditure. Actually at '*Ghusuri*', Bandhaghat, Howrah the first cotton mill was established. Cotton processing industry developed to an excellent level producing cotton thread and weaving cloth both around '*Dhaka*', '*Dhonekhali*', '*Tangail*' and other places long long back as discussed earlier. In fact the very fine quality of cotton thread spun around '*Dhaka*' produced the famous '*muslin*' cloth. Excellent designs were woven on quality silk '*saari*' named '*Baluchari*' in Bankura. Different other articles were produced by processing of agricultural produces like broom-sticks (coconut leaves), bed or '*Godi*' and ropes ('*Kata dori*) (coconut fibrous pulp), '*shon dori* (ropes spun from jute fibre), '*chot*' (cloth from jute ropes) which later initiated establishment of 'jute mills' along the banks of '*Ganga*' river in Hooghly and Howrah districts. Bamboos were processed to produce – '*Darma*', '*Fence*', '*Jhuri*' (basket) in Maldah, house and roof structures, '*Ghuni*' (fish traps), scaffolds ('*Macha*') for creeper crops '*Dhuchuni*' '*Khnocha*' etc. Forest creeper – '*Bet*' (cane) was used to make '*Dhama*' (large container), '*Kunke*' (small), chairs, stick etc. *Tagetes* flower stalk was split and woven into mats ('*Madur*') while '*sitalpati*' was woven into '*pati*' or matters as in Coochbehar. *Hogla*-an aquatic plant was woven into shade structures extensively in 24-Parganas. Leaves of Palmyra and Date palm were used to make 'Handfans ('*Hatpakha*') as in Raghunathpur of Tamluk, hat, containers etc. In Purulia *Babui* grass leaves were dried and used to make different articles. Another important case was with the ripe shells ('*khol*') of vegetable-bottlegourd ('*Lau*') in '*Pushpur*' of Jangipara, Hooghly used to build the main container for making string musical instruments like – '*Ektara*', '*Surbahar*', '*Tanpura*', '*Setar*', '*Vina*', '*Do-tara*' etc. Wooden musk of West Dinajpur and paper musk of Puruliya were great.

(c) 'Haats : bazars (markets), 'melas' (fairs) and festivals (parabs)

'*Haats*' and '*Bazars*' as also '*Melas*' and '*Parabs*' constitute very powerful and widespread network of agricultural trade in rural Bengal. Farmers get fair price of their produces in such places. Farm families living close to such places carry themselves their produce to such places denying any middleman in between. This infrastructure grew by its own strength much earlier than British or Mughol period but subsequent spread and modernisation has not been satisfactory. Large number of *'mela'*, *'utsav'* and *'parab'*s centering round different *'parban'*, *'pala'*, *'puja'*, etc. are going on since long both at the family and public places and initiatives. *'Melas'* across religions, castes and communities are assemblage of large populace of villages and other places being held round the year in different places all over Bengal. As a result a congenial situation for sale and purchase of agricultural and household commodities, handicrafts, agril. implements, potteries etc. is created. Small business persons earns some money and as their profession they move from one *'mela'* to another round the year all over Bengal. Leaving aside the markets in cities and towns the development of *'Haats'*, and *'Melas'* in different district of Bengal as available in some publications may be summarised.

In Darjeeling district the time of establishment of *'Kalimpong Haat bazar'* is not exactly known. Possibly it was owned by someone that later came under control of municipality. Sellers are to pay some cash 'tole' and commodities sold reached distant places. *Sukhiapokhori* (Nepal border) market was established in 1838. On Fridays farmers from distant places (even Nepal) bring potatoes, maize, *'jira'*, other spices and vegetables to sell. The market is daily and sellers were to pay Re 0.50 as 'tole'. Bijanbari *'Haat-Bazar'* started since 1840 having *'Haat'* on Fridays and market (bazaar) round the week. Brisk sale of potatoes, ginger, *'Kalai'*, *'Jira'*, orange and vegetables goes on in respective seasons. *'Mirik bazar'* is of 1924 with *'Haat'* on Sundays and *'Bazar'* on all other days. Common items sold are ginger, *'jira'*, maize, orange and vegetables and *'tole'* charge for each seller is Re1.0. Commodities come from *Aalgarha, Pedong, Lava, Geet, Tista* and *'Rambi'*. Another market at Kalimpong sends produces like ginger, *'jira'*, maize, potatoes, oranges and cacti to Siliguri, Kolkata, Delhi, Amritsar, Kanpur and other places. At *'Rangli-Rangliot'* of this district *'Tistamai'* *'mela'* in the last day (*'Sankranti'*) of *'Paush'* month that attracts many people and trading goes on.

Six big markets namely *'Dhupguri'*, *'Belakoba'*, *'Maynaguri'*, *'Alipurduar'*, *'Falakata'* and *'Kamakhyaguri'* were the main marketing centres of *Jalpaiguri* district, established from 1848 to 1902. Most of these are 'markets' but turns into *'haats'* on Tuesday and Friday or Saturday. Belakoba, Kamakhyaguri and Maynaguri used to sale pulses, oilseeds, vegetables and sugarcane while Dhupguri used to sale betel leaves and Falakata betel leaves and tobacco. This area of western *'Dooars'* on *'Bhutan'* border is an evergreen forest area full of rivers rivulets and canals having people of *'Rajbangshi'*, *'Mech'*, *'Rava'* communities.

11.13 Roads, Transport and 'Hat-bazar' (markets)

(a) Roads and agriculture in ancient Bengal

Roads were built much earlier than some transport launched on them. Of the many roads built one major west bound road in early days was from *Tamralipti* to *Buddhagaya*. Huen Sang came by this road, and he described his route from *Varanasi* to *Pataliputra* via *Baishali* and then to *Pundrabardhan* via *Kajangal*. Another important road was *Samatat, Karnasubarna* to *Odra*, *Kangad* and *Kalinga*. From north-east – one road crossed *Brahmaputra* river from *Gauhati, Bogura-Santahar-Ishwardi* to Kolkata. On many of such roads later railway lines were established. Another was from *Jagannathgaunj-Sirajgaunj-Ishwardi* to Kolkata. Roads reaching places outside Bengal include road from *Pundrabardhan* to *Champa* (Bhagalpur) via *Mithila*, then proceeded to *Pataliputra-Buddhagaya-Kashi* and *Ajodhya*. Another from *Tamralipti* to *Rajmahal* via *Karnasubarna*, then to *Rajmahal-Champa* and *Pataliputra*. From *Tamralipti to Ajodhya* is another north-west bound road. There was road from *Jalpaiguri* via *Darjeeling, Sikim* and *Bhutan* to reach *Yunan-Sojehoan* of China through 'mountain-pass' in *Himalayas*. The road that was used for transport of silk and silk-products from China also in use today served to transfer opium-all carried on the back of animals and animal carts. In those days many such roads developed initially for different purposes for instance one from Ganga-sea confluence (*Ganga sagar*)-passing through *Roydighi, Chhatrabhog, Kalighat, Howrah,*

Hooghly, and northward, called *Dwarik Jungle Rd* (*Dwarik dacoit* used to pass through this road on '*Ronpa*'), from *Piyali* river to Kolkata through Baruipur – Mograhat – Kolkata (Canning Road), Falta – Debipur Rd., Diamond Harbour Rd., Kolkata to *Petrapole* via *Barasat, Habra, Gaighata* and *Chandpara* or Kolkata to *Barasat* - via *Berachampa-Baduria-Ramchandrapur, Katiahat – Shresthanagar – Ghojadanga* – Bangladesh and Kolkata to *Gaurangadihi-Adra* – via *Raghunathpur-Bokaro-Ahalyabati* (Varanasi). Later during *Sher-Saha's* time *Benaras* Rd. and the famous *Shahi Sarak* or G.T. Road from Kolkata – via Howrah – Hooghly – *Barddhaman-Ranigaunj-Asansol-Barakar* to reach *Punjab* that has changed name and shape number of times. *Dinajpur-Maldah* Rd. passes from *Maldah Ghat* to *Sankrole* or *Rohanpur* to *Parbatipur* (Bangladesh). The one that is NH 34 now passes from Kolkata through 24-Parganas, Nadia, Murshidabad, Maldah and Dinajpur. Niharranjan Roy, 1947 emphasised the roads leading to *Tibbat, Tripura-Manipur, Chattogram-Arakan, Tamluk* to *Karnasubarna* and others that were used in trade.

Waterways in Bengal were powerful ancient ways of transport. For a long time the 560 km long south-east ward *Ganga* river as also river *Saraswati* were very strong and widely used navigable waterways of Bengal over centuries. *Saraswati* however has dried up and *Ganga* has changed its course, *Rupnarayan* provides 80 km long navigable waterways. In north Bengal, river *Tista* provides in the plains 13 km long navigable water ways through '*Bashiganj* and *Coochbehar*. In south Bengal, *Bhairabi, Jalangi, Churni* in Nadia, *Jalangi* in Murshidabad, *Ichhamoti, Vidyadhari, Matla, Thakuran, Kalindi, Raymangal, Gosaba* etc. in 24-Parganas being navigable are water-ways for long time. *Saptagram* and *Tamralipti* were connected to Patna, *Kashi* and Allahabad through river. In north east from '*Karnasubarna*' to '*Kamrup*', on rivers *Brahmaputra* or *Meghna-Surma-Brahmaputra* busy transport existed. During rainy season boats used to come from eastern Bengal and reached Mango-orchards of Maldah for purchasing mangoes. All these road and water, ways were used for trading jute, paddy, rice, '*Gur*', paddy-straw, earthen pots like *Hanri* and *Kolsi* etc. Items like bamboos, logs and animals like goat, cows, etc. are transported by floating on boats or swimming in water. Bengal water fleet (*'Saptadinga'*) used to go to *Simhal* (Sri Lanka), *Bramhadesh* (Mayanmar) and even Crete and Greece by waterways. Historians named *Bengalis* to be *'Samudrasayan'* (living in seas). Railways came later, first possibly from *Howrah* to *Pandua* in 1854. East Indian Railways started running trains from Howrah to Hooghly and from *Seorafuli* to *Tarakeswar* in 1884. Bengal Nagpur Railways started between *Tikiapara* to *Kharagpur* extending later to Howrah in 1905. Thus railways developed in stages to support transport of agricultural produces also. Transport helps in development of agriculture through creation of better marketing facilities. All these reveals how in ancient Bengal water and road transport and much later railways extended and strengthened agricultural marketing. Suburban train services between Sealdah-Baharamputra via Ranaghat, to Shantipur and Lalgda on the north and Sealdah to Diamond Harbour, Lakshikantapur, Badge Budge, Canning were created in British period. This in its turn inspired production increase of agricultural commodities and cast enormous influence on Bengal agriculture.

(b) Transports in ancient Bengal

Large number of rivers, canals, *'khal'*, *'bil'* are common in Bengal. In addition large mighty rivers across Bengal, other States and countries along with the sea-coast have incited Bengalis of ancient times to use them in expeditions, tours, trade and even warfare. As a result they learnt to construct boats, ships etc. of different types, sizes and shapes made of natural resources like wood, bamboo, trunk of palmyra palm. They built smaller water vessels like *'Dona'*, *'Duni'*, *'Dingi'*, *'Bhela'*, *'Pansi'*, *'Balam'*, *'Chhip'*, *'Bozra'*, *'Mayurpankhi'*. They also built larger vessels like 'ship' (*'Jahaj'*). Niharranjan identified in olden day publications the terms like – *'Naubat'*, *'Naubitan'*, *'Naudandak'*, *'Nabat Kshena'* etc. that are water-vessels. *'Charshageeti'* has mentioned different components of a Bengali boat namely – *'Dnar'*, *'Hal'*, *'Mastul'*, *'Pal'*, *'Logi'*, *'Nongor'*, *'Kaachi'* and elsewhere exclusive acts like *'Guntana'*, *'Pal tangano'*, *'Logimara'*, *'Hal Dhora'*, *'Dnarbaoa'*, *'Pare bherano'* etc. The boats were more necessary in eastern and southern part of Bengali life like *'Pundrabardhan'*, *'Samatat'* or coastal areas for having more water-bodies. The large ships that were constructed some 2500 or more years back could carry 700 people and it is said that *'Bijay Singha'* used such ships in his navy troop to defeat *'Lanka'* rulers.

During *'Buddha's* time', *'Tamralipti'* was a big port. The ships of Bengal and *'Magodh'* used this port under the management of one *'Nabdhyaksha'*- a staff of the ruler. Four hundred years after birth of *'Jesus Christ'*, *'Fa-Hien'* traveled from *'Tamralipti'* to China on a ship. *'Kalidas'* in his writings claimed that the *'Pal-kings'* of Bengal used large number of armed ships to win battles as found in *'Khalimpur order'* of *'Dharmapal'*. Whether in war or in trade Bengal usually moved with at least 14-16 boats that were well decorated. The fleet moved through *'Ganga'* and reaching the sea they proceeded to different island countries. *'Chand-Sadagar'*s *'Madhukar'* ship had 1200 *'Dnar'* making it high-speed. Rulers of number of Parganas in south of Bengal like *Kedar Roy* or *Pratapaditya* had powerful navy fleet (Haraprasad Shastry, 1947). The ships made in *Chattogram* during 18th cent were quite big. People used to pack their commodities in gunny bags to take to nearby *'haat'*s or markets as head-load on men and women. *'Bank'* (a piece of long bent stick on one's shoulder from two ends hanging strings) carrying commodities like butter, curd, *'chhana'*, 'eggs' etc. taken door to door for sailing. Initially animal power was engaged for carrying different agricultural produces. Selection of domestic animals for the purpose always depended on the locally available animals, considering the historical course of development from *'sledge'* to cart on rolling discs of *'Syrians* or *Sumerians* (4000 BC) and *Sindh valley* (3500 BC) reached two-disc chariots by *Greeks* and *Romans* and later by *Indians*. In Bengal bullocks and ass were initially common, later strengthened with small horses. Evidently in 1520 AD *Chaitanyadev* had to walk on foot at least partially to reach *Nilachal* (Puri) through *Shantipur, Barddhaman, Cuttack* and *Bhubaneswar* from *Nabadwip*. Rich and powerful people of society used to move on *'Palki'*, carried by humans. It is said that after a 'strike' by *'Behara'*s (carrier of Palki) Brown Low in

Calcutta (early British period) fixed tw pairs of discs under the '*palki*' to convert it into car pulled by horses. After roads took shape different horse-carts were developed namely '*Judi*', '*Choughudi*', '*Dughudi*', '*Chhakra*', '*Lando*', '*Fiton*' etc. '*Ekka Gadi*' was very attractive. Some of the horse-cart were used for sending letter etc. from Calcutta to outside in 1825. In 1830, an 'Omnibus' was run as transport from Calcutta to Barrackpur. Subsequently transports like Tram etc. started plying first as horse-pulled, then steam powered, and electricity powered in 1902 and all these had influence on villages around. While such transport vehicles slowly spreading around, railways started developing (1889) even in district *Puruliya* through Asansole, Adra, Puruliya and Chakradharpur. Evidently since 1872 people used to move by 'Push-Push Cart' ('*Thelagari*') in *Puruliya*. During British period such Bus-services started to operate in medium and small towns. But village-life continued with bullock-cart, having horse-drawn cart (faster) in some areas. All these were responsible for transport of agricultural produces. Later from the large-sized '*haats*' all over Bengal to distant places and '*Karo*', '*Toto*', '*Limbu*', '*Bhotia*', '*Lepcha*', '*Saontal*', '*Onrao*' and '*Munda*' community. '*Sadri*' language in use here is a product of '*Bhotbormi*', and '*Mundari*' language mixing. In this area small markets to the extent of 50 around numbers were viable till middle of 19th cent. The local festivals of these people creates a situation favouring very small trading of different commodities. But a larger festival started in ancient times called '*Shibratri mela*' at the famous '*Jalpesh*' temple. In those days '*Bhutia's* used to come to this '*mela*' to sell wool, blanket etc. Besides the '*mela*', a regular market continues.

The oldest '*Haat*' of Coochbehar established in 1730 at *Mekhligaunj* managed jointly by Government and businessmen. Besides running a daily market there is '*haat*' on Mondays and Fridays where main commodities are paddy, rice, jute, tobacco, mustard, and vegetables. Commodities come from '*bhotbari*', '*jalpaiguri*' and '*jorpokhri* and from here transported to Kolkata, Odisha, Jalpaiguri, and Assam. *Haldibari Haat* was established in 1750. Besides the daily market, '*Haats*' function on Tuesday and Saturdays where paddy, wheat, rice, jute, oilseeds, chilli, tobacco, eggs, chickens, cows, sheep – all are available for sale against a *tole* ranging Re 0.50 to Rs. 2.0. Commodities come from *Berubari, Ghughudanga, Deyanganj, Hemkumari, Deyabari* and *Shovarhat. Mathabhanga hat* established in 1850 has a daily market and *'Haats'* on Mondays and Fridays mostly handles agricultural produces and a separate *'Goru Haat'* (cow market) for selling different animals. *'Tole'* payment is compulsory for only *'Goru Haat'*. Besides large *'Haats'* are there at *'Chourahaat'* *(Dinhaata), Tufangaunj, Bashirhaat, Changrabandha* and *'Choudhurihaat'* among the majors. Some of these are accompanied with festivals (*Melas*) of which the *Mela* at *Madanmohan* temple is quite big. The markets of Uttar and Dakshin Dinajpur are big and mainly send *'rice'* to distant places. Chillies of these districts are also exported to different places. *Biddalhat* was established by *Jamidar* of Harishchandrapur in 1880 that sold produces like rice, chilli, paddy, onion, mustard, *'Gur'*, and vegetables. *Dhankail Haat* was also established by local *Jamidar* that did not collect *'tole'* from sellers. This *'haat'*, famous for *'Citilanka'* functioned every Mondays. The typical dress *'Chhauta'* used by *Rajbangshis'* were sold here. Before *Kaligaunj* was rail-connected people used to come on *boats* over *Srimati* river. Now that *Kaliganj* town has grown, this *'haat'* has lost its importance. *Bishnupur haat* of *Hemtabad* on the border of East Pakistan (now Bangladesh) on every Thursday was originally established by *Chaudhury* jamidars. Both paddy, rice, wheat and vegetables (quite cheap) are available. At *Itahar* Durgapur jamidar family established on the sandy coast of river *Nagor* in 1930 a very large *Durgapur haat*. *Porsahat of Itahar* is on Mon and Thursdays selling paddy, rice, jute and the commodity unique of the area i.e. bamboos and quality 'bamboo-baskets' (*Jhudi'*). Another *'haat'* – *'Patiraj'* (1930) on every Sunday arranged to sell paddy, jute, chilli, cow, goat, sheep etc. Main purchasers of this *'haat'* were people of scheduled caste and scheduled tribe class.

Kamalabari haat of *Raiganj* PS used to function on Fridays and has changed its site to avoid high *'tole'* rate. Besides other *'haat'*s like *'Kaskihaat'*, *Mallikpur haat, Dalkhola, Sahapur haat*

(*Goalpokhor*), *Debijhora haat* (tea garden) etc. '*Pir*'s mosque is situated beside *Kamalabari haat* where on the first Thursday of new year '*Pir's Mela*' is a big festival when large number of people assembled, enjoyed and sell and purchase commodities from local agriculture and distant places.

In Maldah district '*Samsihaat*' was founded in 1840, '*haat*' operating on Thursdays only but the market ('*bazar*') goes on regularly and sale and purchase of commodities like jute, wheat, peas, oilseeds, mangoes, eggs, as well as cows, buffaloes and hides of these animals takes place. Purchasers and commodities come from *Ratna, Chnachal, Kamdevpur, Nurpur, Harishchandrapur, Manikchak* and purchasers have to pay Rs 1.5 tole. In addition for cows and buffaloes agent is paid Rs 5.0 as commission. Commodities reach even Kolkata, Malda and Siliguri. At *Tulsihaat*, Harishchandrapur (1872) commodities were jute, paddy, peas, potatoes, wheat and chicks, eggs and bamboos etc. This '*haat*' was used by people from *Kusida, Harishchandrapur* and *chnachal* and commodities used to go to *Malda, Samsi* etc. areas. The international trade centre is known as *Kashimbazar, Khagra-Gorabazar*. The income from *Katra-market* was used to meet running expenses of *Katra mosque*. Others were *Jama mosque haat* of *Aurangabad, Suti, Dhulian (Farakka)* High Madrasa '*haat*' and *Trimohani* High Madrasa '*haat*' of Nouda were important. Income from all these '*haats*' were to meet running expenses of adjoining mosques. Small '*haat*'s in the villages include *Jafrabad, Raninagar, Bhabanipur, Rukunpur, Raypara*, and *Ghoshpara (Jalangi)* '*haat*'. The oldest market of the district are *Jiyaganj* (1750), *Kandi* (1750), and *Lalbag Panchraha* (1972). Market cum *haats* are *Lalgola, Mianpur* (Jangipur), *Jalangi, Gokarna, Islampur, Salar, Raghunathganj, Mirjapur, Aurangabad, Bhabanimati, Nayansukh* (Farakka), *Beldanga, Dhulian, Domkol, Panchthupi, Paddiar, Aamtala, Patkebari, Mahalandi, Ranitala,* and *Akheriganj*-all during 19th cent. Most of the '*haat*' functioning start in the morning or noon and end in the evening around 8.0 p.m. Largest '*haat*' is *Beldanga* (16 acre) attracting maximum people. *Mahalandi kalitala* of '*Kandi*' and '*Tangramari*' are only for animal trading ownership of the '*haat's* are diverse like personal, groups of different types, '*Bazar-Samiti*', religious institution or government. During '*Beda Vasano*' festival in the district a huge mass of people assembles attracting trading. In '*Lalbag*' Muslim boatmen and fishermen community ('*Nikiri*'), '*Khaja-khijir's* (gods of water) are honoured '*Vela*' (float) made of banana pseudostem with a coloured paper shade over it large number of '*pradip's* (small lighting device) are sailed on '*Ganga*' river full to the brim in '*Bhadra*' reclining the entire monsoon. The whole scenario is something rare and extremely attractive. In the south of Nadia on the bank of river *Jamuna* is *Nagarukhra haat* at Haringhata. Mostly jute, paddy, rice, '*gur*' and vegetables are sold and purchased. Jute produced here are in high demand of jute mills in Hooghly on the other side of Ganga river. But in all the 16 villages under Haringhata Block separate '*haats*' functioned, but unlike *Nagrukhra* these did not have any permanent shops. There were many small rice-mills as also household indigenous weaving machines ('*Tant*') and dress-materials like '*lungi*', '*gamchha*' etc. were available in such '*haats*'. Quality '*saaris*' were woven around '*Shantipur*' and '*Shantipur haat*' was famous for that. Besides *indigo (Nil)*, utensils and related articles made of '*brass*' *(Petal)* and 'bell-metal' ('*Kansha*') – all manufactured in local '*Kamarshala*' (black-smith shops). Commodities like coconut, '*gur*', spices, salt etc. were exported. At different places on river bank in '*Shantipur*' '*haats and bazars*' namely '*Kuthirghat*', *Matiganj, Baktarghat, Nrisinghapur,* '*Baganchda*', '*Haripur*' etc. grew up. '*Pirerhat*' of '*Harbandar*' was ancient. Of the '*haats*' or 'markets' *Lakshmitala bazaar* beside the settlements of '*Potua*' and '*Chukidars*' was also old. Besides *Krishnanagar bazaar* and *Gohat* established in 1785, *Mazdia* (1880), *Boda Anduliya* (1908); *Chapda*' (1930), *Badkulla* (1850), *Najirpur Tehatta* (1890), *Chakdah* (1900) and *Bethuadahari* (1975) developed one after the other. Krishnanagar market was daily but *Gohat* was only on Thursdays and there was '*tole*' charge in all the places. *Jagadhatri Puja* coincided with *mela* at '*Pirerhaat*'. Later *Jagadhatri puja and mela* spread to *Krishnanagar*. At *Bethuadahari* on the last days of '*Shraban*' *Brahmanitalar mela* caused huge assemblage and trading activities. Very rich Khan Choudhuri family were famous weavers (*tanti*) and they started *Shantipur 'Rashmela'* and procession. They used to export *'muslin'* and other woven clothes. In 1726, the famous temple of *Shyamchand* was established and *'mela'* organised was well-known all over India attracting 30-50 thousand people. Next comes *'Bhanga raser mela'* that also used to attract masses. *'Rash Utsav'* is also celebrated in *Nabadwip* that started festivals of different folk culture that attracted huge no. of people and the trading activity continues for quite long period. At *Chapra 'mela'* for Christmas from 26th of a year and continues upto 1st January. *Christian* populated area of *Chapra* gets dressed-up, relatives of families, guests and people from other lands gather and Bengali sweet dishes like *Pithapuli, 'Payas'* etc. are in great demand and admired ultimately becoming a good time for sales. In *'Dolpurnima', 'Satima's* mela at Ghoshpara, Kalyani also attracts visitors from vast areas outside Bengal also and brisk marketing of diverse commodities goes on for a week. *Jhaldahat* of *Puruliya* was established in 1820 and sale and purchase of different domestic animals goes on. *Kashipur haat* is on six acres land area. During *'Bhadu'* festival people gathered reaches 60 thousand mark and sale of all articles from earthen pots to animals continue. In different seasonal festivals all daily requirements-broom-sticks to fruits are sold here. In Barddhaman district *Kalna haat* was established at the initiative of *Taranath Bachaspati*. There were rice hulling machine as also business with timber. Other *haats* in Barddhaman were *'Koichar, Durgapur*, *Katoa*, *Nadanghat* and others. Another well-known *mela* i.e. *Agardwip mela* on the other bank of Ganga river at the premises of *Gopinath temple* that is near *Dnaihat* station on *Ekadashi of 'Chaitra'* month. People from both sides of the river assemble. Similarly *Goshala mela* at *Domohani* also created similar marketing facilities and stone sculptors of *'Dnaihat'*, or wood craft artists of *'Natun Gram'* get a market interested to purchase their works. *'Haat's* like *'Shunukpahadi'*, *'Basulihaat'* are pretty ancient and sale of many commodities were common. Besides cows, buffaloes, and goats, jute ropes, items made of *'Babui grass'* and many agriculture produces are also sold in these markets. *'Khatra haat'* sales horses and many other domestic animals. Other *'haats'* of *Bankura* are *Aasuriya,*

Deulivir, Lakshmisagar, Simlapal and finally *Kotulpur*, that is famous for *'Gur'* from *Datepalm sap*. In *Birbhum Dubrajpur haat* exists since 1802. Other *'haats'* are *Amedpur, Bolpur, Murarai, Mahammadbazar, Nalhati, Sainthia, Rajnagar, Rampurhat, Mallarpur, Lavpur, Keernahar* and *Ilambazar* functioning round the week as *market* (bazaar) and on identified dates as *'haat'*. At *Mahammadbazar* sale of flowers goes on day and night. Near *'Siuri' Datapir's* starts on 10th *'Chaitra'* every year. One very large *'mela' is 'Joydev-Kenduli'* that brings people from all quarters to participate in *'Kirtan'*, *'Fakiri'*, *Murshidi*, and songs of physical relations of humans under open sky and on grassy land. In *Hugli* district there are about 300 *'haats'* of which important ones are *Sheorafuli, Singur, Chnapadanga, Dhonekhali, Dashghara, Mogra, Mayapur, 'Khanakul', 'Jirat', 'Jangipada', 'Seakhala', 'Chanditala', 'Pandua', 'Polba', 'Begampur', 'Jegur', 'Bandipur', 'Vasara', 'Khanpur'*, etc. *'Go-haat'* of *Mayapur* functions on every Sunday where on normal days animals like goat, buffalo, duck, chicken are sold and on 'festive day' (*parab*') camels are also sold. Hide and skin of domestic animals were also sold. In winter dried fish, 'gur' from Date palm sap, earthenwares and articles made by blacksmith were sold in the 'markets' or *'haat'*s. Again in the *'haat'* itself welding works (*'rang jhal'*) are going on and fixing 'iron cap on hoof of drought bulls (*Khure naal poraro*'). There is cow-market (*'Gorur haat'*) in *Tarakeswar*. Here vegetable sellers have to pay Re 1.0 as *'tola'*, hide-seller @ 50 paisa per piece, cloth sellers – Rs 2.00 per day, and 50 paisa per piece for duck and chicken. Price of a cow is usually determined through *'code word'*. *'Haat' of* Pandua including *'Gohaat'* functions on G.T. Road (now NH2). *'Gohatt'* is male managed *haat*. The *'Kartik puja'* of *Chuchura* and *Banshbere* extends upto *'Katoa'* with participation of mass. In the month of *'Aghran' 'Nabanna'* or harvest festival is celebrated all over Bengal. Interestingly at *Kestopur* near *Adisaptagram* there is a *'fish-festival'*. In *Howrah* district also there are many *'haat-bazar'* namely *Jagatballavpur* (1596), *Manikara* (1800), *Tajpur* (1852), *Balguhati* (1700), *'Nijbolia'* (1752), *Munsirhat* (1822), *Dhulasimla* (1845), *Sandhyabajar* (1850), *Chakkashi* (1889), *Boubajar* and *Shashati* (1892), *Uluberia* (1893), *Chatterjee haat*

(1876), *Panchla* (1950), *Khatirbajar* (1951), and many others. *Howrah haat* or *Mangalahaat* founded in the beginning of 19th Century at the initiative of *Matilal Sil* is famous for *Tant-woven* and other cotton cloth where quality cloth from *Hooghly, Barddhaman, Nadia, Medinipur* and *Bankura* brought for sale here. These are taken by wholesalers from *Odisha, Bihar, Assam*, and western part of the country. This '*haat*' functions on Tuesday and the very big (two sq. km area) '*haat*' turns into *bazaar* (market) on other days with stable shops and fresh produces. On each Saturday and Tuesday on the bank of river *Damodar* at *Shyampur Deoantala one hat* exists. By the side of the '*haat*' on the bank of a large pond is situated the house of *Deoan Saheb*. On 1st of '*Magh*' a festival ('*Mela*') is organised. This market sells rice, pulses, fish, meat, potato, parwal, leafy vegetables etc. and on another side clothings etc. or sickle, spade, *machate*, '*snadashi*', '*khunti*' etc. and different earthen utensils and articles. In *Medinipur* district 100 year old '*Khakurda haat*' on every Sunday and Thursday is held and '*mela*' is organised on *Shib Chaturdashi*. In the temple there is one idol of '*Shiva*' made of '*makda*' stone. Little away there is '*haat*' for selling '*Goru*' (cow), '*chhagol*' (goat) etc. Popped rice ('*muri*') is a major commodity sold in this '*haat*'. The '*haat*' used to sell clothes, mosquito-net, shoes, umbrella, stationery articles, spices, paddy, rice, pulses etc. '*Jhudi*', '*Chupdi*', utensils made of gun-metal, brass and aluminium are also sold. Earthen articles sold include '*handi*', '*Kolsi*', etc.

Even commodities like betel leaves, fresh vegetables, dry fish etc. are also sold here. Truck-load of green and dry coconuts are brought to this market from '*Kanthi*', '*Digha*' and other areas. *Mohanpur haat* is adjoining *Jagannathdev* temple of *Dnatan* where different commodities including vegetables are sold from permanent and temporary shops. Shops for selling fish, meat, coconut '*chira*', fruits etc. are part of the stable market while vegetables come only on '*haat*' days. The district has many more '*haats*' namely *Radhamoni, Samra, Ramtarak, Panchkhali, Boligeria, Bhandarchandi, Dora* etc. '*Haats*' of 24-Parganas include *Jibanpur, De-Ganga* (1751), *Sarapul, Swarupnagar* (1700), *Gopapur, Haroa* (1750). *Rajarhat* (1802), *Pnudabazar, Badudia*

(1750), *Berachampa* (1835), *Basirhat* (1940), *Hingalganj, Kamdevpur* (1890), *Bongaon* (`1908), *Habra* (1902), *Bagela* (1918), *Dhonpota* (1930), *Aamtola* (1970) and many others like *Gosaba, Basanti, Jhinki, Maibibi, Jabanmandal, Nepalganj, Joynagar, Hedobhanga, Jamtola, Dhola, Kakmari, Bhangar, Bhojerhat, Latghat, Taldita, Dnadia, Baruipur, Raydighi, Mograhat, Kakdwip* etc. On '*Haatbar*' (Haat day) commodities are mostly transported via boats through rivers and rivulets and bullock-carts on land. Inside '*Haat*' there are sections according to commodities like – '*Maachhaata*', *Sabjihaata, Murgihaata, Bichalihata, Brashhata, Gamchhahaat, Shalukhata* etc. The '*mela*' on last day of '*Paush*' at *Gaighata* runs for one month. Then on the fullmoon of '*Magh*' *Swarupnagar* celebrates '*Deoa*' or '*Yamuna*' mela, *Thakurnagar* celebrates *Barunimela* or *Chaitra ekadoshi* ending with *Ambubachi mela* at *Banpur matiari* in '*Ashad*' month. Persons roam from one *mela* to another with their commodities. This roaming for trading goes on round the year except two monsoon months and is called '*parambulating trade*' by Sudhir Chakrabarti, 1996.

Thus innumerable number of '*haats*' and '*bazars*' all over Bengal are functioning for over three centuries or more. During this period some of '*haat's* are transformed into daily markets (*bazaars*) and some other acted as the centre for development of towns or even city. For obvious reasons some have gained strength and some others weak and deserted. Possibly '*mela*', '*parab*', '*puja*' were older than the '*haats*', and assemblage of large number of people to attend these festivities incited the 'trading' aspect and exchange has been the principal chord that tied mass of people assembled in such places.

11.14 Variety of food from different communities in India

Indian continent has been a land of multiple culture and community. Having long-established principle of 'unity in diversity' Bengal, it is evident from its history, with a open welcoming culture always tried to gain from others in food-habits, clothings, music and many other aspects of culture. Even communities that invaded Bengal, have also settled, mixed and mingled by which Bengalis gained some characteristics that built modern Bengalis. Along with other characters, Bengalis imbibed some of their food culture too. Evidently invasion of Bengal by Marathis from Maharashtra, visit and settling by Marwaris from Rajasthan for business, Punjabis for jobs etc. and Gujaratis for business, and Telegu people to Kharagpur through railway services are behind the migration and settlement of such people that caused cultural admixing. While '*marwaris*' came to *Murshidabad* during '*Nababi*' rule, others possibly came to Bengal during first part of British rule when Calcutta was capital of India. Bengalis as a community grew up all along imbibing culture of different communities to the 'core' in Bengalis and the Poet's couplets read like – '*aamar shonite roycchhe dhwanite taari bichitra sur*' (my blood [genome?] sings the song of that diversity). How food-culture of these communities has penetrated Bengali food culture may be examined, knowing that the raw materials for food preparations coming from agriculture could be a limitation.

(a) 'Marwari' *food culture entered Bengal*

A group of people from Marwar, Rajasthan (mostly from Jodhpur kingdom) came to Bengal, first time in *Jiyagaunge*, Murshidabad during Nawabi period. They were mostly business people and invested in money lending and earning interest out of it. In 18th century Jagat Seth introduced a kind of Private Banking System in Murshidabad with rulers in their clientele. Later 1930 onwards there was a wave of migration from Shekawati and Bikanere to Calcutta particularly *Barabazar* to engage in wholesale business of different commodities e.g. quality '*saaris*' from different parts of India, or potatoes etc. ('*Posta*') from different parts of Bengal and UP or '*Chhana*' ('*Chhanapati*') from Tarakeswar and other places. They settled in Calcutta and some of their food preparations like '*Kheech*' of wheat grains (on '*Akshay Tritiya)* or '*Bati*' (another wheat prepn.) that is based on wheat dough dumplings or '*Churina*' i.e. '*Bati*'s broken into pieces, ground and dipped in '*ghee*' or even '*Gawar Badiyon ka Saag*' made with *mungdal*. Inspite of the standing complain about their speculation, hoarding, and adulteration practices or hoarding cloth, wheat etc. (1917-18) and anti-marwari movements in some adjoining states they were stable in Bengal. Community contributed *'papad'*, *'Chapati'* preparations of *Bengal gram* (black chickpea) and sweets like *'peda'* (from milk), *'laddu'* (mung daal and sugar) and different kinds of snacks made from pulses.

(b) 'Gujarati' *food culture reached Bengal*

'Gujaratis' also came to Calcutta during British rule in the interest of business and these Gujaratis were mostly *'muslims'* and *'Parsis'*. Many Gujarati *Brahmins* also came to Calcutta mainly in respond to *'Rajas'* and *'Jamidars'* of Bengal. *'Memory'* of Gujarat (muslims) came to *Chitpur* through water-ways and settled in *Chitpur*, Calcutta. Another group of Gujaratis came from or via *'Surata'* and are known as *'Surti'* and settled in *'Kolutola-Pataldanga'* area which later was named *'Surtibagan'* that was situated on the west of present Presidency University. Gujaratis are essentially vegetarians and use yogurt (*Dahi*), butter milk (*mattha*), coconut, groundnut, sesame seeds, lime juice, sugar etc. in food preparation that is a highly distinctive Indian cuisine and generally diverse wheat breads and sometimes rice also are staple. Crisp spicy fried *'farshans'* (snacks), most common *'chioda'* or plethora of sweetmeats, chutneys and pickles have already been in the purchase list of Bengali housewives. *Gujrati* families prepare and enjoy *Dalparantha, Chakli, Khaman, Khichu, 'Toor Dal', 'Kadhi', Maslapuri* and *'Bhangi Bata Bhaaji'*, but has not yet entered Bengali kichen.

(c) 'Punjabi' *food culture in Calcutta*

On Sept. 26, 1914 the ship *Komagata Maru* approached Calcutta with 376 passengers mostly Sikhs organised by Baba Gurdit Singh with the desire to meet the British ruler at Calcutta. They were prevented and taken to Budge Budge. Their attempts to meet Governor and hand over a copy of *'Granth Sahib'* was foiled and many were killed by British bullets. But this made rest of them interested in Calcutta. Their settlement was in south Calcutta and with time they started publishing 'Sikh Review' edited by S. Saran Singh. One Punjabi novelist Mohan Kahlon was in Calcutta. Subsequent developments included establishment of Bhowanipur Gurudwara, Khalsa School etc. and another group settled in Baranagar area. Slowly Punjabi cuisine with immense range of dishes using-unique-spices led to establishment of Punjabi restaurants and one pulse preparation – '*Tadka*' became popular. Generally sweet dishes used lots of '*Ghee*' and wheat is their staple food and rice taken in festivals. Later they brought in road side '*Dhaba*' culture in Bengal mostly to serve the people driving from long distances.

Punjabi foods are both vegetarian and non-vegetarian. Their spice use range is also wide from minimal to high. Home cooking is different from restaurant-cooking e.g. they use sunflower or any such oil in home but lots of '*desi ghee*', butter and cream in restaurant. Traditional *Punjabi thali* contains varieties of breads – tandoori roti, lachha parota, Kulchha and naan. Dry *tawabaked* '*chapattis*' and *jawar ki roti*, stuffed *paranthas* and different milk products are in their food list. *Rumali roti* is another unique Punjabi food that were either present in Bengali kitchen or adopted from Punjabis. Their deep fried '*puri*' is '*Luchi*' of Bengali food. '*Bhatoora*' however is not adopted though egg-curry and bhaji are common. Non-vegetarian foods like *Murgha kari* (chicken curry with tomato), butter chicken or chicken tikka are enjoyed by Bengalis in restaurants. '*Murg masollam*' is prepared in Bengali ceremonies. Punjabi vegetarian preparations like *Ahegobi, Alumotor, Dalmakhani, Dal fry, Jira rice, Mokki Di Roti* etc. are also popular. Sweet dishes like *Carrot Halwa, Gulab jamun, Kalakand, Soanpapdi, Sooji Halwa, Kaju barfi* etc. are well taken in Bengali food list, some of which might be already in Bengali-sweet list may be in a little different form.

(d) Madrasi food culture in Bengal

During 1022-1044 AD Tamil King Rajendra Chola advanced through Odissa and defeated Mahipal in 1023 AD. He never tried to occupy Bengal; on the contrary being pious he renovated many temples in Bengal. The culture of high-fly racing Madrasi pigeons attracted Bengalis.

But Madrasi food was initially not very favourite of fish-eating Bengalis but for their being very healthy, nutritious and good for stomach. It slowly gained admiration of Bengalis.

Some of the preparations like '*Meduvadai*', '*Idli*' and '*Dhosa*' became widespread and very much liked by Bengalis. Idli and

Dhosa entered Bengali kitchen along with *'Upma'* – a salty preparation of *'suji'* that was already in Bengali kitchen – as sweet dishes like – *'Halua', 'Payas'* etc. With time *'Idli'* started to be accompanied by *'Sambaram'* and so-called *'Aachae'* in Bengali preparations.

(e) Bihari food preparations in Bengal

'Bihar' has been for sometime at least, a part of greater Bengal but the language, food habit and culture show strong grounds of differences. Bihari cuisine, it appears, is widely popular in the country and outside. These have similarities with north Indian dishes and basic differences with Bengali dishes. Unlike Bengali-dishes they are predominantly vegetarian, based on ingredients like *Dahi, Mattha, Butter, Ghee, Lassi, Mustard oil, salts* etc. *Bihari* preparations with unique characters include *Sattu paratha* (*parathas* stuffed with fried chickpea flour), *Chokha* (spiced mashed potatoes), or *Litti* (ball shaped wheat powder dough baked in mildfire), *Chokhaa* (mashed brinjal, potatoes and tomatoes), *'Saaj', 'Kosta', 'Veg Korma', 'Bhaswan Karela', 'Piyanj parota'* etc. very little of which could enter in Bengali food system. However *Bihari thali* has rice, *roti, aachar, chaatni, Dal*, etc. with similarities. *'Khichdi'* and *'Ghugni'* are very common in both food cultures not being clear about origin of these foods. *'Bhujia'* is clearly a Bihari or north Indian origin. Non-vegetarian dishes like fish curry is not only common in Bengal but it is prepared in unlimited varieties in Bengal. *Bihari kabab* is made with mutton and *'Taash'* of Champaran is one grilled mutton dish that has developed independently in these two adjoining areas. To get a strong aroma Bihari practice of getting chillies, smoked has been adopted in Bengali kitchen in very limited occasions. Similarly use of *'Panchforon'* (saunf, mustard, *methi, jowan and mangracel)* is quite common in both cooking practices.

11.15 Natural calamities and agriculture

In Bengal generally two types of natural calamities that affect agriculture are encountered namely flood and drought. But between the two, continuous rain flooding have been more frequent and destructive. In earlier days, irrigation facilities being very limited drought was more destructive. In addition cyclones and destructive highwind usually destroys the shelters more. Hailstorms destroying crops are also not very common.

Floods have been destructive to Bengal agriculture very often. With passing of time the flooded area has grown. Being an area under monsoon rule, Bengal had many rivers, rivulets, natural canals and large number of small to large water bodies and swamps locally known in the names of '*Khal*', '*Bil*', '*Jolabhumi*', '*Pukur*', '*Daha*', '*Bheri*', '*Jolkar*', '*Nala*', '*Oar*' etc. Long back they were capable of holding huge volume of water. Over last fifty to hundred years silt deposition and failure to excavate such waterbodies has led to fast decline of water carrying capacity of these natural waterbodies. In recent times the floods in 1978, 2000 and 2006 in Bengal have destroyed very large agricultural crop area. Bengal is largely located in lower-gangetic plain and in West Bengal portion of this plain there are 17 major rivers, four drainage basins – together making up 21 large water-shed areas. North and west of this land are not plains including a part of mountain range – *Himalaya* and its foothills and part of *Chotanagpur–plateau* area in west. The huge volume of water from rains over four months (average rainfall 1459 mm and 2705 mm in Himalaya foothills) floods spread over 21.8 lakh ha area in the plains. The drainage sub-basin in East Medinipur and South 24-Parganas comprises of basins of *Keleghai, Pichabhanga, Rasulpur* and *Haldi* rivers that spread over 6.9 lakh ha. Rest of flooded areas are in the districts of Uttar 24-Parganas, Nadia, Murshidabad, Maldah and the two Dinajpur on one side of *Ganga* and Howrah and Hooghly lower Bardhaman on the other side of the river.

Farmers of Bengal out of their long experience go for contingency cropping after flood havoc following unique technologies. A system of free supply of seeds or seedlings to such farmers has been developed over last three decades in Bengal.

Drought ('*Khora*') creates a still harder situation for the farmers. Drought prone areas in West Bengal are *Puruliya, Bankura, Paschim Medinipur*, and portions of *Birbhum* and

Barddhaman districts. Drought in other districts sometimes results from failure of monsoon. Agriculture in non-irrigated areas is affected when drought or rainless spells before and after '*summer*' occurs. During this extended summer period if there be one or two spells of rainfall the drought is not aggressive. These short spells of rains, on failure creates drought situation. Besides when there is delay in arrival or early receed of rains drought may result. Once drought affected, the crop can never be revived or saved. Due to lack of moisture in soil contingency cropping can neither be planned nor implemented. However spread of minor irrigation over last four decades have caused decline in drought-prone area. Cyclone and destructive high winds come in spells at the end of summer in Bengal i.e. in months of *Baisakh-Jaistha* and popularly known as '*Kaal Baisakhi*'. Mostly in the afternoon along with spells of rains the cyclones arrive duration of which is often a short spell. But it destroys all crops and trees in the field as also domestic animals and houses of the farmers. When it has origin in sea, the coastal areas of South 24-Parganas, North 24-Parganas, East Medinipur are much damaged. Coastal dyke (mud) breached at number of places and saline sea water inundates crop fields making cultivation on such lands impossible for years. One example is '*Aila*' of recent times. Heavy untimely rains also destroy crops. All the hazards do occur in other districts too to destroy crops.

11.16 Publications in Bengali on agriculture

Publications like books, magazines, papers published from Bengal in late 19th and early part of 20th century were on progress of agriculture and efforts to make farmers more knowledgeable about methods and techniques of agriculture, and cover larger number of people for developing awareness in agriculture. Most of the publications to be discussed here are published in the first half of 20th century. Among the many publications, many were published in English and Bengali languages in the first two decades that included the famous and first Indian volume '*Handbook of Indian Agriculture, 1901*' by Nityagopal Mukerji followed by another valuable book on '*Sericulture*' in 1919. Besides many leaflets in English and Bengali languages on crop pests and other aspects. Publications in third decade also included many bulletins, books, leaflets and one that needs to be mentioned is '*Sabji Chaas*' by Manmathanath Mitra published in 1925. This Bengali book described commercial and amateurish agriculture, general methods of vegetable growing and characteristics and cultivation methods of 76 different vegetables that includes roots and tubers, stem and leaves, flower-vegetables, fruit vegetables and seed vegetables. This was published by *Bharatiya Krishak Samity* established at Calcutta in 1897. '*Samity*' used to publish a monthly named '*Krishak*'. During this period *Basumati Prakashani*, Calcutta published one book "*Grihastha Darpan*" (1900) by *Fakruddin Mahammad Choudhury* of *Barishal*. This landlord collected to grow in his home garden many crop plants including flower, fruit, medicinal and spice crops and described them. Besides food, daily activities, treatment of diseases and food for patients (*Pothya*), rules of food intake, and discussion on 'seasons' were there. In the appendix part details of crop cultivation in 26 districts (including Tripura) of Bengal in those days have been summarised. In the fourth decade of 20th century publication number has increased enormously. All these publications show the increasing interests of people in agriculture. Different crops, their cultivation and protection methods, rearing methods of different domestic animals, their healthcare, treatment of their diseases etc. were published in the forms of different booklets, leaflets, bulletin etc. Many regular publications were coming out. '*Samachar Darpan*' (1818), '*Gram Barta*', '*Gardners Magazine*', '*Krishak*' were in the frontline being regular. One interesting book, '*Hazar Jinish*', compiled by Upendranath Mukhopadhyay and Satish Chandra Mukhopadhyay was an unique publication possibly at the end of 19th century included one Chapter '*Chaash-Abad*' that consists of discussion on cultivable land, soil, seed, water, manure, pesticides over 323 pages and descriptions of about 30 vegetabels, 14 fruits, 31 flowers and cacti, and 24 fishes. Most important to note is very brief description of *Ipomoea* (*Kalmi*), '*Hinche*', '*Bramhi shak*' etc. plants. '*Juin*', '*Mallika*', '*Chameli*', '*Kunda*' flowers or fishes like '*Khayra*', '*Gurjaoli*' etc. reminds the glorious past of Bengal.

12

Agriculture in Modern Times (1947-2010)

The partition of India and Bengal alongwith, during independence of the country from British rule, has achieved sovereignty and full authority to determine the policies to rule the nation. Hence growth of agriculture under self-rule of Indians at national level and Bengalis in West Bengal has been placed under independent rule of the country named modern times. Considering the period upto 2010 the progress of agriculture over 60-62 years has been generally impressive. Large number of peoples' demand and need has brought an all out change in agriculture along with other sectors. Both the country as well as state has many more requirements from agriculture. The entire changing situation is difficult to be totally brought within a small chapter in a book. The entire period has been divided in two stages only for convenience of presentation taking freedom of some amount of overlapping or crossing the border of the two stages.

12.1 First three decades after independence

India became independent on 15th August, 1947 and the country was partitioned. Bengal was also partitioned that brought a terrible shock both geographically, economically and socially. A large population had to leave East Pakistan (now Bangladesh). These people were offered land in Andaman islands and '*Dandakaranya*' area. Many of these people of a high rainfall, humid, fertile land area could not accept this and tried to find space in West Bengal, already densely populated. They were compelled to take shelter in different places in Bengal – mostly low land swamps and worked hard to live and earn their bread. This resulted in a very hard and complex situation for economic, social activities and agriculture. For example, jute mills were mainly on the banks of river *Ganga* in West Bengal and the crop in those days was mainly produced in East Pakistan area. Large number of skilled farmers were to stay in small space in colonies and camps having no scope to apply their skill in crop cultivation. They simply had to spend this part of their life to come out of the crisis of their existence. People of West Bengal accepted them as own people but nation i.e. the Union Government remained almost non-chalant. Those who could find a space doing agriculture, contributed their ideas and skills inspite of their limitations. West Bengal as a tailored state, inheriting the memory of 'Bengal Famine' of early forties as a state of independent country started its journey as a food-deficit state. Indian agriculture too was not strong with good irrigation system or satisfactory fertiliser-use in the midst of many agriculturally developed country. Some of the states having no pressure of population and through quick development of irrigation facilities started developing agriculture fast. Bengal agriculture, besides this, had another difficult problem i.e ownership of agricultural land. 'Permanent settlement' – guarded landlords (*'Jamidars'*) and money-lenders (*'Mahajans'*) to continue to exploit farmers, share-croppers, and farm labours who were not allowed to plan, implement crop cultivation with full freedom. The entire village atmosphere having infightings, litigations, conspiracy, engagement of muscle and money power-spoilt any positive programme to develop agriculture.

It was so destructive that even scientifically planned projects of Department of Agriculture could not be implemented satisfactorily. For example, in 1961 one such 'fighting' in Kulpi-II Block of South 24-Parganas may be remembered. Owner of very large land area failed to show in crop agriculture and allowed passage of saline water into such land for *'Bheri-fish culture'* that favoured the large farmer to get adjoining small farmers' lands inside his '*Bheri*' since flooding covered all these land. SDO gets AEO's advice to cut open the mud-dyke to drain out the water. But next morning landlord's paid '*lathials*' again built the dyke to keep the '*Bheri*' intact. Looking at the progress of world agriculture one could realise that good agricultural practice with fertiliser use could increase production and independence has created opportunity for all these. In the circumstance, West Bengal had to devote in restructuring of the state, physical and mental rehabilitation of a very large population of refugees within its limited space and resources.

On the other hand at the beginning of 1947 the gazette for removal of the system of 'landlordism' was not placed in the legislature for approval. An ordinance was promulgated that later in 1953 took the shape of Abolition of Jamindari Act, 1953 provided 60 per cent of produce to '*Bargadars*'. An order in 1958 prevented removal of '*bargadars*' from the land they cultivated without the knowledge of court of law. Landlords continued to hold land area above ceiling as orchards, '*bheri*', estate of God, or in the names of children, even in the name of domestic animals. In forties, there was food-crisis all over the country and during 1942-43 a large number of Bengalis died out of hunger. Realising the importance of food production the independent Government in the First Five Year Plan (1951-1956) emphasised agriculture. Number of major irrigation projects namely Bhakra-Nangal, Damodar Valley etc. were started, and of these projects Damodar Valley was to develop irrigation in West Bengal and Bihar.

(a) Weather and agriculture

From the beginning or middle of eighth decade of last century (20th) the four different rainfall areas as considered in those days are (i) 2000 mm or more annual rainfall in the hilly and Himalaya adjoined area with heavy rainfall for seven months from May to November, (ii) 1000-2000 mm annual rainfall area in the large plains, (iii) 500-1000 mm annual rainfall in relatively dry western area, and having no extremely low (less than 500 mm annual rainfall) rainfall area in some western pockets in West Bengal. In 1988, Planning Commission constituted a Regional Agro Climatic Planning Cell in its own office. Sardar Patel Centre for

Economic and Social Research, Ahmedabad and proposed agricultural planning be done according to regional agro-climatic situation and that was accepted by Planning Commission. Following this principle Planning Commission divided the country in 15 agro-climatic regions and accordingly 15 Regional Agricultural Planning Teams were constituted with Vice Chancellors of 15 concerned State Agricultural Universities as chairman.. Thirteen districts of West Bengal constituted the Zone III. Lower Gangetic Plains, three districts namely Darjeeling, Coochbehar and Jalpaiguri were included in Eastern Himalaya Zone and Purulia was included in Eastern Plateau and Hilly Zone. The districts of Lower Gangetic Plains and others were subdivided into six to seven subzones like Hilly (Darjeeling), Tarai (Jalpaiguri and Coochbehar), *Barind* (North and South Dinajpur and Maldah), Alluvial (Murshidabad, Nadia, Hugli, Bardhaman, Howrah and Medinipur) coastal saline (North and South 24-Parganas), *Rarh* (Birbhum and Bankura) and eastern plateau (Puruliya) (Guha and Ghosh, 1997). This procedure actually has linked geographical and soil characteristics of the region concerned. Subsequent developments in regard to global warming coinciding with deforestation, uncontrolled exploitation of minerals and their use and chemical agriculture all over the world – all resulted in 29 per cent decline of rainfall and increase of air temperature. On an average annual soil erosion (5300 Cr. ton) from 32.7 per cent land and 24.78 per cent land area was desertified (Current Science, 25th Nov., 2009; IAASTD Report, 2004). All these had adverse effect on agriculture. In West Bengal average temperature has increased and rainfall declined. Besides, sudden rise in temperature now and then, heavy rainfall anytime, cyclones in coastal areas, land slides in hills, spread of flooded area, increase in saline soil area in the coast, decline in duration of winter etc. are important destructive events of climate change and all these have effects on agriculture.

(b) Institutional activities

In British period, Department of Agriculture, Govt. of West Bengal was located at *Dhaka* and Dept. of Veterinary and Animal Husbandry at Calcutta. Hence state govt. had to establish one Department of Agriculture at Calcutta. Mr. S.K. De, ICS, became the first secretary of the Dept. of Agriculture and Community

Development, who also worked as Director. Mr. M. M. Basu, ICS was the next secretary when Dr. H.K. Nandi, the famous plant breeder joined as first Director. He was Dy. Director, Agriculture in Odissa. In early Dept. of Agriculture's structure at its upper level was Higher Agricultural Service and West Bengal Agricultural Service. In the lower level agricultural extension work was done by personnel of Sub-ordinate Agril Service Class I and Class II and Director was assisted by one Joint Director, and two Deputy Directors. Later, officer posts at District levels and Superintendent posts for Agricultural Farms were created. Upto this stage Animal Husbandry was within the Dept. of Agriculture. One separate Department of Animal Husbandry, Dairy and Veterinary was created in West Bengal in 1959.

(c) Agricultural Research

In 1936, Indian Central Jute Committee was constituted centering that Jute Technology Research Laboratory was developed at Tollygaunge in 1939 to conduct researches on different use of jute fibre. The Institute under ICAR has been developed further and renamed as National Institute of Research on Jute and Allied Fibre Technology. In 1946-47, Jute Agricultural Resarch Institute was established at Nilgaunje, Barrackpur wih Dr B.C. Kundu as its first Director. Subsequently with development of number of sub-centres at Sarbhog, Assam and Pratapgarh it spread its activities and later named as Central Research Institute for Jute and Allied Fibre (CRIJAF). In the same year (1947) Central Inland Fisheries Research Station was also established initially at Calcutta and later (1959) taken to Barrackpur. One station of Central Soil Salinity Research Institute of Karnal (ICAR) was established at Canning, South 24-Parganas to examine the soil salinity problems and crop cultivation on such soils. In seventies of last century National Dairy Research Institute, Eastern Zone was established by ICAR at Kalyani. The Regional Fertiliser Testing Laboratory was also established at Kalyani in nineties of last century.

In the mean time Prof Prasanta Chandra Mahalanabis, returning from Rothansted Research Station, England, established Calcutta Statistical Laboratory that was subsequently developed into Indian Statistical Institute, Baranagar and opened up the road to application of statistics in agriculture that was appreciated worldwide. By 1961, one Crop Science Unit was created under ISI to pursue this research and the unit was finally renamed as Agricultural Science Unit. Indian Institute of Technology was established at Kharagpur in 1952 with one Agriculture and Food Engineering Department to study and conduct research in the discipline. Prof A. Basu, Prof Sunit Mukherjee and others led education and research in Food Science and Chemical Engineering in Jadavpur University.

(d) Agricultural research through All India Coordinated Research Projects

Initially number of All India multilocation research projects on food crops were launched and during 1969-70 Rice Research Project was under the co-ordinatorship of Freeman and SVS Shastri, Maize project and Wheat projects were started and Chunchura was made a station of rice research. One yearly workshop was arranged for getting scientists from 12-14 stations all over India (at Hyderabad, first two yrs) to discuss progress, to plan next year's programme, make recommendations and arrange exchanges of experiences. Dwarf paddy variety was created from '*Dee-Ge-oo—Gen*' and one of the first batch was Taichung Native-1. Variety IR-8 was brought from IRRI, the Philippines and Joya, Bala and Ratna were developed through Co-ordinated Project System. Some others brought from IRRI are IR-20, IR-22. The project research system put all varieties from different areas in Initial Evaluation Trial and Varieties like IET-826, IET-1444 (*Rasi*) etc. finally reached farmers field. In 1973-74, All India Wheat Improvement Project had Kalyani Station initially under control of State Agriculture Dept. and later under BCKV and this AICRP produced *Kalyan Sona, Sonalika, Janak, UP-2338* varieties. AICRP-Maize, Jowar, barley, etc. though did not have any Station in West Bengal, produce varieties like *Decan* and *Megha*, *Swati* and M*ugti* and *Manjula* and *Geetanjali* respectively. During this period varieties of wheat obtained were Joy, Vijay, Motia that are very good for food industries. Varieties of malt-barley selected were *Rekha* and *K-551*. AICRP-potato has produced *Kufri Jyoti, K. Chandramukhi, K. Badsha, K. Sindur* etc. True Potato Seed (TPS) was produced and popularised during these researches. Many other varieties of different other crops came from the co-ordinated Research Project system like IPC-937, 93-5 of chickpeas, NDM-88-14 of *Mung*, NDU-888 of '*Kalai*', BDA-88-29 and PDA-88-33-1 of Pigeonpea. At Kalyani Station soybean varieties like *Brag. Clarke* etc. were selected. Oilseed project has produced S-42, P6FH-67 and *Jwalamukhi* of Sunflower, *Girnar-1* of Groundnut, DCS-9 and DCH-30 of Castor, Co8028 and CoLK-9101 of Sugarcane, LS-6 of sugarbeet, *Anjali, Purnima, Jyoti* of cotton, hybrids of cotton like *Kirti, Hybrid-4* etc., JRO-632, *Rupali*, of olitorious jute and JRC-321 of capsularis jute.

All India Co-ordinated Research Project on vegetables has also produced high yielding varieties of brinjal like *Arka Nibi, Arka Nilkantha, A. Keshab,* of *Bhindi* namely *A. Abhoy, A. Anamika*, or of Beans namely *A. Joy, A. Vijay* of Bottle Gourd namely *Pusa Nabin, A. Bahar,* of Bitter gourd Hybrid *Priya* and BG14, of carrot namely *Pusa Meghali*, of cowpea namely *Sel-263*, of Peas namely JR-83, of cabbage namely *Sri Ganesh Gol*, of cauliflower namely *Pusa Hybrid*, of chilli namely *Panniyur*-1, of *Sem* namely *Arka Joy, Vijay*, of *Amorphophallus* namely '*Kavur*', *Kusum* etc. have changed the scenario of crop fields.

Project on flowers and ornamentals produced varieties like *Swapna, Mira, Najrana, Punam, Jwala, Gajal, Agnirekha, Suchitra, Mayur* and *Kohra* of *Gladiolus, Usha, Arjun, Chitra, Dr. B P Pal, Begum Sikandar, Aloke, Mahara* of *Bouganvilla Basanti, Purnima, Shefali, Taruni* and *Indira* of Chrysanthemum. Hybrid T-Group varieties like *Raktagandha, Anurag, Arjun, Dulhan, Bajran,* Floribunda group varieties like *Aakash, Nortaki, Ajij, Chitachor, Jantar Mantar* and Miniature group varieties like *Delhi Pinkparle*, Delhi white parle, etc. Varieties of *Juin* and *Bele* are *Co.P. Chi* and *Pali Mullai*, of tuberose are *Rajatrekha, Swarnarekha*, and Hybrid variety are obtained. New variety of Chinarose are *Fulkari, Benajir, Chitralekha* and *Srimati Indira Gandhi*. Similarly *Niharika* of Lantana, *Jhumka* and *Ratnam* of

Portulaca were popularised. Among spices *Sudarshana, Subarna, Suguna* of turmeric, *Co-2* and *UL* of coriander, *PGS-35,* Wainad Nandan *Suruchi, Surair, Potangi* of Ginger, KS69, *HP-732, 813, Srikara Shavakara* of Black pepper are high yielders. Among furits *BMA39-4, Hybrid 24* and *Jhargram* of *Cashew, Pathankot* of sweet orange, *East Coast tall* and *Chandrasekhar* of coconut, *Promali, Vikram* of lemon, *PKM-1* of *Sapeta, Co-1, Governor*, of Banana, *Hybrid-1, L49, Harija*, of Guava, *Arka Aruna, Arka Anmol* tc. of Mango are some new, high yielding varieties. In addition *Kew* and *Queen* of pineapple, *Kolkattiya* of Litchi, and Monoecious or Gynandrocious varieties of papaya are good selections and contributed towards progress of agriculture of the state.

(e) Agricultural education

In 1949, one College of Agriculture was established under Calcutta University at Jhargram in Medinipur. Within a short while (1953) Dept. of Agriculture, Govt. of West Bengal established at Ranikuthi, Tollygaunge offering a three year B.Sc. Agr. degree and the Jhargram College was closed down. This State Agriculture College was shifted from Tollygaunge to Mohanpur, Nadia in an excellent building and the college was named Birla Agriculture College in the name of donor family. In 1960, a new University – 'Kalyani University' with Agriculture College as its first faculty was established and the first batch of graduates (B.Sc. Ag.) of this University came out in 1961. Since 1962 post-graduate studies in disciplines of agriculture started with Plant Pathology and others like Agronomy, Soil Science, Agril. Chemistry, Genetics and Plant Breeding, Entomology, Agril. Extension, Agril. Economics from 1963 and Agril Statistics, Animal Science and Soil and Water Conservation subsequently. Calcutta University also offered postgraduate degrees in Horticulture and Agril. Botany and later Agronomy and Soil Science. From late seventies Palli Siksha Sadan, Visva Bharati also started offering B.Sc. Ag degree. In 1956, a branch of National Bureau of Soil Survey and Land Use Planning, Nagpur was started at Calcutta which later in 1974 became a Regional Centre of NBSSLUP.

(f) Agricultural University

The first state agricultural university (SAU) was established in September, 1974 at Mohanpur, Nadia with the wiseman of the east Prof Sudhanshu Bhusan Chattopadhyay, as its Vice Chancellor. The Agriculture Faculty offering four year B.Sc. Agr. Hons degree course, and Veterinary and Animal Husbandry Faculty offering five year BVSc and AH degree course and four year B. Tech. Dairy Technology degree course. Both the Faculties offered two year Masters degree in different disciplines and research project based Ph.D. degree programme. Under the Directorate of Research besides having its own research scientists in Agronomy and Soil Science, number of All India Co-ordinated Research Projects and six Zonal Research Stations at Hills (Kalimpong), Terai (Poondibari), Old Alluvium (Maldah), Red Laterite (Jhargram), New Alluvium (Gayeshpur), Coastal Saline (Kakdwip) and number of substations. Besides number of agricultural farms were developed all over Bengal for production of quality seeds of different crops as also providing space for different research programmes. Directorate of Extension Education was responsible for training, extension education and demonstrations of modern varieties and technologies in collaboration with Directorate of Agriculture, Govt. of West Bengal. To meet the increasing demands of training a Farmers Training Centre was established at Kalyani. The establishment of a Central Library at Mohanpur that is largest in eastern India was important.

The desired object of creation of SAUs since 1960 in the country was to provide agricultural education-research a free and sovereign environment that only could bring out innovativeness in scientists and teachers to workout new vistas of agricultural development in a state. The second object was to organise agril universities and regional research stations to act as centres to supply technologies and technical personnel to the state department of agriculture. The entire concept of agricultural development demands through this system agril extension network of the Govt. Dept. of Agriculture shall receive technologies and expertise from the agricultural university system. But in West Bengal apathetic relation of Dept. of Agriculture with SAUs has failed the above concept. The memorandum of understanding between Agril Univ. and State

Dept. remained non-implemented. A campus of agricultural education and research at Poondibari, Coochbehar created under BCKV later became a separate Agril Univ. i.e. *Uttarbanga Krishi Viswavidyalaya* with initially two faculties namely Agriculture and Horticulture later strengthened with Agricultural Engineering. Three of regional research stations at Kalimpong, Maldah and Poondibari were transferred under UBKV.

(g) Agricultural Extension and Development

Initially agricultural extension in the country or in Bengal emphasised second crop in agriculture. From the beginning of fifties of last century extension programmes included 'vegetable garden for home consumption', 'kitchen garden' or 'Homsted Garden' etc. In 1952, 'Community Development Programme' was started in some areas of West Bengal. The objectives of CDP were – all out improvement in village life in the spheres of agriculture, village industries, cooperatives, village engineering, animal rearing leading to an all out development of village life. Later this programme was modified and developed into National Extension Service in 1953 to bring larger rural population under the programme. This aimed at faster agricultural development with lower investment. To start with about 50 NES Blocks were developed in West Bengal. During second five year plan (1957-1962) entire rural area of the state was brought under NES Blocks. In the block area number of projects aimed toward increasing crop production. To build up minor irrigation infrastructures programmes of building dykes, excavating ponds and canals, and digging wells were taken up. Use of swing basket (*Siuni*') or '*Don*' to raise water to uplands increasing irrigated area were popularised and use of '*pail*' ('*sora*') to moisten crop fields getting water from channels in the field. These however were quite common in ancient Bengal farming practices. All these made second crop in Rabi season possible but also provided life saving irrigation to the first crop when necessary. During this period Dept. of Agriculture used to celebrate '*Vana Mahotsav*', that later became a programme of Forest Department, through distribution of saplings. Lord Boyed sometimes back assessed progress of agriculture on behalf of the Government. Following that 'Grow

More Food' campaign was taken up in 1952 in the midst of food crisis in West Bengal. Food grain ration system was functioning in cities, towns and surrounding areas. Rice grains obtained from different states that often on distribution invited different troubles and skirmishes for the food grains being spoilt. Since mainly wheat was produced by most north Indian states, food supply through ration shops included wheat also. Bengalis were not used to consuming bread etc. made from '*Atta*' (ground wheat) the non-availability of enough rice compelled them to consume bread in the evening (supper) or as breakfast. In the villages in pavements of cities and towns, railway platforms and in many official (camps) and unofficial settlements of poorer refugees (migrating from East Pakistan) were seen to cook broken rice grains ('*Khud*'), leafy and root-vegetables and poor quality bold rice grains or rice grains full of broken stones ('*Kankar*') (often mixed by unscrupulous traders) once a day to survive. Some people consumed '*Dalia*' (broken maize or wheat grains), 'mailo' etc. to live. From fifties to beginning of sixties of last century there was a supply of wheat grains from USA under PL480 programme against only the carrying charge of ship to meet the requirement of food for poor Indians. Shortage of rice led to banning sale of rice grains in open market (except in ration shops) and any rice selling was termed locally as '*black*'. For earning some money refugee women used to purchase rice in villages in small packets (non-ration area), carry them in local trains to enter Calcutta (cordoned area) and sale at a relatively higher price. State administration represented by police created trouble and harassment and sometimes risk of life from moving trains. This continued upto the end of seventies. For refugees State Government offered settlements in Andamans or '*Dandakaranya*' (MP) and Sisal Farm in Birbhum (suitable crop for drought prone area). People coming from high rainfall areas of East Pakistan did not have any liking for living and cultivating in such dry areas.

Another important area of agricultural extension in those days was to popularise chemical fertilisers among farmers that started in West Bengal also by offering chemical fertilisers

(Ammonium sulfate) free of cost for arranging demonstrations in farmers' plot as also in Govt. Farms. Side by side programmes to demonstrate importance of organic matter and humus in production increase as also building up of soil fertility. Using road side space programme of composting was taken up using green materials like *Eichhornia* (*Kachuri pana*), grasses and other succulent weeds, chopped, mixed with cowdung to make 'heaps' covered with clay coating and allowed to rot for two to three months to get organic manure. '*Dhaincha*' (*Sesbania*) seeds in small packets were distributed free or against nominal price to farmers for growing as green manure crop. Then programme at district or subdivision level to lend chemical fertiliser on credits, that the farmer could repay in cash or kinds. First fertiliser factory was established at Sindhri, Bihar and later number of fertiliser factories came up in different states including the one at Durgapur, West Bengal.

Japanese method of paddy cultivation was a big campaign in West Bengal in sixties developing Ranaghat Farm as the training centre where some Japanese experts lived to develop the farm into a Japanese Paddy farm and trained personnel and made demonstrations. In this programme fresh agricultural graduates were employed initially only for Aman paddy season as Food Production Assistants (FPA). The campaign made a mark on the production of paddy in the state. For popularising technologies in agriculture, Dept. of Agriculture started publishing and distributing leaflets, pamphlets, bulletins, posters, charts etc. in Bengali and use. Department also started publishing a Bengali periodical on agriculture named '*Basundhara*'. To increase production of pulses a programme of distributing quality seeds of different pulse crops among farmers was started. But due to the poor quality of the seeds collected, the programme was withdrawn. For increasing sugarcane production training programmes for farmers were taken up to select seed-canes, treatment of setts etc. But these programmes did not meet much success. But farmers became aware of the techniques through these programmes. In fact results of these programmes were not scientifically analysed to understand their impact on the growth of agriculture in the State. Practically over three decades following the programmes particularly on compost making, spread of *Dhaincha* as green manure crop or production of sugarcane or pulses not much impact could be felt and the sugarmills in Ahmedpur, Birbhum or Palashi, Nadia became sick and finally closed down.

In fifties of last century central project on crop protection was launched. The demonstrations on use of pesticides attracted farmers. The project initially used organochlorine products like DDT and BHC as insecticides and perenox (copper compound) as fungicide, agallol, ceresan and agrosan GN (all mercury compounds) as seed treating fungicides. In early days, Bengal farmers commonly used ash from '*Chula*', water from '*Hookka*' ('*Hoonko*') containing tobacco extracts, and ash mixed with kerosene oil were applied with hands or broom sticks or with a bunch of straws. Use of kerosene-soaked rope, kerosene-emulsion and tobacco decoction might have started earlier than British rule. But progress in plant protection activities have been very slow. At the beginning of 'Modern period' of agricultural development programmes on soil conservation have been taken up especially in the districts prone to soil-erosion. Areas included hilly areas of Darjeeling district, Birbhum, Bankura, Puruliya and West Medinipur where land surface was hilly, rolling, wavy and with slopes.

By the end of fifties eight 'Gram Sevak Training Centres' were established at Maldah, Coochbehar, Kalyani, Narendrapur, Balurghat, Kalimpong, Barddhaman and Fulia to train in agriculture the staff of Dept. of Agriculture and those who were interested to work under the Department. The centres were later named Agricultural Training Centre and trained staff were called '*Krishi Prajukti Sahayak*' instead of '*Gram Sevak*'. After partition of the country and the state the vast jute area remained in East Pakistan ('Bangladesh') and most of the jute mills were located in West Bengal on the bank of river '*Ganga*'. As a result there was definite programme for increasing jute area after independence in West Bengal. Department of Agriculture recruited Union Agricultural Assistants and Jute Field Assistants and one Jute Development Officer was appointed to supervise their works. Side by side the set up of staff like Agricultural Demonstrator and Agricultural Inspector were abolished slowly in sixties. Thereafter since sixties the responsibility of agricultural extension work was assigned to staff recruited as Agricultural Extension Officer (AEO) (Block level), Asst. AEO, Sub-divisional Agricultural Officer (SAO) at sub-division level and District Agricultural Officer (DAO). Initially the leader of a Development Block was an Administrative Officer BDO whose leadership guided the extension activities of AEO, Veterinary Surgeon (VS), Panchayet Inspector (PI), Lady Social Welfare Officer (LSWO), Co-operative Inspector (CI) etc. assembled in BD Office. Through this system villagers in a block area were used to receive expert-advices in different spheres. However, the essential principle of such village extension work was a resource survey of the village or the Block area in the first year of Block activity called 'pre-extension stage' that unfortunately was rarely taken up failing to realise its importance. By this local character and resources were ignored in framing a plan for agricultural development of the village or block concerned. Later many more changes in the action-programme of agriculture in a block area took place.

After the West Bengal Panchayet Act was passed in 1956, '*Gram*' and '*Anchal*' panchayets were constituted through indirect election. As a result no devolution of power and direct participation of village people in Panchayet system was effected. However by 1963, 50 per cent of the villages and 60 per cent of villagers were covered by this panchayet system. Then in 1963 the '*Jela Parishad*' Act was enacted. As a result a four-tier panchayet structure – *Jela Parishad, Anchalik Parishad, Anchal Panchayet* and '*Gram Panchayet*' came into being. This panchayet system was formally inaugurated in 1964 but no devolution of administrative and economic power from State Government took place. The Government of the village did not take shape. Like many other Govt. Depts., Agriculture Dept. was also growing. The Agricultural Statistics wing was converted to Socio-Economic Evaluation branch. The collection of data about crop-wise area cultivated, production, productivity etc. were made. In 1962,

Bardhaman district was selected for Intensive Agricultural District Programme (IADP) and it was started. Object was to increase production of rice for economic upliftment of the farmers. This project of S. Ijonson and funded by Ford Foundation aimed at introduction of extensive changes in paddy-culture technology. This was followed by launching of similar project in 16 agricultural districts of the State. DAO's were made Project Executive Officer (PEO) assigning additional responsibility. In nine of these districts nine Joint Directors of Agriculture were placed to lead the entire programme of the district. Number of technical experts like agronomists, soil and fertiliser chemists and plant protection specialists were posted to strengthen the activities. Attempts were made to initiate partial mechanisation and bring in modern agriculture. To organise the entire state-wide programme the state was divided into four ranges and run the programmes. Along with soil tests done at State Agricultural Research Institute, Tollygaunge were also merged with this programme. Farmers utilised this service although farmers of the entire State could not be served. Next programme was Intensive Area Development Programme (IADP) in 1964 for agriculture development in the State.

In 1964, National Dairy Research Institute, Eastern Regional Centre (NDRI) was established at Kalyani, Nadia mainly to conduct researches on animal nutrition. In 1963, another agricultural education institution was started at Visva Bharati, Birbhum through establishment of *Palli Siksha Sadan* at Sri Niketan. In 1962, State Dept. of Animal Husbandry and Dairying established one Institute for teaching Dairying as one year Diploma course at Haringhata, Nadia.

(h) Development of major irrigation programmes

Government of India enacted in 1948 to constitute Damodar Valley Corporation – a multi-object project with flood control, irrigation, electricity-generation and conservation of natural environment as the objects. The project created irrigation-potential of 3640 sequence km area/ '*Bundh's* erected were '*Tilaiya*' on Barakar river in 1953, *Maithon* in 1957 and *Panchet* in 1959. Besides *Durgapur barrage* was erected on *Damodar* river in lower flow area in 1955 to control water release. Many irrigation canals were dug alongwith. Bihar Government erected *Tenughat* dam on *Damodar* river that is now in *Jharkhand*. Hydel electricity projects were developed at *Tilaiya, Maithon* and *Panchet* with a potential of 144 MW electricity generation.

DVC is capable of producing 2745 MW electricity at *Chandrapura, Bokaro, Durgapur* and *Mejia*. DVC's irrigation potential is spread over Bihar and Bardhaman and Hooghly districts in West Bengal. Electricity is supplied in lower Damodar areas like Bardhaman, Hooghly, Howrah, Bankura and part of Puruliya in West Bengal.

Mayurakshi irrigation project was developed in 1955. This river is generated from *Trikut* hills and passes through Jharkhand and Birbhum and Murshidabad of West Bengal to merge in Hooghly river. *Canada* Dam was erected on this river at *Massanjore* to control flood and irrigate agricultural fields. *Tilpara* barrage construction helped irrigation of six lakh acres and generated 2000 kW electricity. Finally it appears that 'floods' could not be checked particularly on east bank of *Bhagirathi* in Nadia, Murshidabad, and North 24-Parganas where actually floods have increased.

Kangshabati project was taken up during Second Plan period by erecting one bund at *Khatra* in 1956 on the *Kangshabati* river. Irrigation of West Medinipur, East Medinipur, Bankura and Hooghly was arranged with water from *Shilabati* and *Bhairav* rivers and one *Anicu Dam* constructed in 1872 has been used along with.

The largest and most complex river bund project is *Tista* project building of which was started in 1976-77. This project was started to irrigate 9.22 lakh hectare agricultural land in six districts of North Bengal and generate 67.50 MW of electricity. Till date in three phases project components like *Tista* barrage at *Odlabari*, Pick-up barrage on *Mahananda* at *Fulbari* and at Jalpaiguri were built. Pickup barrage is already constructed on *Dahuk* river at *Chopra*, Uttar Dinajpur. Excavation of *Tista-Mahananda* link canal and the next-stage canals, minor and sub-minor canals are mostly completed. The main canal from *Dauk barrage* has also been completed as also the *Tista-Jaldhaka* canal. Some more works remain to be completed. Thus in many areas in West Bengal, bunds, barrages and canals have extended river-water use in irrigation. But unfortunately failure in regular reclamation of water reservoirs and canals particularly in case of a large project like DVC has led to decline in utility of such projects. On the other hand failure to develop field-channels in such project areas caused extensive wastage of irrigation water. Wastage of irrigation water is also a result of distributing irrigation water on the basis of supply duration (hours) leading over use of water.

(i) Change of varieties

At Chunchura Paddy Research Station, B.N. Ghosh identified *Lathisail* as one day length independent short duration variety that succeeded in cultivation in short-day periods in winter. The breeding programme in South India (*Adhuturai*) by crossing '*Japonica*' and '*Indica*' subspecies of rice produced high yielding varieties (HYV) like '*ADT-27*', '*Masuri*' of rice of which *Masuri* was accepted and released in West Bengal. Locally developed varieties upto end of fifties, were '*Satika*', '*NC-1526*', '*Dhairal*' and '*Dular*' among direct sown '*Aus*' paddy, '*Charnak*', *Marichbuti, Bhutmuri, Bankura-6*, '*Jhanji-34, CH-45* and NC-918 among transplanted aus. '*Dular*' and *NC 1626* were also transplanted. For selection of '*Aman*' varieties adaptation to soil conditions were important. For uplands of silty clay soils varieties like *Churnakathi, Lathisail* and *Badkalamkathi*-64, for medium and medium low lands *Rupsail, Sitasail, Patnai-23, Bhasamanik, Jhingasail, Nagra, Kalma-222, Raghusail, Indrasail, Dudhsar, Dahijira, Kumragode, Nigersail, Bamati-370, 'Kataribhog'*, *Randhunipagol* and *Tilakkachari* were selected. For medium up land of red soil area varieties selected were *Churnakathi, Badkalamkathi-65, NC918* and *NC517* and for medium lowlands varieties chosen were *Rupsail, Bhasamanik, Ajan-246, Dahijira, Jhingasail* and *Patnai-23*. For medium and medium lands of saline area varieties selected were *Patnai-23, Sitasail, Rupsail* and *SR-26-B* while varieties selected for medium uplands of hilly area were BSAB-4 and for medium low lands varieties were

Ramtulsi, Adde, CH-988 and *CH-4*. Two more varieties for low saline tract were *Matla* and *Hamilton*. Varieties selected for flood-prone areas were *RD-19* and *Jalplaban*. Most of these varieties were actually selected through cultivation of these and many other varieties in ancient Bengal. In his book NG Mukerji, 1901 has discussed large number of paddy varieties some of which may be quoted. In early days Bengal was full of *'Khal', 'Bil', 'Daho', 'Jola', 'Pukur'* and many other water bodies as also swamps and flood lands that required selected paddy varieties for growing. Some are *'Oti Rang', 'Sadaora', 'Meghi', 'Rupsal', 'Ova', 'Lalora', Sankhchura, Kadurtupi, 'Bhut Kaurabi', 'Pashakathi', 'Soura', 'Paromananda', 'Aaman', Nadonghata', 'Muktashal', 'Sambora', 'Kalashal', 'Nilratan', 'Nilkantha'*, etc. Some of these varieties yielded even 45-50 *maund* per acre. He named for some other lands in Bardhaman varieties like *'Kanakchur'* and *Harinakhuri* producing quality *'Khoi'* (popped rice). *'Knejurchari'* produced panicles that are similar to the bunch of Date-palm. *'Pakshiraj'* grains appeared winged and its rice had some medicinal properties. *'Paramannasal'* emitted sweet smell on cooking and this alongwith *'Randhunipagol'* were scented but not fine grained. Scented and fine grain varieties are *'Gobindabhog', 'Khasghani', 'Bashmati', 'Benafuli', 'Kamini'* and *'Badshabhog'*. Grains of *'Hatishal'* were large and bold but yield was not so impressive. High yielders giving 45-50 maund grains per acre were *'Otirang', 'Sadaora', 'Meghi', 'Ora', 'Bonkamal', 'Chilerangi', 'Uttar Kalma', 'Lalora', 'Tuki-Lata-Mol', 'Uri', Lakshmibilas, 'Sindurtupi', 'Bhut kourabi', 'Pashakati', 'Soura', 'Ratiramshal', 'Kalboyra', 'Panikalma', 'Sholpana', 'Aman', 'Nadanghata', 'Sambara', 'Kalshal', 'Metekuji', 'Nilkantha'* etc. Mukerji, 1901 claimed many more varieties that were high yielding. There was a devastating flood in Bengal in September 1900. Plants of varieties after being submerged under water for 12 days produced normally are *'Kapursal', 'Kelejira', 'Samudrabali', 'Mohanbhog'*, etc. In those days *Boro paddy* area was very small though it was done following one of two methods, namely incubating soaked seeds in wet gunny bag to sprout and sowing them on soft, claye soil in just drying *'Bil'* called *'Baran aman'* (varieties with tall stem) and raising seedlings and transplanting called *'Rayda'* that was harvested later.

In case of *wheat* variety like '*Dudhia*' was produced to get flour. Varities '*Jamali*' and '*Gangajali*' were used to produce '*Suji*' and '*Aata*'. Other varieties of wheat grown in Bengal are '*Kheri*', '*Piusa*', and '*Namibia*'. '*Jamali*' was an early variety that matured and harvested in *February*. *Maize* however was grown in house-yards or on the bank of ponds as kitchen crop, grains on cobs roasted and consumed. But different pulses were grown in other districts usually in small pockets to meet household requirements only. '*Chola*' or '*Boot*' (Gram), '*Khesari*' (*Lathyrus*), *Mung*, '*Kalai*', '*Arhar*'. '*Motor*' (Peas), '*Masur*' (Lentil) etc. and the scented mung variety – '*Sonamung*' was also a pride of this land. Varieties of different crops have changed with time – slowly but unchecked.

(j) Progress of agriculture

During 1965-66 high yielding dwarf varieties namely *Taichung Native-1, Taichung-65* and *Tainan-3* and later from the Philippines – IR-8 varieties of rice were introduced in India and West Bengal. In case of wheat *New Pusha* group of varieties from IARI were replaced with dwarf HY-varieties like *Sonora-64* and others brought from Mexico. All were aimed at production of food grains initiated through import of record quantity of seeds. During this five to six years food production in the country increased by four to five per cent and population by two per cent, making the country self-sufficient in food production and this period of agriculture is termed '*Green Revolution*'. Through this a procedure of variety release took shape like acclimatisation of imported germ plasm to local climate, development of new variety by crossing imported germ plasm with local promising variety and releasing the best variety obtained through these steps for use by farmers. This is how rice varieties like Jaya, Ratna, Bala or wheat varieties like Kalyan Sona, Sarbati Sonora, Sonalika came into being. During 1966-1970 Central Variety Release Committee and State Variety Release Committees were constituted who were responsible for studying and analysing all the experimental data for the varieties proposed and decide to release the variety to farmers for cultivation.

The programme of releasing high yielding varieties was taken up in 1966 offering seeds of varieties, fertiliser required, opportunity for irrigation and machinery use and modern crop protection measures for best production. Small and marginal farmers faced problems for arranging all these. Hence ICAR came forward with *'minikit'* of HYV-seeds etc. for farmers which increased farmers' participation in the programme very fast. *'Minikit'* programme was adapted for post-flood or post-drought situation for Bengal farmers and became very popular among small and marginal farmers i.e. most of the farmers in West Bengal. Department of Agriculture utilised this concept in different areas of farming to receive positive response. In 1968, Department created Agro Industries Corporation to cater quality seeds, fertiliser, machineries and plant protection chemicals that slowly spread in the villages. Light tractors and power-tillers became popular among a section of farmers and to extend loans agencies like Small Farmers' Development Agency (SFDA) and Marginal Farmers and Agricultural Labour Development Agency (MFALDA) were constituted. The programme started in the districts of Darjeeling, Hooghly, West Dinajpur, Nadia, Murshidabad, Maldah and Coochbehar but not many of the farmers were prepared for this since their existence on the land they cultivated was not strong and deep-rooted. The responsibility of disbursing loans was assigned to nationalised banks in 1969. Short, medium and long-term loans were permitted and even for building infrastructure such loans were available. In 1970, the Village Development Department of the Central Government launched *'Gramin Jibika Mission'* through *'lead bank'* projects. Provisions were made through NABARD, Reserve Bank and nationalised banks for village youths taking loans with priority to develop processing plants for agricultural produces as also other fields in villages.

Saline tracts in Sundarban were difficult for crop production in *'Rabi'* or winter season for salinity and absence of irrigation facilities. In dry hot season accumulation of white salt powders on soil surface in patches was common. Hence programmes for growing salt-tolerant crops like cotton, sugar beet etc. were attempted. Short duration varieties of cotton could produce *'boll'* before onset of monsoon and give good production. But absence of ideal variety and pest problems failed the programme. Later a programme of '*Nimpeeth Asram*' raising seedlings in polybag and planting them in field showed the road to success. Growing sugarbeet and establishing one alcohol producing plant to utilise sugarbeet raw material also failed for lack of strong will on the part of the developers. Number of such attempts were made for first three decades after independence. Side by side pressure of a very high population density as also shortage of food grains created extreme discontent among poor rural people and such food crisis here and there erupted in 1967-68 at '*Nakshalbari*', North Bengal in the form of a violent 'farmers' revolt' that was with arms' against the administration. One local communist leader Charu Mazumdar in the process deserted communist party to form a new revolutionary party and changed the slogan of 'ownership right on the land' to 'revolution to oust state power', though not successful but has shaken the state power all over India. At the beginning of seventies of last century Dept. of Agriculture created its Agriculture Meteorology Section and different areas of the State Weather Stations with modern equipments measuring rainfall, wind velocity and direction, maximum and minimum temperature, humidity, evaporation rate, bright sunshine hours and issue forecast the weather conditions to help farmers in their cultivation practices. In drought prone districts like Puruliya, Bankura and Medinipur extension of irrigation projects and aforestation programmes were started. The Accelerated Food Production Programme (AFPP) based upon irrigation programmes was quite popular among farmers. In 1974, 'Minor Irrigation Corporation' was created with the support from World Bank and extensive installation of deep and shallow tubewells, river lift irrigation (RLI) programme, creation of 'Dug-wells', erection of dykes ('*Jore Bandh*') etc. implemented through Agricultural Engineering section of the Department. Thereafter a separate Dept. of Minor Irrigation was created. In 1976-77, this project was further expanded to include dry farming, soil conservation, survey of groundwater etc. and loan giving institutions were strengthened to fund all such programmes, extension of horticultural crop cultivation and finally multiple crop programme were taken up.

Crops included photoperiod independent varieties of rice, pulses, oilseeds, or vegetables as second crop. In hilly areas centrally funded programmes of soil conservation, development of fruit gardens and cultivation of winter flowers were taken up. 'Sundarban Development Board' was formed in 1970 to launch all out development of the area including construction of roads and transport for communication, digging of ponds that ultimately helped agricultural development, cultivation of salt tolerant crops like cotton, safflower, sugar beet, watermelon etc. were encouraged. Growers in this area used to cultivate salt tolerant paddy variety – SR 26 as also bitter gourd and chilli. 'Land shaping' – by digging ponds and using the soil to build its banks to harvest rain water (sweet water) to be used in growing crops in *Rabi* season also became popular among people of Sundarbans.

Beginning in 1974 Comprehensive Area Development Project (CADP), implementation of the project started in 1975, coming out of all limits of Departmental activities it started village development works over an area in a comprehensive manner. The programme included agriculture, seed production, poultry, fishery, cottage industry, building of roads and ultimately poverty-alleviation. This power of comprehension and collectiveness made an impact on rural development and economy.

During fifth plan period (1975-80) for judicious use of 'bundh' irrigation water 'Command Area Development Programme' was started mainly in Barddhaman, Bankura, Birbhum (Seuri area) developing infrastructure for taking '*Bundh*' or barrage water to agricultural fields for irrigation. Side by side in 1975 itself in five districts namely Bardhaman, Nadia, Murshidabad, Maldah, and West Dinajpur – deep and shallow tubewells, river lift irrigation programme were slowly started to spread irrigation to a greater extent.

Agricultural marketing system development was started alongwith supply of inputs to farmers in the form of creating three wholesale markets and 200 'Agro-service centers' as models. This programme started with the support of 'International Development Association and was not continued in other areas of the state although these were quite helpful to farmers as also for agricultural development.

(k) Seed production programmes

During British period in 1929 as per recommendation of "Royal Commission on Agriculture", attempts to increase agricultural production were made through seed production. Department of Agriculture later took special initiative to establish 'Seed Farms' from 1957. Original plan was to establish one 25 acre Seed Farm in each Block. Some such farms after establishment started producing seeds that met a part of requirement of the Block area. However for different reasons not much success was achieved by the Department through this programme. For instance seed potato production in Darjeeling district was banned after detection of wart disease due to intervention from Directorate of Plant Protection and Quarantine, Govt. of India. Later lack of technical initiative allowed to continue this embargo even after the Joint Wart Survey detected and declared presence of the fungus (*Synchytrium*) only in a very small pocket. Again even after repeated advices and recommendations of Jute Research Scientists of the SAU and ICAR, serious initiatives and programmes of jute seed production in the State were not taken up. However production of rice seeds by farmers, Seed Farms of the State Govt. and the SAU was satisfactory. Production of hybrid maize seeds started as early as in 1961. According to Nayban, 2001, the seed-demand of the state is fulfilled 16 per cent by Government Farms, 18 per cent by private farms and 66 per cent by farmers. This is true for field crops particularly rice. But considering the requirements of other crops including wheat, jute, vegetables, flowers etc. a large part is brought from outside state.

National Seeds Corporation was constituted in 1963 to provide leadership in seed production in the country involving and encouraging State Seed Corporations. State Seed Corporation, West Bengal was however constituted much later in 1980. The first Seed Act was enacted in 1966. This Act provides that variety of seeds selected by scientists are first notified for inclusion in the seed production programme. Usually such varieties are identified by the scientists of All India Coordinated Research Project of the concerned Crop, ICAR-institute, SAU or others who supply the pure seed which is multiplied under his care to produce 'Foundation Seed'. The FS is multified by selected farm or farmer under NSC or SSC concerned to produce 'certified seed' to be distributed to growers. Sometimes such seeds may be produced under the supervision of a SAU or research institute that is not certified but called Truthfully Levelled seeds which also can be distributed among growers.

This procedure of seed production is followed in case of major food, oilseed, etc. crops but seed production for rest of the large number of crops rest with producer farm or company. Farmer members of Primary Agricultural Cooperatives can also take the responsibility of quality seed production and enter seed business as it has been done by Gontra PACS, Nadia successfully. This has taken shape with technical support of BCKV and Dept. of Agriculture since nineties of last century and has given rise to a 'Seed Village' and the concept of Seed Village has taken a shape in West Bengal.

Seed scientists have identified districts like Birbhum, Bankura, Puruliya and West Medinipur for production of paddy, wheat, maize, jute, groundnut and potato seeds. Murshidabad, Birbhum and Nadia were found good for production of seeds of pulses and oilseeds. Hazra, 2006 identified four areas of vegetable seed production. They are Darjeeling, Kalimpong and Kurseong for medium-late cauliflower and capsicum seeds, and for early cauliflower, tomato and chilli seed, Haldibari, Maynaguri, Dhupguri, Falakata and Coochbehar are suggested. For onion, early cauliflower, bhindi, bottle gourd, sweet gourd, cucumber, ridged gourd, bitter gourd, brinjal, chilli, tomato seeds areas like Ajimganj, Baharampur, Beldanga, Krishnanagar, Ranaghat, Bongaon, Habra, Kalna, Katoa and Kelpur are suitable for production. At the end of last century production of hybrid seeds of maize, paddy etc. have been started by different seed production agencies. Frequent floods and droughts used to incur great loss to food grain production. Hence production of seedlings or plantlets, saplings, grafts etc. was also in practice. Infact tree plantings created green cover and shades that lowered atmospheric temperature through transpiration. Such tree lots used to supply fruits, fuel, fodder etc. simultaneously. Production of grafts of different kinds, air layering, budding etc. are continuing in different areas as private enterprises for pretty long period. In nineties intellectual property right in case of seeds entered the premises of Indian agriculture. At the beginning of 21st century the era of Genetically Modified (GM) seeds through the GEAC approval system came to India. One step of great importance during this time period was the 'National Commission on Agriculture' and publication of its valuable report in volumes (1976). An analysis of Indian agriculture, its progress and impact on people's health, nutrition as also future of agriculture as would depend on conditions of farmers in the country.

(l) Few more institutions

During British rule 'Agri-Horticultural Society' was established in 1820 at Calcutta. Rev. William Carey, learned teacher and well-wisher of India started teaching agriculture with botany at Serampur College, Hooghly and later developed the Society for effecting economic upliftment of farmers. Initially society opened branches at Delhi, Bombay, Madras, Lucknow, Cuttack, Punjab, Agra, Allahabad and even in Sri Lanka and Singapore to spread scientific agriculture. On the one hand East India Company and on the other the society with support of large number of people started campaigning for agricultural development in the country. The programme covered crops like cotton, linseed, sunhemp, sugarcane, wheat, maize, tobacco, cinchona, potato, paddy, tea, ginger, arrowroot, cocoa, different fruits, vegetables, flowers and ornamentals through spread of their cultivation and import of improved varieties from abroad. Society organised training for use of agricultural implements, silk culture, and exhibitions and advisory services, on such subjects. In the last five to six decades of last century society built up its own garden at Alipur, Kolkata and a collection centre for many ornamental and flower producing plants. In the last few decades it has emphasised in its activities on flowers and ornamentals. In 1894, Percy Lancaster became its secretary and unto 1960 hoisted the society to the peak of its glory through his merit, skill and perseverance. Besides many others he made an excellent collection of Canna at this garden.

The other famous Institution was Bengal Veterinary College. During British period during 1774-1838 trainings were offered to develop Vety physicians at Belgachia, Kolkata by the Dept. of Veterinary and Animal Sciences. In 1839, Veterinary College was established at Belgachia and since 1898 Diploma were offered after a longer duration of study and training and researches on animal health and treatment was initiated. Thereafter from 1953 after modernisation of infrastructure a Veterinary College and Hospital was developed and a graduate course in Veterinary and Animal Husbandry under Calcutta University led to B.V. Sc. and AH degree. The hospital was constituted of Cattle ward, Dog ward, Horse ward etc. In 1974, with the creation of Bidhan Chandra Krishi Viswavidyalaya this college was made a faculty under the University to offer a five year degree course and subsequently M.Sc. degree in different disciplines of Veterinary Sciences and Animal Husbandry. A college of Dairy Technology was also created under this faculty to offer four year degree course as also post-graduate degrees in Dairy Bacteriology, Dairy Chemistry and Dairy Technology. In 1995, taking this part of BCKV, West Bengal University of Animal and Fishery Sciences was created with three Faculties namely Veterinary and Animal Husbandry. Dairy Technology and Fishery Science offering for the first time a degree in Fishery Science also in the State.

At Coochbehar, Pundibari the BCKV campus was converted in 2000 to a full-fledge university called Uttarbanga Krishi Viswavidyalaya (UBKV) with two faculties namely Agriculture and Horticulture offering four year degree courses and post-graduate courses. This University retained three Regional Research Stations at Kalimpong, Mohitnagar and Ratua-Manikchak. Later they started to offer degrees in Dairy Technology, Home Science, Fishery Science and Agricultural Engineering.

BCKV further developed (1998) Faculties of Horticulture and Agricultural Engineering offering four year degrees as also post-graduate degrees in different disciplines under these faculties.

One Farmers' Training Centre was created in its Kalyani Campus.

(m) Agriculture Cooperatives

Based on Bengal Co-operative Act, 1940, first agricultural cooperative was registered in West Bengal. Any seven *'ryot'* or farmer could jointly apply for formation of an agricultural cooperative to the Asst. Registrar at district town in a form taken from the same office. Usually the District Cooperative Inspector conducts the enquiry at the place where the cooperative has to function and being satisfied recommends for approval. In 1955, Govt. of India Constituted a Committee for drawing policies for agriculture, forests and fisheries that recommended that state Governments should start large-farm agriculture at least two per districts as public and joint or cooperative ventures. This proposal was approved in the 14th and 15th Conferences of the registrars of the cooperatives. Planning Commission also justified importance and necessity of co-operative farming in their First and Second plan documents and promised all inspiration, support and help from Planning Commission. Actually they aimed to drag small and medium farmers in this programme. In 1958, four representatives of Govt. of India went to Israel for gaining experience about co-operative farming. Allocation was only Rs 50 lakh in first plan and it was increased in second plan.

In densely populated West Bengal, land holdings were small from earlier days. During fifties the holdings were below nine bighas for 12.5 lakh small farmers out of 17.7 lakh farming families suggesting that over 70 per cent of the land holdings were below 9 bighas. Another problem was that the number of land holdings of the same family were often located at different places. Of the four classes of co-operatives, the one that was preferred by the members was picked up for implementation. The co-operative for supply of inputs like agricultural loan, seeds, irrigation, fertiliser, plow and other agricultural implements, bullocks, etc. on the one hand. Marketing of produces and transport of all these articles also could be brought under its purview. Besides these no other area of agriculture was considered for cooperative development in West Bengal. The Cooperative Department of Govt. of West Bengal decided to develop 508 number of Primary Agricultural Cooperative Societies (PACS) during second plan period. But only 97 in 1957-58 and 160 in 1957-58 were actually developed. These however included all four classes of co-operatives, for example, Makorkole-Dhuapara Society, Bankura, 'Trifasali' of Hooghly, Madanpur of Nadia and Kumarsanda of Murshidabad tried to cultivate land pieces together under cooperatives. Joint effort of Depts. of Cooperative and Agriculture arranged training of 23 people for enabling them to act as cooperative managers (Radharaman Goswami, Co-op. Dept., Govt. of W.B.). In West Bengal development of agriculture and villages through cooperative activities in Gosaba, South 24-Parganas by Daniel Hamilton, and at Shilaidaha (Bangladesh) and Surul (Birbhum) by Rabindranath Tagore in different aspects.

In this time period, what we call second phase of Modern agriculture in Bengal, co-operative agriculture has not met with much success. In fact the cooperatives of sugar and sugarcane or cooperative of fertiliser producer IFFCO are all co-op organisations of rich people making influential business with success. However, the Milk Cooperative (Amul) in Western India is a great contribution of V. Kurien to building a model of 'Milk Federation' subsequently followed in some other states like Punjab, West Bengal and others. However, Cooperative Banks in West Bengal have been very helpful to farmers and till date they extended loans to 16 lakh cultivators in a unique context of nationalised banks not so eager to extend loans to farmers in Bengal. Above all 18.81 lakh farmers in West Bengal received no loans from any quarter.

Another achievement has been development of one PACS (Gontra, Nadia) into a seed (mostly paddy) producing and marketing Co-operative with the leadership of scientist from Bidhan Chandra Krishi Viswavidyalaya. Another PACS at Tarakeswar, Hooghly has started producing 'potato seeds' and marketing.

(n) Poverty, failed agriculture and famine

M.S. Swaminathan once uttered – "In our country also seeds of partisan system has been sown against poor section of people".

It is true that there have been no famine after independence of the country. But before that there have been number of 'food crises' and a few 'famines' in the country. Nityagopal Mukerji, 1901 has stated – "Famine is not a new thing in India. 'Famines' excepting those in civilised countries, have been mass-killer in other countries. India has achieved self-sufficiency in food but poors being unable to purchase food and had to go for '*suicide*'. It is a shameful event and matter of grief. The pages in his book where he dealt with famines has recorded famines in Emperor Akbar's time (1596) even. During 1615-16 famine was accompanied with plague epidemic. Famines were not uncommon during the rule of Shajahan or Aurangjeb. One crore people died in Bengal during 1770 famine. The famine of 1784 was also widespread and highly destructive. Nityagopal in this chapter in his book listed famines during 16th to 19th century. He tried to determine the cause behind these famines, description of relief work and some recommendation to combat and oppose such events. A very sad picture has come up about the human sufferings, weak administration that remained indifferent to such a catastrophe. His description is revealing the poverty of people and their food crisis that led to famine and on some occasions the famine was there all over the country.

Incidentally the situation in Ancient India was also not very bright according to Sukumari Bhattacharya, 1998's "Hunger and food during the period of '*Vedas*". 'Veda's were composed during 15th B.C. to fifth AD. Bhattacharyya has clearly said that there were definite poverty, food shortfall and a section of people that are poor. In '*Rk-Veda'* it is said that people used to repay to god *Indra* for food. The prayer says "Oh *Indra* and *Agni* we are praying for food": Or "Oh. God accept our claim on food". *Brahman Bamdev Rishi* said "I have cooked the elementary system of dog to eat in absence of food. None among the gods helped me and I had to tolerate insult to my wife". The other '*Veda*'s also mentioned about different degrees of hunger.

The last famine in India was the Bengal Famine of 1942 in which 35 lakh people died in the famine. The report of 'Famine

Commission' of Sir John Woodhead was published in 1945. It is noteworthy that Bengal was food exporting state till 1927 as also during 1929-1933. In fact in 1940-1941 production of Aman paddy declined. Production of *Aus* and *Boro* paddies taken together the total production was little less than the state's total requirement. But there were other reasons behind the Bengal Famine, 1943. In 1943 food grains was brought to Bengal from other state much late. The second world war (April, 1942) led the closure of roads after fall of Burma. Calcutta was bombed in Dec. 1942. Hoarding of food grains by dishonest traders also contributed. Government made unusual delay in requisitioning food to Central Government. The administration of Bengal Government sent message requisitioning food grains in end of December, 1942. According to Amartya Sen, 2000 the informations available with us about few 'famines' all on analysis suggest that people of only some profession are affected and abolished, leaving others with some or no injury. In fact the unequal access to market snatches food from one group of people and they are vanquished".

12.2 Bengali Food Culture takes shape

A. Home-made and street shop snacks of Bengal

(a) Bengal is famous with its snacks-trio namely *'Khoi'* (puffed rice), *'Muri'* (sand-fried or parched rice) and *'Chira'* (bitten or pressed boiled rice) that are in Bengali homes since ancient times. Over long period of time demand for these food articles increased very fast. Characteristics of these food items are their relatively long storability, flexibility of being consumed in different ways and ability to satisfy different appetites. These snacks are versatile raw materials for developing different other food items that carry their own characteristic taste and flavour, different from the parent materials. For over long time Bengali farmers selected specific varieties for each of these snacks and some such varieties have earned reputation to be used to make such snacks. For example *'Khoi'* from *'Kanakchur* variety etc. *'Chira'* from *'Indrasail'* etc. variety or *'Muri'* from *'Jhingasail'*, etc. variety.

Fast increasing demand for these snacks gradually initiated commercial production interest, and ultimately led to development of cottage industries in subsequent centuries.

(b) *'Ruti'*, *'Luchi'* and *'Parota'* are three others made from wheat powder, former from *'Ata'* (coarse ground) and the other two from *'Mayda'* (fine ground). Incidentally broken grains of wheat of coarser kind makes *'Dalia'* and of finer kind makes *'suji'*. *Suji* has been very common in earlier days and its boiling in water adding sugar etc. produced *'Halua'* a very popular and common snack-dish in Bengal. At this stage it is to be made clear that *'Ruti'* (hand made bread a flat-round stuff, baked on a *'chatu'* (iron plate) has been most common in Bengali families while *'Luchi'* ('Puri in north India ghee dip fried) and *'Parota'* that oil or ghee-baked respectively were special preparations. In Bengal one *'puri'* is *'Dalpuri'* made by putting a *'pur'* inside the small ball-shaped dough (*mayda*), turning them flat and oil baked on a *Chatu*, the other being smaller in size and dip-fried in oil called *'Kachuri'*. There was another *'Khasta kachuri'*, made from a *mayda*-dough that is mixed with enough *'ghee'* (*moyan*) while making and product became very crisp. This kind of high *'moyan'* dough was often been used to produce of *'nimki'* of different kinds. They are usually deep-fried in *'ghee'* and besides being home-made they are commonly produced and sold in sweet-shops. Sometimes small balls of *'mayda'*-dough made into thin round flat stuff, halved on the *'Chaki'* with a knife and each half folded into a 'tri-cone' container like in which previously cooked dry curry (*'pur'*) is packed and the tri-cone is sealed, deep fried in oil or ghee to get *'Singhara'* that is so popular. This *'pur'* in a *'singhara'* (*samosa* in Hindi) is often changed like curry of potatoes, cauliflower, meat, etc. as per season. There were *'Dhakai Parota'*, *'Alur Parota'* etc. although *'Lachha Parota'*, *'Rumali Ruti'* etc. are modern time additions.

Different pulse grains like *'ehola'* (gram), *'Khesari'* (*Lathyrus*) *'mung'*, *'musur'* (lentil), *'arhar'* (pigeonpea), *'Kalai'* etc. were boiled in water adding salt and spies like a thick soup that is consumed with *'Bhat'* in a Bengali family. Different *'dal'* with different ingredients, preparations and tastes were second to rice only. Different specialised preparations like *'tetor dal'*, *'toker dal'*, *'gadur dal'*, *'macher mathar dal'*, *'hing-kalai dal'*, *'Bhaja muger dal'* etc. were delicacies.

Pulse grains (mainly '*Khesari*') were ground to produce '*beson*' (pulse powder) which then is used in so many food articles like '*pampar*', '*telebhaja*', and different other snacks. Pulse grains are fried dry to be used in preparation of '*Chanachur*', '*Dal bhaja*', '*Chhatu*', etc. Pulse grains are soaked in water, made into paste with '*shil-nora*' (stone grinder of ancient design) and used for preparation of different food article like '*dhonka*', '*boda*' etc. that are made components of different foods. Such pulse paste is used to prepare '*bodi*' of different sizes and shapes from different '*dal's* like '*motor*' (peas), '*musur*' (lentil), '*kalai*' etc. by dropping in small quantities on a cloth or on oiled surface of a plate or so and allowed to dry in sun for days together to become storable. An excellent quality of '*bodi*' layed in beautiful designs particularly in Medinipur called '*Gayna bodi*' and it is very soft and crisp to taste after deep fry in oil. Besides pulse grains, mainly '*Chhola*' and '*motor*' are soaked in water overnight and cooked by boiling with salt, spices etc. to produce a dish called '*Ghugni*'. It is also prepared and sold in street-shops or by hawkers. Soaked germinated pulse grains ('*motor*', '*chola*' etc.) are mixed with salt, lime juice and chopped onion makes mouth-watering dish served in small '*shaal-pata*' dishes.

Most traditional dish from potatoes is '*Alukabli*' where boiled, peeled potatoes are sliced, and dipped in tamarind water with salt to serve in a '*shaal-pata*' dish with a prick to pick up and eat. Potato is a major component of different curries with or without fish or meat or boiled egg. The multiple use of potato in different food preparations in Bengal is unique. Boiled potato with pinch of salt, mustard oil and pieces of chilli is a delicacy. To serve a quick meal in Bengal washed potatoes are put in boiling rice so that along with '*bhaat*' one gets boiled potato also. That is why the term '*Aaloobhate*', so popular in Bengal means boiled potato. All such boiled foods like '*Dim bhate*', '*Kanchkola bhate*', '*Bhindi bhate*' etc. are simply the item boiled in '*Bhaat*'. '*Aalu bhaja*' has been the traditional oil-fried preparation of potatoes, having no '*chips*' concept in those days.

Another class/snacks ('*Telebhaja*') that are of course not home-made but are oil-fried generally in the afternoon by housewives or their husbands coming out of home in the afternoon and on a street corner sits with a '*chula*', a thick '*beson*' (pulse powder) made fluid, thin slices of brinjal, sweet gourd or a spiced boiled, smashed potato – all dipped in '*beson-gola*' and deep-fried in boiling mustard oil stands in high demand from Bengalis across age-groups. Three kinds of '*telebhaja*' mentioned above are '*beguni*', '*kumdoli*' and '*Aalur chop*', but varieties of them are sold round the year to some extent influenced by the season. The primary one was definitely '*Fuluri*' made of '*beson*' with heavy pumping in of air (*Fetano*') with hands. Large number of others namely pianji, '*pokouda*', '*dalboda*', '*sliced egg chop*', '*Chingdir chop*', '*Mochar chop*', '*Fulkopir chop*' etc. served with sprinkled salt on them.

One preparation named '*Moglai Parota*' was popular from 19th century and prepared in many places using 'egg' and '*moyda*', given a flat shape and oil fried on '*chatu*' or '*Tawa*'. One prepared in *Asansol* (Valley View Hotel) or in Calcutta (Anadi, Esplanade) were delicious. '*Kachuri*' and '*Aalur Chop*' of different tastes were also crowd puller be it '*Hinger Kachuri*' of Naihati or elsewhere. Many such snacks in the name of '*mutton chop*', '*vegetable chop*', '*Omlet*' (?), '*Kabiraji*', '*Roll*' etc. ruled Bengali restaurant for decades.

B. Sweet dishes in Bengal

(a) Bengalis are generally fond of sweets made out of milk, flour, rice, coconut, bottle-gourd, pulses, different fruits like mango, tamarind, ber, hog-palm, wood-apple, amla etc. all with sugar or '*Gur*'. While sugar or '*Gur*' are primary components, mixing of non-sugar components are also quite common. Boiling, frying, baking and dipping in sugar-syrup etc. are followed. Interestingly in Bengal every home or every village and many towns and cities had their own culture of sweet-meat making and many have attained speciality status to become famous all over Bengal, some acquiring national and international fame.

(b) Home scale specialities

'*Payas*' or '*Paramanna*' prepared by cooking scented rice or '*suji*' (broken wheat) or even pieces of peeled potato in milk with sugar or date-palm '*gur*'. Another is '*Halua*' made of cooking '*suji*' fried in '*Ghee*', along with sugar, water or milk and sometimes enriched with '*Raiasin*' ('*kismis*'). A third one '*Nadu*' of different kinds namely grated coconut pulp and '*Gur*' or sugar, powdered '*mung dal*' (fried) with sugar, '*muri*' with '*gur*', '*chira*' with '*gur*' and '*khoi*' with '*gur*'. All these after cooking were made into small round ball-like using palm of both hands. Very often '*khoi*' (popped rice) was made into '*Mudki*' cooking with '*Gur*' or sugar. Sometimes flour mixed with '*Ghee*', pinches of salt and '*Kalojira*' and sufficient water to make a dough which is then made into a *chapati* like, round flat shape using '*chaki-belun*' and finally cut into small pieces with a knife. The pieces are deep fried in '*Ghee*' (later vegetable oil, hydrogenated). These '*nimkis*' are often dipped in sugar syrup, alkalinated (*Bij Mara*) with little sodium bicarbonate ('*Khabar soda*') to turn into a sweet, crispy snack article.

Another sweet dish prepared and included in daily meals as one late-served course named '*Chatni*'. Using generally cut pieces of peeled fruits like unripe mango or tamarind, or hog palm or 'Chalta' (elephant apple) or *jalpai* etc. the things are cooked with water, sugar/*Gur*', '*Kalojire*', and a pinch of salt. There were however varieties of '*chatnis*' made of tomatoes, sweet potatoes, pineapple, date palm, and even fishes like '*Hilsha*' or '*Mourala*' in a Bengali kitchen. Even using mango fruit at different stages of its growth, variety of '*chatnis*' of diverse taste and flavour were excellent sweet dishes of a Bengali kitchen.

Another preparation of sugar only called '*Michri*' (country sugar cube or candy) was pepared in some families peparing a relatively thick solution of sugar and laying it on a flat, raised edge metal tray with nucleus of cotton thread or pieces of '*michhri*'. '*Batasa*' and '*Michhri*' were so common in a Bengali family having so many use in any odd hour.

(c) Cottage scale production

Besides '*batasa*' and '*michhri*' already mentioned, another important group of sweet-meat in early days were '*Nadu's* ('sweet ball') of different ingredients. Practically in the early days every such sweet produced were only to satisfy requirements of family, relatives and neighbours and not for sale. However the products remaining same to avoid repetition production for sale taking place only in late 19th century is also mentioned along with.

'Batasa' and *'michhri'* were produced for home use and later in 20th century only the idea of selling them came initially through 'grocery' in the nearby and later by packing in polypacks. *'Chira'*, *'muri'* and *'khoi'* production in homescale possibly dwindled as soon as they reached grocery shops for sale after being produced in mass-scale by some enterprising families.

Few other sweet preparations include *'Payas'* (*'Paramanno'*), *'Rosbora'*, etc. were very common household preparations in those early days. *'Pitha'* (*'Pithe'*) is a class of unique mostly sweet-preparations that adored any Bengali family during winter (*'Paush'*) and has been a signature sweet' for a Bengali family. Starting with *'Raser pitha'*, *'Bhaja Pitha'*, *'Aaske Pithe'*, *'Siddha Puli'* (taken with *'Nolen Gur'*), *'Khirpuli'*, *'Puli Pithe'* boiled in *'Payas'* and so many others. *'Malpoa'*, *'Patisapta'* and few others were prepared almost round the year and developed a special admiration among family member. *'Payas'* is made of different stuff e.g. scented rice or *'suji'* or *'sabu'* or *'potato pieces'* boiled in milk with sugar and *'Kismis'*.

(d) Sweetmeats famous with name of the area or maker ('Moyra')

Many of the sweetmeats of a particular area in Bengal have earned fame for the excellent taste and flavour of the sweetmeat concerned although the same is produced in many other places in Bengal. An attempt for recollection of such names is being made. Like *'batasa'*, *'kadma'* of Domohani bazaar, Asansol was very famous. *'Rosogalla'*, *'Kodapak Sandesh'* and *'Rabri'* are three from Kolkata itself. *'Sitabhog'* and *'Mihidana'* of Bardhaman, *'Sarpuriya'* and *'Sarbhaja'* of Krishnanagar. *'Talsansh* sandesh' of Chandannagar, *'Lengcha'* of Shaktigarh, (Bardhaman). *'Pantua'* of Arangghata (Nadia), *'Chhanaboda'* of Ranaghat (Nadia), *'Moya'* of Joynagar (South 24-Parganas), *'Monohara'* of Janai (Hooghly), *'Morobba'* of Siuri (Birbhum), *'Aamsatta'* of Maldah, *'Tilkuto'* of Konnagar, Hooghly and *'Gupo sandesh'* of Guptipara (Hooghly), *'Jilipi'* of Mecheda (Purba Medinipur), *'Sada Bonde'* of Kamarpukur (Hooghly), *'Doi'* (Curd; Mollarchak), *'Amriti'*, *'Labongo Latika'*, *'Goja'*, *'Kanchagolla'*, *'Sadabonde'*, *'Makha sandesh'*, *'Nikhuti'*, *'Dorbesh'*, *'Jivegoja'*, *'Kalakand'*, etc. from different places are famous with person or producer (*'Moyra'*) like *Rasogolla* of KC Das, *'Rabri'* of *Dwarik*, *'Kodapak Sandesh'* of Bhimnag, *'Taalsansh* of Surjo Modak, *'Chakasandesh'* of *'Ramchaki'*, *Dulaler' 'Talmichhri'*, *'Ledikeni'* of *'Nitai moyra'* etc. *'Jilipi'* of Asansol was also famous as was *'Baborsha'* of *'Khirpai'* (Hooghly) and *'Muger Jilipi'* of Medinipur.

(e) *'Nadu* were another class and one called *'Anandanadu'* was prepared only in ceremonies like 'marriage' or in wearing sacred thread by Brahmin boys. Mixing rice powder, sesamum grains and *'gur'* made into small balls and dip fried in mustard oil. There were many *'nadu's* in Bengali family mostly by mixing *'Gur'* with any of grated coconut, sesamum, peanut, *'chira'*, *'muri'* etc., cooked on a oven, and after taking down from oven small balls are made with hand while the material remaining hot.

Sometimes stuff like *'muri'*, *'fried mung grains'* etc. were ground into powder, mixed with *'gur'*, cooked for sometime to make 'balls' or *'nadu'*. *'Mihidana'*-another Bengali sweet is often made into round balls to get *'laddu'*. Another is *'bonde'* mixed with *'Khir'*, *'Ghee'*, *'Pesta'*, *'Kismis'* and made into round balls i.e. *'Darbesh'*. Other sweets of fame were *'Chomchom'*, *'Danadar'*, *'Kalakand'* made from milk and *'Jivegoja'*, *'Balusai'*, *'Kuchogaja'* etc. from *'mayda'* (flour). *'Macha Shandesh'* of *Beletod* was also common in *'Shatoda'*, *'Chhatna'* or *'Mejia'*. Another ancient sweetmeat made from sugar only was *'Chinir Monda'* of *Barddhaman-Katwa* area (*Nigon*). In these areas sweets like *'Rosomalai'*, *'Khirkadam'*, *'Labongalatika'*, *'Malai-chomchom'*, *'Rosakadamba'*, *Nikhuti*, *Chhanar murki*, were also famous.

E. Spicy dishes in Bengal

Large number of spices (*'Fodon'*) are used in Bengali cooking singly or mixed, in whole or powder form, dry fried or oil-fried or sand parched. Some unique processes of cooking besides boiling, steaming, dry frying, oil-frying, deep frying, roasting etc. are *'santlano'*, *'chnuke deoa'*, *'Bhaate deoa'*, *'Fordon Deoa'*, *'Vapano'*, etc. are followed in Bengali cooking.

While use of table salt, mustard oil or 'Ghee', and sugar or gur are quite common, use of 'spices' is a strength of Bengali cooking and commonly used well-known spices are *'Dhone'*

(Coriander), *'Jira'* (Cumin), *'Halud'* (Turmeric), *'Aada'* (Ginger), *'Pianj'* (Onion), *'Rasun'* (Garlic), *'Lanka'* (Chilli), *'Sorse,* (Mustard), *'Choto elach'* (Small cardamom), *'Bodoelach'* (large cardamom), *'Labanga'* (Clove), *'Darchini'* (Cinnamon), *'Methi'* (Fenugreek), *'Joan'* (*Trachyspermum*), *'Mauri'* (Fennel), *'Posto'* (Poppy seeds), *'Kalojira'* (Black cumin), *'Tejpata'* (Bayleaf) etc.

Other uncommon ones that are used in preparation of some selected dishes are Black pepper (*'Golmarich'*), Tamarind (*'Tentul'*), Aesafoetida (*'Hing'*), *'Amada'* (Mango flavoured Ginger), *'Randhuni'* (Ajmud), *'Jaiphal'* (Nutmeg Kernel), *Jaitri* (Nutmeg gynaecium) etc.

In addition *'Chaal mogor'* (Ash gourd seeds), *'Kesar-methi'* (young leaves and tips of Methi), *'Karipata'* (Curry leaves, *Murraya*), *'Gandal leaves'* (*Geodaria*), *'Palta'* (Pointed gourd leaves), *Neem leaves* (*Azadirachta*), though not spice, are used to add flavour or bitterness required in some preparations.

Some spice mixtures like *'Panch Fodon'*, *'Garom masla'*, *'Dhone-Jire'* are very common in use. While *'panch fodon'* is a mixture of *Kalojira, Mauri, Methi, Jira* and *Rnadhuni*. *'Garom Masla'* is a combination of *Darchini, 'Labango', 'Chota elach'* and *'Kalojira'*. *'Dhone-Jira'* is another combination of two spice used mostly in almost all vegetarian preparations (*niramish*). *'Garam Masla'* is often used in non-vegetarian preparations (*Aamish*), *'Panch Fodon'* is a primary spice mixture that is fried in little mustard oil followed by pouring the boiled *'Dal'* or *'Tarkari'* in it (*santlano*). Besides one very common spice-powder *Jira* used in most of the Bengali cuisines – vegetarian or non-vegetarian except possibly in *'chatni'* (sweet) or *'shukto'* (bitter and sweet). Again in most of the non-vegetarian preparations chopped or pasted onion is very common in use.

Some special spice combinations are in standard use e.g. *'Sorse', 'mauri'-posto* and *'Aada'* pasted in *'Shukto'* a bitter dish served in the beginning. Some selected vegetables like *'Sem'*, *'Mulo'* (Radish), Sweet Potato, *'Kanchkola'* are used with drum stick or bittergourd or neem or *'shiulipata'* to add bitterness. Sometimes *'Kalaidal'* is cooked with *'Mauri'* and *'Hing'* to add an excellent flavour, *'Hing'* is also used in preparing *'Alur Dom'*. *'Ghugni'*, *'Hinger Kachuri'* etc. *'Randhuni'* is also used to prepare *'Shukto'* and *Randhuni, Aada, Mauri* and *Sorse* pasted together and used to make a preparation called *'Paturi'* (covered with banana leaves) made of fishes as also few vegetables.

'Lanka' (hot chilli) is used both as unripe, ripe or dry chilli mainly to add heat (*'Jhaal'*) in different degrees to the preparations. *'Aamada'* is used only in *'Chatni'* preparation to add a kind of mild mango flavour. The juice from *'Aamada'* is used in *'Sandesh'* – a kind of milk-based sweet-meat. While *'Posto'* pasted is used in a potato curry (*'Aaloo posto*), potato mixed with *Jhinga* (ridged gourd) (*Jhinga posto*). However *'posto'* paste is used in some *'chatnis'* (unripe tamarind fruits) or paste is made mixed with hot chilli and boiled a while to make a very tasteful chaat preparation. Even *'peel's ('Khosa'*) of potato fried with posto is a delightful preparation. *'Kesar-methi'*, dried, fried and stored for its use in many curry like preparations to add a beautiful aroma.

Preparation of different fishes like *'Ilish'*, *'Tengra'*, etc. are hot favourite of Bengalis when the main spice in it is mustard paste. In fact *'Mustard paste'* is called *'Kasundi'* in Bengali and is used in preparation of curry of brinjal, sem (*Dolichos*), bhindi and even drum-stick. *'Oal'* (Amorphopballus) *bhate* when mixed with mustard paste with a pinch of salt is mouth watering. Another food item called *'Gota'* selected small-sized vegetables in their whole size are cooked usually in winter that demands a special combination of spices called *'Gotar Masla'*.

F. Vegetarian preparations and Bengal widows

Widows were in large numbers in this period due to the very unfortunate social provisions of practices in the name of religions, like *'Kulin'* and *'Bahubibaha'* system among very old Hindus as also *'talaq's* among Muslims. Some of these deserted women belonging to teen to middle age groups were prevented from taking non-vegetarian foods mostly fishes in this area. But they were to share heavily the works in the households from cooking to cleaning and what not. Under the circumstances widows responsible for cooking devised newer recipes in the vegetarian category using different vegetables, spices in different combinations and cooking process. Bengali widows used to undergo '*Ambubachi*' on 7th day of '*Ashada*' continuing for three days. Widows do not cook for these three days and they do not eat any cooked (in fire) food and depend on '*sabudana*', or '*mungdal*' soaked in water along with some fruits and sweets. '*Ambubachi*' literally means beginning of monsoon. Such social taboo's were only a kind of torture while exploiting her through simultaneous hard labour.

Besides widows were to undergo '*upabas*' (fasting) on '*Ekadashi*', '*Amabasya*' etc. The culture of taking vegetarian food preparation was also among other members of a family – irrespective of sex particularly on auspicious dates. Very poor class of people in the society who could not afford fishes also depended on vegetarian preparation, sometimes even depending on twigs of plants that are available in wilderness. Taking this entire group of people across families some common, popular and excellent preparations by Bengali women, some vegetarian preparations may be discussed.

'***Shukto***' - is possibly the most popular vegetarian dish of Bengal cooked with different spice combinations (sorse-posto paste in west of the state and 'joan' in east), the ingredients like sem, drumstick, sweet potato, *kanchkola* and some other bitter components like bitter gourd or '*palta-pata*' remaining common.

'***Dhnoka***' – *Pea-daal* (*motor dal*) soaked in water overnight, made into paste next day, vapour cooked, layed on a tray and cut into pieces to be fried in oil and made into curry with pieces of boiled potatoes. '*Motordal*' preparation is often mixed with chopped and boiled '*mocha*' (banana inflorescence) to get '*mochar dhnoka*'.

'***Mankochu bata***' – Green, peeled *Alocasia* ('*mankochu*'), pasted with salt etc., oil fried on '*Kodai*' with '*Kalojira*', '*Mankochu*' is mixed with grated coconut paste making a tastier food.

'***Mochar Ghonto***' – Banana inflorescence of fruit – banana (*paka kola*) varieties are used picking up flowers, eliminating their androecaeum, chopped and boiled in water with little salt and then cooked into '*Ghonto*' with spices etc.

'Aalur Dom' – Boiled '*Nainital*' variety potatoes whole or halved cooked into curry with spices, chilli, salt etc., very often using '*hing*' to get a flavour.

'Kumdor chhakka' – Cut into cube like shapes, '*Kumdo*' (sweet gourd), soaked gram and potatoes and cooked into curry adding spices, chilli, little sugar etc.

There are so many dishes and these are only few examples.

G. Fish based food preparations of Bengal

The geo-ecological location of the land and its unique network of rivers, ponds ('*pukur*'), '*Khal*', '*bil*', and different other water bodies and their flooding in monsoon remained a compulsion for people of this land to depend on water-fauna also that include primarily fishes. People of this land were long back assigned the designation of '*Samudra Shayan*' for their undisputed command on water bodies. Bengalis were skilled in running ships, boats and different kinds of vessels ('*Shalti*', '*Chhip*', '*Bojra*', '*Jahaaj*', '*Saptadinga*' and so many others).

Having flowing to standing sweet-water bodies, brackish water bodies and coastal sea water, cold water and warm water that created a natural situation that were full of all the different kinds of fishes, Bengalis – primarily the fishermen and women developed all kinds of fish harvesting 'nets' and traps, of different types and designs. All these created a very congenial situation in which they slowly developed the habit of consuming fishes. Over time women folk of Bengal also slowly developed method of cooking fishes using spices, mustard oil etc. Innumerable number of fish-based cuisine are developed that are unique.

1. Fish preparations

Besides large number of unique and excellent 'special dishes' the fish preparations were of five different categories namely (i) Fry, (ii) Curry, (iii) '*Jhal*', (iv) '*Jhol*' and (v) '*Soup*'.

'Fry' : Fries were quite common and made as deep fry in mustard oil, plain oil frying being not uncommon. Fishes selected for such frying are *'Ilish'*, *'Maurala'*, *'Punti'* and a few others. A practice of coating the fish with paste of pulses (*'Besan'*) or rice (*'sabeda'*) make the fry more tasteful.

'Curry' **:** Usually the fishes are fried and then mixed with a vegetable curry to final cooking. Some of the famous dishes are *'Lau Chingdi'*, *'Inchod-Chingdi, 'Bhetki-Fulkopir Dalna'*, *'Kumro Chingdi'*, *'Chingdir Malaikari'*, *'Katlar Kaliya'* etc.

'Jhal' **:** The fish is cooked after frying with little water, chilli, turmeric and mustard oil. This way *'Jhal'* of *'Maurala'*, *'Punti'*, *'Kachki'*, *'Pabda'*, *'Tengra'*, *'Parse'*, *'Koi'*, *'Ilish'* etc. are made. Some of such preparations are made with *'mustard paste'* and are called with a prefix or suffix *'sorse'* like *'sorse Ilish'*.

'Jhol' **:** A more or less similar preparation with watery-gravy being larger in volume often with vegetable pieces like potato, brinjal, plantain etc. and pieces of chilli. Some well-known *'Jhol'* were – *'Ilish-Begun'*, *'Katla / Ruier Jhol'*, *'Singhi'r Jhol'*, *'Magurer jhol'*, *'Tengrar Jhol'*, *'Parser Jhol'* etc.

2. Special fish dishes

Bengali fish preparations are famous for their taste and aroma but are not taken or tested world wide simply because of the bones and spines (*'Kanta'*) are difficult to manage while eating. But their spread over non-veg areas of India over last seven decades shows that once people are used to separate them from the fish while eating, it is going excellent. Mouth-watering dishes are – *'Ilisher chanchra'*, *'Lotta makha'*, *'Lau-Chingri'*, *'Koi-Ganga Jamuna'*, *'Daab Chingri'*, *'Ilish paturi'*, *'Bhetki paturi'*, *'Telkoi'*, *'Chitaler muthi'*, *'Kachushak-Ilish Ghanto'*, *'Vapa ilish'*, *'Chingri malaikari'*, *'Mankochu chingri Bata'* etc. Using *'tentul'* (Tamarind) unripe or ripe number of *fish-tok* like *'Ilisher tok'*, *'Mauralar tok'*, etc. are prepared.

3. General components of daily meal (lunch) in Bengal

This daily meal widely varied as per economic conditions of people. For a very poor family, always unsure for even one mid-day meal arranges *'Fenabhat'* (cooked rice with starchy fluid) and a pinch of salt once a day only. The *'Fenabhat'* in a well to do family is consumed with *'ghee'* and salt.

But the common mid-day meal of a middle income (*'Madhya Bitta'*) family includes an appetiser (bitter tasty item) like fried *'neem leaves'* or *'bitter gourd'* or neem leaves with brinjal pieces (*'Nimbegun'*) or fried leaves of pointed gourd (*'Palta'*) or *'Brahmi'* or flowers of Drumstick is starter. This is followed by *'bhaja'* (oil fry) of any of different leaves or twigs (*'Shaak'*) like *'note'* (amaranthus) or *'palang'* (*'palak'*), or *'kalmi'*, or *'Punarnava'*, or *'Helencha'* or *'Kulekhada'* etc. Then comes thick pulse soup (*'Dal'*) of any of different pulse grains e.g. *'mung'*, *'masur'*, *'adhar'*, *'motor', 'chhola', 'khesari'* etc. along with oil fried pieces of brinjal or pointed gourd or *'Kumro'*, or sweet potato, or potato, or *'Bhindi'* etc. Sometimes, *'bhaja'* is replaced with different *'Charchadi'* (*'Kumro'* or *'lau'*, 'shak' and stem pieces, pieces of potato, *'kumro'*, ridged gourd, *'sem'*, *'borbati'* (cowpea), leaves of cauliflower, cabbage, radish etc.) or a *'tarkadi'* (similar to *'charchadi'* except the stem pieces). Then comes *'macher jhal'*. The penultimate dish is *'chatni'* with little sweetness and concluded some amount of homemade *'Tok Doi'*. Some are fond of taking a betel leaf with pieces of arecanut, little lime and *'Khaer'* and some *'mouri'* to chew. There were great many combinations of such food items.

H. Home-made beverages of Bengal

Early Bengali family used to rear one or two cows and few goats mainly for milk. Milk has been a regular drink for all members of a Bengali family. Excess milk produced was converted to *'Chhana'* with lime juice and the watery portion (*Chhanar jol*) was a favourite drink.

The natural cream (*'sor'*) formation on boiled milk surface was collected in a stone-pail for a week and at the week-end made into butter (*'Noni'*), the leftout water (butter milk) was a good drink adding little salt and lime juice.

Converting milk into *'Doi'* using a starter culture (*'Sajo*) was a common practice. A drink called *'Ghol'* was often prepared mixing *'Doi'*, sugar and cold water stored in a *'Kunjo'* (earthen pot with porus wall) and particularly served to persons completing a laborious job or to the guests visiting. This was sometimes substituted with glass of *'sarbot'* made in some cold water mixing lime juice (*'patilebu'*), sugar and little salt. Another substitute in a poorer family was '*muri bhejano jol*' which sometimes was used as a relief for stomach-upset. Juice extracted from ripe mango ('*Aamer ros*' or *Jackfruit ('Kanthaler ros')* were common drinks in families owning garden of such fruit plants. '*Belerpana*' is another common drink made from the pulp of ripe '*Bael*' (wood apple) with little sugar, '*tentul*' (tamarind) and salt.

Some other beverage type preparations were regularly made on requirement for restoration of health from different ailments. They include '*Panchan*' (a drink made of five different stuff boiled with sugarcandy for getting relief from stomach-upset as also cough. Some people being diabetic used to drink extracts of '*neem*' leaves or bitter-gourd fruits or leaves of '*Telakucha*'. From around the time of English rule after establishment of Tea Gardens in Darjeeling, Bengalis slowly became used to drinking hot tea with sugar and milk. Tea extract has become a very common drink sometimes without milk mixed with lime juice or not.

Fermented beverages like '*Hadia*' (boiled rice fermented in earthen pot with sealed cover) or '*Desi mod*' (country liquor made by '*Gur*' fermented and distilled) were common. In western districts sap of palmyra palm ('*Taal*') is allowed to ferment under natural conditions and the drink ('*Taadi*) was nutritious too. Similar drink was developed from sap of Date Palm ('*Khhejur*'). In the hills millets (*Kaon*') were fermented in the hollow of bamboo pieces to get a popular drink called '*Chhang*'.

12.3 Next three decades : (End of seventies to first of 21st)

From the end of seventies of 20th century to the beginning decade of 21st century production rate of crops was 1961-71–2.24 per cent, 1971-81–3.23 per cent, 1981-82 to 1991-92–4.24 per cent, 1991-92 to 2000-01 – 6.75 per cent, 2001-02 to 2008-09 – 6.61 per cent and in 2008-09 – 8.19 per cent. A person requires 167 kg food/year to continue healthy. In West Bengal during 1990-92 the production comes to 170 kg/head and in 2005-07 it is 160 kg/head. Dr Ramesh Chand of ICAR on analysis in 2010 found that in terms of rupees per hectare production was worth of Rs 15,107.00 in 2006-07 turned to Rs 45,735.00 per hectare in 2009-10. Rameshchand rated this success as '*Excellent*'. Fact is that in 14 districts out of 16 in West Bengal production is high to very high.

As per 2011 census out of a total population of 9,13,47,736 persons in West Bengal 6,22,13,676 are villagers. Number of villages in 2001 was 40,782 that came down to 40,203 in 2011. Decline in children population has been 11.4 per cent. During 2008-09, income of villagers from agriculture has increased by 32 per cent (National Academy of Agricultural Science, 2010) and 24.77 of the population were recorded as poor. From 2001 to 2011, a larger number of rural people were engaged in non-agricultural profession. Mr Srikanta Jena, the MIC of Project Implementation Department, GOI made a statement based on one NSS of 2009-2010. "In rural areas poorest of the families (10 per cent) spent Rs 377.05 per head while upper 10 per cent of the rich people spent seven times more i.e. Rs 2394.56 per head. In 2003 the survey of people's indebtedness was 26.5 per cent of village families were indebted. Poverty and indebtedness in villages led to suicide of farmers. The official statement in Lok Sabha in this regard say that during 1991-2004 one lakh farmers committed suicide. However in West Bengal due to sincere implementation of some welfare schemes, no record of farmers' suicide is available till 2010 while according to National Crime Records in 2006, 17060 farmers committed suicide in India. Farmers' suicide took place mainly in Maharashtra, Andhra, Karnataka and a few other states. Considering farming totally non-remunerative, during 1999-2001 about 80 lakh farmers withdrew from farming activity and 40 per cent of the farmers were willing to leave farming getting any alternative job. (Farmers' Commission, 2007).

A. *Farmland situation*

In Darjeeling hills the high slope (6-30 per cent) land were converted to steps across the slope during British rule. The terraces made prevented much of soil erosion particularly during rains. In the plains jungles were cleared, leveling the land by cutting raised portions to make the land a better plain that actually started during *Gupta* rule. This has progressed very slowly. The land being fertile, with good rainfall and large number of rivers and rivulets, density of population has been more since early days. As a result people always felt a shortage of land. Even up to the end of British period the *'ail's* separating land pieces were quite broad to be used as path for the farmers to move inside their crop-field. A long practiced custom among Bengali farmers was to use a spade to cut with only one strike on *'ail'* so that land remains the same in dimension. In days to follow the broad *'ail'* was gradually made narrow and walking on it has become impossible to meet the requirement of land. Farmers often have more than one piece of land, at different levels that could be brought together by exchange of land, but farmer did not opt for this for reasons best known to farmer himself. Actually a farmer is full of a kind of anxiety and fear as to what this attempt to change in document (*'parcha'*) would bring for him? Or he may be afraid due to some black-custom or culture that prevented this change. It is true that land in Bengal is flat plain compared to the lands in many other Indian States, but they could be made still more plain and level using plow and ladder they use in cultivation. This would have made distribution of nutrients more uniform leading to increased production.

Natural processes going on through wind, water flow, flood etc. cause erosion but the same natural process appears from another angle is the development of land that is taking place for example the eroded soil is taken to a lower level land that very slow silting develops into a land better for agriculture. The process going on for over seven-eight decades have filled up marshy lands in districts Hooghly, Nadia, North and South 24-Parganas and even Maldah and many wetland has filled up, deep wetland has become shallow wetland and deep water body, less deep. This way ups and downs of land is corrected and becoming flat-land. The depth of soil of the upland has declined as also filling up of waterbody have been harmful for agriculture and environment. Again in coastal saline area and in western districts land-shaping programmes by excavating large number of tanks and ponds to collect and conserve rain water has also brought change in land shape. In the coast particularly rivers at their confluence with Bay of Bengal silting and deposition of dead aquatic flora and fauna as also dropping of mangrove plant parts is constantly creating new land surface. In course of large rivers like '*Ganga-Bhagirathi*' and others development of number of '*Char-land*' or '*Diara land*' as in many districts that are brought in use for agriculture. The same rivers destroyed large land areas in districts like Maldah, Murshidabad, and Nadia and many villages and agricultural land were lost. Altogether 2081 thousand hectare land is degraded that constitutes 29 per cent of total agricultural land area. As per Dept. of Agriculture the degraded land comprises of 820 thousand ha of saline and alkaline soil, 666 number of ravenous gully erosion and 594 thousand ha are flood land. In addition Medinipur, Hooghly and South 24-Parganas have 173.4 thousand ha. land with extreme drainage problem while in 24-Parganas, Nadia, Murshidabad in the South and Jalpaiguri, Coochbehar, Medinipur, Howrah and Hooghy has 2443.3 thousand ha with general drainage problem. In Barddhaman, Birbhum, Howrah, Maldah, Dinajpur, Medinipur and Puruliya has 1747.5 thousand hectare with wrong drainage plan.

(B) Agriculture policy, plan and development

In modern India, National Agriculture Commission was constituted and its report was submitted in 1976. Report narrated the basic aspects of Indian agriculture and recommendations were made as per the need of Indian people, agriculture and the country. Discussions and visions were there that could show the future course of development of agriculture in India. Thereafter in 2000, National Agriculture Policy has been declared by Govt. of India. But the policy did not consider the economic conditions of the farmers of the country. Sometimes back GOI stopped production of fertilisers in its number of factories with the notion that imported fertilisers are cheaper than those produced in the country. Again globalisation and signing of WTO created a situation when seed business is also encroached by multinational seed companies that are strengthened by newer Seed Acts. For food crops, however, National and State Seed Corporations has been playing major role while responsibility for seeds of vegetables, flowers and saplings of fruits were with the private business houses. But in case of hybrid and GM varieties multinational seed business houses became the main players. Besides the policy withdraws any subsidy to farmers on irrigation, electricity etc. On the other hand to get reasonable price for his produce determination of Minimum Support Price (MSP) and its proper, timely implementation is not done meticulously on behalf of the Governments. It is often failing to play role leaving the farmers at the mercy of agents of unscrupulous businessmen. All these are resulting in large number of farmers' suicide. Although Govt. of West Bengal with a different policy till 2010 was alert and did not fail to arrange purchase of the produces like paddy, jute etc. at MPS so that there was no farmers' suicide in West Bengal.

Another development at International level was the massive assessment work by a body called International Assessment of Agricultural Science, Technology and Development and its Report (IAASTD, 2004) giving an account of agriculture all over the earth in last 50 years that identified the fact that agriculture has become dependent on 'chemicals'. In 2007, National Commission on Farmers under the Chairmanship of M.S. Swaminathan published its Report that pointed to the resource poor Indian farmers, the price rise of agricultural inputs and commodities for the rural people and a dull market for sale of farmer's produces etc. with a recommendation for granting farmers a soft-loan (4 per cent interest). The report has also drawn attention to the situation that given a better job, farmers wanted to leave farming. State Agriculture Commission, West Bengal (Chairman R.N. Basu) in its report (2009) analysed the success of land reform, problems of agriculture by small and marginal farmers, necessity of mixed farming, need of such farmers to receive soft loans from Government, requirement of organised marketing network and proper and timely implementation of MSP for agricultural produces. The nation has passed through eleven five year plan periods and facing the 12th. From the very first five year plan – judicious use of natural resources, development of irrigation system, provision of subsidies in agriculture and enough support to farmers were the objective of development of agriculture though it faced many disasters like flood, drought etc. In the sixth plan target was to increase production in both small and large farms. During 1989-91, there was no plan-wise development programme. Evidently in eighth Plan also (1992-97) agriculture made highest contribution in GDP of the country and two-third of the workforce are employed in agriculture. Agriculture production was declared to make the country self-sufficient. The main object of Ninth Plan was to develop villages and bring a stability in price situation. In the Tenth plan (2002-2007) target was judicious use of the agricultural land, agricultural development and food security. Budgetary allocations were 3.9 per cent in agriculture, 6.8 per cent in irrigation and flood control, 25.5 per cent on electricity generation and 8 per cent in rural development. Eleventh Plan (2007-2012) aimed at fast inclusive development, with emphasis on road and transport development and spread of irrigation in greater area. Keeping allocation of 3.7 per cent in agriculture a growth of 4.1 per cent was expected in agriculture. Besides allocations of 8.3 per cent for rural development, 5.8 per cent for irrigation and flood control and 23.4 per cent for electricity generation. But agricultural production target could not be reached in last four-five years. Growth in agriculture of the country is 2.5 per cent in Ninth Plan, 2.47 per cent in Tenth, and 2.2 per cent in 11th. Possibly failure to spread irrigation is the prime reason since about 50 per cent of agricultural land in India is rain dependent till today.

On the other hand in West Bengal irrigation could be spread over 70 per cent of agricultural land and hence cropping intensity has reached about 200 per cent. The agricultural policy adopted in India includes contract farming through non-government participation, National Agricultural Insurance, providing assured market and reasonable prices for agricultural produces. Timely supply of sufficient input, rural electrification, and building up of agricultural processing centres etc. are included.

In West Bengal emphasis has been given on irrigation water, electricity, subsidy in fertiliser, seed, irrigation water etc. for small and marginal farmers, increasing crop diversity, cropping intensity etc., use of modern techniques and varieties and reducing cost of production through use of organic manure and balanced fertilisation has been the key factors to enhance production. Mixed farming with inclusion of animal rearing like poultry birds, goat, bore and sheep farming, fish cultivation in water bodies, beekeeping, silk farming, lac cultivation etc. all in home scale to increase income of farmers. Rural electrification, development of roads and communication, other infrastructure and encouraging processing of agricultural produces along with spread of education and public health facilities were other important areas. All these ultimately aimed to increase capability of farming families.

(c) Control on land and agriculture

During Emperor Akbar's rule (1601) registration of all agricultural lands with the Government was started. By this ownership of the land and tax collection against land could begin. Some rules and regulations for this were framed that were included in *'Ain-i-Akbari'* but they were not promulgated by Akbar. But the regulations were so perfect that British Rule also followed the rules. On analysis it appeared that Government control over land was liked by Mughals for tax-collection and Britishers for their business and trade. While land was being controlled in this manner British rulers enacted land requisition act in 1894. In fact land acquisition was required for different purposes. In 1820, land was acquired for establishing coal mine at Raniganunj etc. After this for laying of railway line was initiated in 19th century alongwith laying telegraph line, establishment of cotton mill, jute mill land acquisition was going on. The Forest Act of 1865 simultaneously prevented spread of agriculture. Similarly mining, establishment of tea-gardens, establishment of industries, major irrigation project and laying long roads required acquiring of many land. Acquisition of land was done by paying the price of the land plus 15 per cent of it as solacium. The solacium was enhanced to 30 per cent in 1984. Along with this besides acquisition for Government need for public purpose and industry was also permitted since 1984.

1. Land Reform : Take over and distribution of land

Land acquisition as a step toward land reform, acquires ceiling surplus land of a person or family which does not change character of land as happens in other cases. Surplus lands above ceiling, possessed by a person is vested as per West Bengal Land Ceiling Act, 1955 to Government and the Govt. can utilise or allocate to some other person as per provisions of Act. The vested land may be utilised to build school or college or University or Industry etc. or may be distributed among landless villagers. The villager receiving such land through a deed (*Patta*) is called '*Pattadar*'. *Pattadar's* land is inheritable to his heir(s) but the land cannot be sold without Government permission. In the last three decades (1980-2010), about 30 lakh landless families received (i) patta land and (ii) registration of '*bargadars*' (share croppers) awarding them right to the land they have been cultivating as a share-cropper. All these caused 84 per cent of land under small and marginal farmers ownership, all India picture being 43 per cent. The existing law of the country permits equal right to sons and daughters and that results in further splitting of land holding of the family. Thus holdings of small and marginal (within two ha) class have increased. The progress in 'service' and 'industry' sectors has been quite slow failing to accommodate rural people, thus continuing to depend on agriculture. As per policy of State Government, other landless villagers (six lakh) were awarded 16 *kottah* of house building land (five kottah for house building and rest for vegetable growing) in the last three decades.

Side by side in West Bengal urbanisation and growth in service sector has drawn many rural people to a workplace other than agriculture (NSS 61st Sample Survey, 2008-05). On an average 12 per cent of rural people are leaving agricultural to join any non-agricultural job. The highest rate (70 per cent) of this shift is in Darjeeling followed by Howrah district (60 per cent). NSS 59 the sample survey has claimed that in West Bengal 90.43 per cent of agricultural land is owned by land owners of one ha or lower size holding.

2. Land acquisition for urbanisation and infrastructure development

Land acquisition for purposes of urbanisation and building of infrastructure changes the character of land from 'agricultural land' to land for other purposes. Civilisation in its natural course transforms villages into towns, but much of it depends on population increase and economic capability of these people. Different activities, surplus agricultural production and their trading and financial affluency attracts people to the advantages of town life. With decline of dependence on agriculture rural non-agricultural professions grow and through all these and related activities the town-life facilities are created in the lifestyle of these people and some of such villages turn into towns or even cities. Along with markets, bus stoppages and terminus, railway stations or river jetties, development of schools, colleges, small or medium industries roads and preliminary transport turn the place into an agglomeration census-town like area and a small town. Urbanisation in West Bengal from 2001 to 2011 is revealed in 2011 census report. These are unplanned towns. The number of cities in West Bengal was 378 in 2001 and 909 in 2011. These developments of agricultural land areas has taken place naturally without land acquisition and change of character of land. Some other areas are also urbanised and having 75 per cent of people employed in non-agricultural job, a minimum 5000 population and 400/sqkm population density. In West Bengal, census towns were 255 in 2001 and 780 in 2011. Besides municipalities, Notified Area Authorities and ULB inceased from 123 to 129. This is why the rate of increase in population is 29.9 per cent in cities and 7.37 per cent in villages. To develop planned cities at Durgapur, Barddhaman, Salt Lake in 24-Parganas, Kalyani in Nadia and Haldia in East Medinipur vast land areas were acquired after independence. In last three decades development of new town ('*Jyoti Basu*' Nagar), Rajarhat on east of Kolkata, and Baruipur, Tamluk, Barasat etc. developed as district headquarters required acquiring of vast land. It was necessary changing the agriculture character of land.

3. Industrialisation and development of Special Economic Zone (SEZ)

Lands taken for such purposes no longer remains agricultural land. At different times and places huge land were acquired mainly by Government and allocated to different industries namely Hindustan Motors, Shaw Wallace (formerly

D. Waldia), Alkali Chemicals, Dashnagar, Haldia Industrial belt, number of industries like Indian Iron and Steel, MAMC, Alloy Steel, Graphite India, Hindusthan Fertilisers, Phillips Carbon etc. in Hooghly, Howrah, Burdwan and other districts acquiring vast land tract. All these changed character of agricultural land. To develop Thermal Power Plants at Bandel (Hooghly), Budge Budge (24-Parganas), Titagarh (24-Parganas), Kolaghat (Medinipur), Saontaldihi, Mejia (Bankura), Sagardighi (Murshidabad), Pumped Storage Plant at Puruliya (Ajodhya Hills) also required East land areas, mostly using agricultural lands. All these were necessary for development of the state.

4. Development of roads and other infrastructure

Before independence to develop roads like Grand Trunk (Sahi Sadak of Sher Shah) Road, Jassore Road, Benaras Road, Barrackpur Trunk Road etc. bridge on rivers like Bally bridge, Howrah bridge, Educational Institutions required use of a large area of agricultural land mostly. After independence, development of Delhi Road, Bombay Rd., Durgapur Express Rd., National Highways No. 36, 6, 31, 41, Haldia Road etc. required land to be acquired. Innumerable number of bridges namely Iswar Gupta Setu, Nivedita Setu, Matangini, Farakka etc. required lands – mostly agricultural. Universities established in Bengal include Bardhaman, North Bengal, Kalyani, Bidhan Chandra, Uttarbanga Krishi, Gourbango, Vidyasagar, Rabindrabharati, Sidhu-Kanhu, Alia, Barasat etc. required acquisition of huge land area that is mostly agricultural. The Special Economic Zone Act was promulgated in 2005 in the country. This permitted industrialists to get large chunk of land which were used by them to establish industries with tax relief for several years at the beginning. However in Bengal no such venture was made except the one at Falta, South 24-Parganas which was already earmarked for industry centre and IT-Complex at Rajarhat.

5. Panchayet system and delegation of power

The Union or Central Government ruling the country and State Governments ruling the states are through 'Parliament' and 'Assemblies' elected directly by the people once every five years. These Governments at two stages act as per the constitution and its provisions. The duties are divided into central, state and functions shared between State and the Centre. In the process of devoluation of both administrative and financial power and authority the stage below state level are the '*Jela Parishad*' (district level), '*Panchayet Samiti*' (Block level) and '*Gram Panchayet*' (Village-level) – all elected as per Panchayet Act. In the cities and towns municipalities and corporations elected as per concerned Act and work directly under state.

After establishment of Left Front Government in West Bengal in 1977, the Act of formation of three stage '*Panchayet's* (two stage for smaller states) was passed and the first election was held in 1978 forming '*Jela Parishad*', '*Panchayet Samiti*' and '*Gram Panchayets*' and delegation of both administrative and financial power was made transferring 50 per cent of finance to these levels. Later in 1992, the 83rd amendment of the constitution was made incorporating the provisions of Panchayet Act. The Act provided that a state or so having less than 20 lakh population shall have two stage Panchayet system all others having three stage panchayet. At village level Gram Panchayet and its '*Pradhan*', at Block level *Panchayet Samiti* and its '*Sabhapati*' and district level and its '*Sabhadhipati*' are all elected representatives ruling the villages and looking after their developments in respective areas. While each *Gram Panchayet* get one '*Secretary*', the BDO is the executive officer of *P. Samity* and District Magistrate is the executive officer of '*Jela Parishad*' and 50 per cent of state budget is used through this '*Panchayeti Raj*' structure to run the development etc. work of the '*Gram*' (village) or '*Block*' or '*Jela*' (district). The policy decisions are taken since 1994 in two meetings in a year of 'voter villagers' convened by the '*Pradhan*' of Gram Panchayet and these meetings called '*Gram Sabha*' are of immense importance. This along with delegation of financial and administrative power to the panchayet the Govt. of the village is established. The Panchayeti Raj Act transfers the power and responsibility of 29 development activities along with the authority to collect some revenue, tax and non-tax income independently. This is actually the way through which rural people of a village has been brought to play the main role in administering and development of the village in West Bengal.

Since 1978 in West Bengal 3354 Gram Panchayet, 333 *Panchayet Samity* and 17 *Jela Parishads* have been constituted through elections held every five years. It has been found that more than 66 per cent of panchayet members were landless '*Kshet Majur*' (farm labour), marginal farmers and small farmers. This percentage of participation of these classes increased to 70.8 per cent since 2003. Again members included 34.1 per cent women and 33.4 per cent persons from SC and ST communities. In effect, women and people from backward community were empowered through this system. In 2003, "Village Development Committees" (Gram Unnayan Samity) were formed selecting person from different categories and stages of village society to help '*Gram Panchayet*' drafting yearly and five year plan papers. Arranging drinking water for the villages, cleaning and sanitary works, public health infrastructure, development, primary education, development roads, culverts and maintenance of all these became the responsibility of *Panchayet*. Maintaining accounts and auditing at this level was arranged by *Panchayet*. '*Panchayet*' also ventured preparing land map of the village showing vested land, land deserving vesting, distributable land etc.

6. Agro-climatic zones, preparing plans and zonal research

In eighties of last century in West Bengal six agroclimatic zones were demarcated by Agroclimatic Planning Team constituted. For implementation of National Agricultural Research Project (NARP), ICAR jointly with Bidhan Chandra Krishi Viswavidyalaya initiated development of six Regional Research Stations and Sub-Stations with support of State Govt. Department making provision of lands. The six Regional Research Stations at *Kalimpong* for Hill area with a sub-station at *Pedong*, at *Poondibari*, Coochbehar of *Tarai* region, at *Ratua Manikchak*, Maldah for Old Alluvial region, at *Jhargram*, West Medinipur with two sub-stations at *Raghunathpur*, Puruliya and *Sekhampur*, Birbhum for Red lateritic region, at *Gayeshpur*, Nadia with a sub-station at *Chakdah* for new alluvium region and at *Kakdwip*, South 24-Parganas for Coastal saline region were being developed. The objective was to identify regionwise problems of agriculture and the specific technologies etc. to overcome them and achieve maximum production.

7. Seeds and agriculture

In India 80 per cent of the seeds used for cultivation particularly for food crops like paddy and some vegetables are farmers' own produce, West Bengal being no exception. However the seeds of flowers and vegetables were purchased from business houses. Farmers themselves produce and preserve some other seeds and exchange seeds with other farmers.

The first Seed Act was passed in 1966 prescribing quality requirements, seed testing aspects, seed certification etc. For implementation of provisions number of seed testing laboratories were established and modernised in West Bengal. Initially nine Seed Corporations including one in West Bengal were established that has taken over the seed certification work. West Bengal Govt. appointed Seed Certification Officers. In 1988, Seed Policy was drafted that contained provisions to meet the terms of World Bank. By then seed production infrastructure with the capacity of producing 20 per cent of seeds required was ready. The new seed policy appeared to destroy this extent of self-sufficiency in the country. Along with Seed Act, 2004, Patent Act, 1970 was amended for the third time. According to TRIPS the Act provided patenting of seeds, plants, microorganisms, cells, GM materials and animals that was not permitted in the original Patent Act. The Seed Inspector as in the Act would supervise seed production by farmers but not the same by multinational companies. As a result the responsibility of the Govt. has been reduced.

Signing WTO terms in 1994 with provision for import of seeds by Open General License (OGL) made the DIP Act, 1914 (Destructive Insect Pests Act virtually defunct changing the quarantine provisions number of times from 2003-2007. This created the possibility of entry of foreign pests and pathogens through seeds. During this period the Post Entry Quarantine (PEQ) which has not been so effective was introduced. Initiatives like 'Gene Campaign' etc. by people, could press to bring in Biodiversity Conservation and Farmers' Right Act, 2001 that recognised both the rights for breeder-creator of seed of a variety and the right of the farmer to produce and sale seeds to other farmers. The interest of people over that of industry of foreign character that was EUPOV Act was aroused to oppose this Act.

The second Agricultural Revolution (Green Resolution) through use of Hybrid seeds was a call of Union Govt. in 2010 (Dept. of Agriculture) that asks Indian farmers usually spending Rs 475 per kg of seeds, to spend for hybrid seeds from multinational company's Rs 76,000 a kg that generally they can not afford. However, hybrid seeds of different vegetables, flowers, fruits and paddy, wheat, maize, pulses and oilseeds of local sources are being brought in cultivation by Indian and Bengal farmers too. India, Bangladesh, Indonesia, Philippines and Vietnam together constituted a '*Task Force*' for necessary exchange of hybrid seeds. Countries like China and Sri Lanka have joined this TF afterwards.

Use of GM seed in India is controlled by Environment (Conservation) Act, 1986 that has 'Rules for the Manufacture, Use, Import, Export and Storage' of hazardous microorganisms and genetically engineered organisms and sales, 1989. The responsibility of application of this Act is vested to GEAC, Department of Environment and Forests, GOI. In West Bengal also attempts for introduction of GM varieties of Brinjal, Bhindi, Paddy etc. have been made. In other parts of the country GM maize, cotton and soybean have been introduced not without problems. Failure of Bt cotton in Andhra, Maharashtra, Karnataka, and Punjab has brought terrible loss to the farmers. Similarly Bihar farmers suffered loss with Bt maize. In most of the places pests that are not susceptible to *Bacillus thuringiensis* toxin or some diseases destroyed the crop. But there were other reasons also of loss of these crops.

Recently introduced 'organic farming' requires certified, organically produced seeds for the produce to get '*organic*' certificate. West Bengal is ahead in terms of fish seed production but most of such seeds are of carp fishes. The arrangement for production of seeds of cat fish, '*Galda*' prawn and Tiger prawn were in growing stage. Seeds of tiger prawn is generally collected by *net's* in coastal rivers in early morning and its production in this state is yet to take shape.

8. Irrigation development

National Watershed Development Project for Rainfed Areas (NWDPRA) works started in Eighth Plan Period (1991-1997).

Rain water on a land area flows through a natural drainage canal and the area is considered watershed of the canal. The watershed areas are called *Miniwatershed* for areas within 1-100 ha, *Microwatershed* for 100 to 100 ha, *Miliwatershed* for 1000-10,000 ha, *Sub-watershed* for 10,000-50,000 ha and *Full watershed* for 50,000 – 2 lakh ha. When the watershed is 2-10 lakh ha it is *sub-catchment*, 10-50 lakh ha it is *catchment* and 50 lakh to three crore ha called *Basin*. Any watershed area that is two crore 70 lakh to 11 crore 30 lakh ha size is called *Water Resource Region*.

In West Bengal the size of *Ganga Resource Region* is 8 crore 20 lakh 10 thousand hectare and includes four *Basins* or 22 *catchments* or 126 *Subcatchments* or 836 *Full watersheds*.

Within this vast *Resource Region* Block areas having less than 30 per cent agricultural area irrigated and 50 per cent of total land area is under cultivation. The programmes of prevention of soil erosion, water and soil conservation, maintenance of natural balance of environment, crop cultivation and animal rearing following scientific methods have started in eighth Plan. The work has continued through ninth Plan and the period thereafter effectively covering 165 Blocks in 16 districts of among the major irrigation projects works in *Tista Project* and *Subarnarekha Project* are continuing. Besides ninth medium projects are continuing in Puruliya districts.

In cases of Minor Irrigation Projects State Water Investigation Directorate (SWID) jointly with Central Ground Water Board has surveyed ground water levels of 269 Block areas excepting the 59 saline and 13 hilly Block areas and reported existence of 2746 crore cubic meter water. According to their data ground water reserve 231 in Blocks are free from any danger, 24 Block areas are in partly danger zone and 10 Block areas are within danger zone. These Block areas are short of ground water, with arsenic contamination, and fluoride and iron pollution. The West Bengal Groundwater Resources (Management, Control and Regulation) Act, 2006 was passed in Legislative Assembly on the basis of which lifting of groundwater from more than 300 places has been stopped. State had 3,844 number of HDTW, 609 MDTW, 3703 LDTW and 13,924 shallow tubewell till 2005-06. In addition there were 3686 number of MRL (from rivers), 102 Midi RL, 1294 Mini RL and number of dug wells.

In South 24 Parganas and North 24-Parganas the saline tracts in 13 and six Block respectively allowed only Aman paddy during monsoon to be cultivated and winter (Rabi) crop was impossible. Starting from seventies at the beginning of nineties of last century chillies and bitter gourds were grown only on 35 thousand ha out of 3.10 lakh ha agricultural land was under *Rabi* cultivation. Then massive programme of pond-excavation to collect rainwater to be used for *rabi* cultivation was launched. Large number of ponds made pond-water irrigation possible when other vegetable crops like tomato, brinjal, cabbage and different flowers were grown. Among the fruit plants only coconut and sapota were grown earlier and pond irrigation made growing of banana, citrus, mango etc. possible.

Together the irrigated area in West Bengal of 810 lakh ha in 1991-92 was made 1,030 lakh ha in 2006-07. The modern concept of crop irrigation is crop cultivation with minimum irrigation water and in this programme Drip irrigation is very effective with not much investment. This irrigation technique could be used in fruit orchards, vegetable crops and flower crops quite successfully. In case of rice, System of Rice Intensification (SRI) as suggested by Mukerji, 1901 long back in Bengal and by Laonel in South Africa recently reduces water consumption to a great extent. This technique has been introduced successfully in the last two decades from North 24-Parganas to Puruliya by Agricultural Officers (Dr S. Sarkar) of Dept. of Agriculture in West Bengal. N.R. Das, 2006 of BCKV showed very elaborately that at least in eight districts of West Bengal, '*paira*' cultivation of '*Kalai*', *Lathyrus, Blackcumin,* Mustard etc. could be grown as rabi season on paddy fields sowing the seeds seven days before harvest of paddy requiring no tilling and irrigation. This second crop was followed with a third short duration vegetable crop without additional irrigation. Farmers' experience in '*Shirkabad*' at the '*Ajoddha*' foot hills in Puruliya with repeated plowing and dew harvest made *sugarcane* growing possible without irrigation.

9. Nutrition of crops and chemical fertilisers

From the last part of forties of last century after Independence, chemical fertilisers were introduced initially giving *ammonium sulfate* free of cost to farmers. Even before this some personalities taking personal initiative brought some quantity of fertilisers from abroad to apply on some crops. Urea, phosphate and potash fertilisers were brought later. The concerned fertilisers were single super phosphate (SSP) and muriate of potash (MOP). Mixed and compound fertilisers came later.

First factory of chemical fertilisers was established by Fertiliser Corporation of India (FCI) at *Sindhri*, Bihar in fifties of last century. A small factory manufacturing phosphate fertilisers (ICI) was there at *Rishra*, Hooghly. In 1974, a nitrogen fertiliser factory (urea) was established at Durgapur, Bardhaman by Hindusthan Fertiliser Corporation of India Limited (HFCL). Gradually 57 large fertiliser factories were established in India of which at *Haldia* one each factory was established by HPCL and Hindustan Lever Ltd. One of the two was commissioned but closed down later while the HFCL plant was never commissioned. To promote fertiliser use among farmers FCI establishd Fertiliser Promotion and Agricultural Research Division at Durgapur campus of FCI. This Institution and later one project namely Indo German Fertiliser Education Programme under leadership of FP and ARD campaigned in Eastern India for enhancing fertiliser use that made an impact.

In West Bengal, total volume of chemical fertilisers used was 66,000 tons in 1950-51, 82 lakh tons in 1969-70 and 143 lakh tons in 1996-97. As a result in 1995-96, 118 kg of fertilisers was applied per ha in West Bengal whereas the average Indian figure was 87.4 kg/ha.

Coming to Soil Testing, State Agriculture Department started this in their Soil Test Laboratory under State Agricultural Research Institute. Thereafter, first Soil Testing Laboratory was established at Barddhaman in 1962. Later FCI established one such ST lab. at Durgapur and started extending this service in the form of a mobile ST Lab.

In the mean time considering the production cost in the country and the cost at which fertilisers were available in International market, Govt. of India decided to close down production in many of the factories particularly in Eastern India and purchase fertilisers from outside. All the factories were brought under four clusters and those in Eastern region (HFCL) were generally closed down. The other side was the acidification of soil due to continuous use of urea and nitrophosphates and the recommendation of agricultural scientists to use lime for correction of acidity of soil was not followed by the farmers regularly. The Fertiliser Control Order was issued by Government of India in 1985 and it provided some instructions in regard to fertiliser business, its price, quality and distribution system. One amendment to this order covered four microbial fertilisers, and three organic manures to make the order comprehensive. To manage and supervise all these, the Central Quality Control and Training Institute was established in *'Navi Mumbai'* alongwith some Regional Fertiliser Control Laboratories in different States, one being in West Bengal at Kalyani.

To generalise it can be said that in West Bengal soil fertility has not improved much. In all the areas soil is deficient in nitrogen and phosphate is fixed in such a way that plants can not absorb. In many areas soil is deficient in sulfur and in acid soil area calcium deficiency is also common. This state of micronutrient deficiency has caused wider use of micronutrient-mixture. There was a time till when use of balanced fertiliser meant use of N:P:K in proper proportions considering the soil and the crop.

Later Integrated Nutrient Management (INM) meant generally use of chemical fertilisers and organic manure in 7:3 ratio, use of main nutrients in appropriate quantity, ratio and requirement of the crop after correcting soil-pH as much required. This is followed by application of the micronutrients that are required for the soil and crop. The entire planning of nutrient supply is done ahead considering the crop and the soil in INM.

10. Organic farming

At the beginning of last century National Project on Organic Farming was given the shape of an Act in 2004. The concept of organic farming stood on a foundation of long history of use of organic manures of different kinds in cultivation and this practice was continuing, though very poor, till the middle of 20th century. In fact in India and in Bengal the era of chemical fertilisers started after this. Over last 50 years of use of chemical fertilisers in agriculture the economic limits of the farmers disallowed balanced use of fertilisers. Along with this chemical agriculture culture moved farmers away from organic manures and due to lack of knowledge they failed to make necessary corrections of soils. As a result soil gradually turned unable to yield expected response to fertiliser use. In the mean time in countries with developed agriculture knowledgeable people and scientists started raising questions on different limitations of chemical fertiliser. As a result 'organic farming' was started in those developed countries.

In Bengal since longtime back rotten plant leaves (leaf mold), compost from excess fish-stock, and oilcakes from mustard, linseed, sesamum etc. were in use for manuring crops. However, the composts were not very scientifically prepared oil-cakes were often made into slurry dipping one-two days in water and then applied. The sweeps from cowshed ('*Goalghar*') containing soiled feeds (straw, grass etc.), cow dung and urine are allowed to rot for a period after which that was put on farm lands taking by bullock-carts. Kitchen refuses were also used in the same manner in kitchen gardens.

'*Composting*' has come through many changes over time strengthened with farmers' experience and scientists' interventions. Faster composted '*vermi-compost*' or phosphate-rich '*phosphocompost*' (with rock phosphate) or the '*supercompost*' enriched with minerals (sulphur and iron from pyrite) appeared one after the other. During composting use of microorganism cultures has also become popular.

As liquid manure use of diluted cowdung or cattle urine or animal blood or starch from cooked rice ('*Fen*') have been in use for longtime. Recent contribution from farmers is by allowing chopped succulent leaves of drumstick, *Mikenia*, *Ocimum* etc. to rot in water in an earthen pitcher for 20 days, diluted thereafter and sprayed on crops.

Different leguminous plants namely flax, *Sesbania* (*'Dhanche'*), *'Kalai'* etc. are grown on a crop field for a short period and then plowed under and mixed with soil for adding organic matter and the nitrogen fixed by *Rhizobium* at their roots come under green-manuring. Young twigs, leaves and even pods of some other plants like Drumstick, Glyricidia, *Leucaena ('Subabul')* are chopped and added to soil to be plowed under. Composts are also made from the wastes of silk culture, mushroom culture wastes and 'coconut pith' for soil application. Sweepings of droppings from chicken, goat, sheep etc. reared in the house are also taken to compost pit or heap. *Azalla*, a fern growing on water surfaces of villages carrying fixed nitrogen (through *Cyanobacteria*) are used besides as animal feeds, of late in transplanted paddy fields to add both organic matter and nitrogen. While during dry season collection of silt from ponds and application in field has been a practice of Bengal farmers from olden days, *biogas plant slury* use as manure is a recent practice and not yet very common. From the end of last century wastes of wine factory, sugar factory, pulse processing mills have been used by dissolving in water and spraying on field.

Survey selection and mass production of *Rhizobium* culture and their application as seed treatment was initiated and run by Bidhan Chandra Krishi Viswavidyalaya. Later mass production of *Azotobacter, Azospirillum,* Phosphate solubilising bacteria (PSB) were initiated at BCKV laboratories and samples supplied. Since eighties one exclusive project was assigned for all these works. In a separate venture identification and production of biopesticide cultures of *Trichoderma harzienum*, *Pseudomonas fluoresence, Bacillus subtilis* were developed and techniques of their mass culture and application on crops were standardised in BCKV. As a result, the microbial products manufactured in the state were sent for testing at BCKV for certification. All these inputs for organic farming, capability of their production was achieved in nineties of last century.

The first organic farm in West Bengal was developed in Bankura after independence by *Satish Das Gupta*. In North 24-Parganas (*Aatghora*) one voluntary organisation SEVA, (Society for Equitable Voluntary Action) experimented on a new way of social change in villages and in the process was pioneer in inculcating organic farming culture among villagers since seventies of last century. Centering round Aurangabad one centre of International Forum for Organic Agriculure Movement (IFOAM) started gaining ground in end of eighties in India mainly through publications, campaign, holding seminars etc. In West Bengal IFOAM is active through SEVA. Some organisations are growing as composite units of farming, processing of farm produce along with resort and tourism development in Puruliya, West Medinipur and North 24-Parganas.

A small model organic farm has been developed at Kalyani under BCKV fulfilling all criteria of organic farming under leadership of *Dr M. Pramanik*. Besides, '*Bio-Paribar*', '*Tagore Society*', and some other individual (*Memari*) and groups are also making efforts. State Agriculture Commission (2009) recommended establishment of '*Biovillages*' in the State and accordingly State Dept. of Agriculture initiated establishment of 'Biovillages' (*Jaibagram*) in eight districts.

11. Progress in cultivation of fruits, flowers, vegetables and spices

In the western part of Bengal mainly in *Red Lateritic* tract development of orchards of pomegranate, sweet orange (*Musambi*), Ber (BAU variety) has taken place in last couple of decades. Commercial cultivation of custard apple, '*Bael*' (Woodapple), cashewnut, guava etc. are traditional crops of the area while '*Kino mandarin*' has been a successful new introduction in eighties of last century. Grapes are grown in a limited scale by some commercial farms.

In north Bengal, pineapple cultivation spread extensively through initiative of Central Bank and Gramin Banks in eighties of last century. It has later stayed for lack of processing industry as also break out of some crop health problem. *Arecanut* was popular since long but *Black-pepper* with it was spread in last few decades. While some intermittent closure of tea-gardens, started in British period, is not uncommon but in a large area small farmers are growing tea and sale the leaves to garden cum fatory holders ('*bought-leaf*). Introduction of *Rubber* in *Dooers* and establishment of some processing establishments are new development along with countrywide programme of growing rubber in non-traditional area to meet requirements of natural rubber.

'Litchi' produced in Murshidabad has been found quite good for export as fresh fruits and its quality has received international appreciation. Mango varieties namely *'Himsagar'*, *'Lakshman Bhog'*, and *'Fajdi'* has been registered as varieties of Maldah gaining advantage in International trade. In eighties large scale cultivation of water melon in coastal districts have slowed down for non-availability of quality seeds and other problems. *Cashewnut* is a traditional crop in West Medinipur but mostly wasted for not having good processing facilities. However development of nut frying industry in cluster has met the problem though cashew apple processing is yet to grow. In the matter of growth flower cultivation has gained momentum particularly in case of standard rose, Chrysanthemum, Sim carnation, Tagetes, and Tuberose. Commercial cultivation of these have increased greatly in this period. Another divident of population increase is increase in demand of other common flowers like *Jasmine, Hibiscus, Gladiolus, Taebermontana, Lotus* etc. Another progress in flower growing is protected cultivation of *Sim Carnation*, chosen varieties of roses and tropical cacti that are appreciated in high value markets.

In case of vegetables spread of onion cultivation beginning with Hooghly district over last three decades and the state is producing a quantity that meet the requirements little more than the additional requirement out of increased consumption.

Newer vegetables like *Broccoli, Brussel's prouts, Chinese cabbage, Asparagus, Cherry tomato, Kartoli, Gherkin, Fababean, Limabean, Coloured capsicum, Baby corn* are being produced in North 24-Parganas, Nadia, Hooghly, Barddhaman and Howrah where domestic markets show demand and offer better price. Hybrid varieties of cabbage has made it possible to produce in some pre and post winter months and smaller size bottle gourds also for prolonged periods.

Among spices cultivation of ginger, turmeric, garlic and black cumin have spread in larger areas and production of black pepper has increased perceptibly. Having mostly a shorter duration on field, prospect of marketing the produce on different dates over a period assures better price.

12. Food crops to commercial crops

A silent transformation of farming practices particularly in regard to crops has began in late eighties initially in some select districts like North 24-Parganas, Nadia, Hooghly and Barddhaman in West Bengal. In eighties, annual rice production was 74 lakh tons that reached 1 crore 26 lakh tons at the beginning of present century. The food deficit state turned self-sufficient in food by nineties. The next target of Bengal farmers, though undeclared, to increase income. Earlier jute was the declared cash crop of Bengal. But with the spread of irrigation in eighties and nineties, '*rabi*' cultivation increased through cultivation of '*Boro rice*' (areawise not much), winter vegetables and flowers mainly. Simultaneous increase of income of farm families, has increased demand for these vegetables right in local markets encouraging these vegetable growing and a 'small-farmers' commercial farming. Unique in its character the transformation was taking shape. Besides vegetables some flowers having demand in the markets around also were grown. Even some fruits like banana, guava and papaya increased diversity of produces and the demand in markets. Small farmers from their own experience started selecting more remunerative crops as also maintaind a '*changing mode*' so that the demand for the produce remained increasing. The search for variety of short-duration vegetables by these farmers not only brought newer vegetables as mentioned earlier but also bringing back once important types or varieties of Bengal vegetables like '*Bunchy onion*' (small bulbs), sweet peas, '*Makhan sem*', '*Bibi kumdo*', '*seedless sem*', '*Lafaa*', etc. These commodities has great demand for their taste (Mukherjee, 2011). Along with demand for '*organic*' produces among well-off people is increasing slowly.

Medicinal plant cultivation was encouraged by grant of Eighth Plan period two research and extension projects funded by Health and Family Welfare and Agriculture and Co-operation

Departments of Government of India that started collection of different medicinal plant species, develop medicinal plant garden, their conservation and propagation for distribution to prospective growers and development of awareness about such plants and their commercial prospects. For this purpose one three hectares medicinal plant garden was developed in BCKV and large number of the plants were conserved. A data base on nature, properties and medicinal use of such plants was built, their selection for different agroclimatic regions and their distribution was made. Training programmes and workshops were held and publications in Bengali was brought out (Ghosal and Adityachoudhury, 1997). This provided additional strength to commercialise small farms.

From eighties with initiative from agricultural scientists as also the fame of some varieties of localities (*Tulaipanji* of Dinajpur, *Gobindabhog* of Puruliya, *Sitasail* of Bankura etc.) farmers turned toward quality and scented rice for commercialisation. *Badshabhog* and *Govindabhog* of Puruliya, *Sitasail* of Bankura, *Tulaipanji* of Dinajpur, *Jirakathi, Dudheswar, Randhunipagol, Balam Lakshmidevda* and *Kanakchur (for chira), Indrasail* (for *Muri*) also fetched good price after re-introduction. (Mukherjee 2005). Similarly *Sonamung* has always a good market for its excellent flavour.

For low, swamps commercial crops like Bamboo, cane (*'Bet'*), *'Pati'* (North Bengal), Tagetes (*'Madurkathi'*, Medinipur), *'Hogla'* (South Bengal), *'Shola'* are good commercial crops for poor lands. Water chestnut (*'Panifoll'*), *'Shaluk'* (*Neelumbo*) and many other leafy vegetables (*'Saak'*) of wetlands have demand in Bengal markets. Leafy vegetables include *'Kulekhara', 'Kalmi', 'Sushni', 'Punarnava', 'Brahmi', 'Bathua', 'Gima'* etc. that have exclusive demand in Bengali market.

13. Fodder cultivation

Due to excessive population pressure after partition of the State, the pastures and grasing lands are mostly occupied for other emergent purposes since fifties. For long time in Bengal domestic animals have become stall-fed affecting their nutrition and feeding. In fact over four decades since independence of the country the entire animal stock of the state has become dependent only on vegetation on unused, fallow lands, '*Nayanjuli*', and such other places and the dry straw of paddy. For a long time '(from seventies) one All India Coordinated Project under BCKV conducted researches and extension activities to promote different fodder crops that became a valuable source of information, technologies and seeds of such crops for farmers. Side by side one small State Fodder Research Station at Nadia also contributed. NDRI, Eastern region came up in *Kalyani*, Nadia much later (seventies).

Ultimately *Coix* found some space to grow on '*ails*' of paddy fields in Southern Bengal, *Paragrass* grew in some Nayanjulis and margins of ponds, *Stylo* on hillocks in Puruliya and West Medinipur. Another class of feeds came from some herbs and trees like *Subabul, Babul*, Jackfruit, Drumstick, through lopping of their leaves and branches.

Besides rice straw (chopped), wheat husk ('*Bhusi*'), Pulse husks ('*Chuni*'), Cakes of different oil seeds ('*khoil*'), many other kitchen wastes, cooked rice starch ('*Fen*') and even pulses (soaked overnight) and molasses in well-off families made animal feeds. Some short duration fodder crops like Grasspea (*Gaimung*'), '*Kalai* etc. have been grown exclusively as fodder.

14. Crop protection

In 1967, Expert Panel of FAO for the first time talked about Integrated Pest Managemnt (IPM). Keeping in view the environment and depending upon natural rise and fall of pest and disease pressures, the management practices for restraining incidence of and incident pest and diseases is IPM. Data reveals that in India 2330 tons of technical grade pesticides have been used in 1950 and in 1990-1991 it became 75,000 tons. According to WHO since 1999 to 2000 out of 546 districts, 10 districts selected from five states reported 1176 cases of agricultural pesticide toxicity of whom 247 persons were dead mainly in Karnataka, Haryana and Andhra Pradesh. The report also revealed that poisonous chemicals above tolerance level were present on more than 25 per cent of food samples. Such above tolerance level of chemical was recorded against world average at 1.2 per cent. Side by side the production cost in the areas of fertilisers, seed and pesticides increased at very high rate. This context in India necessecitated integrated management programme or IPM.

IPM started in India in eighties of last century and was progressing quite slowly. Evidently in 1999-2000 it spread only over 10 per cent area. But due to lack of guidance and control by Government officers and scientists the programme of IPM – its extension, plan of implementation and components was under indirect control of pesticide producer companies. Starting with the Operational Research Programme on paddy at Panduah, Hooghly conducted by the Scientific Officers of State Agriculture Department in eighties, the IPM of paddy was successfully designed and implemented by them through organising training programmes. But gradually the traditional practices of use of tobacco-decoction, kerosene-emulsion, sprinkling of ash mixed with kerosene or neem decoction were substituted by systemic pesticides empowered by strong campaign.

The Chandannagar Center of Central Plant Protection and Quarantine Directorate also participated and added microbiopesticides in the programme. State Plant Protection Officers conducted elaborate camping to make farmers aware of 'predator-parasite' relation with pests, their identity and their existence in field to balance pest-population. Scientists of BCKV also joined the programme as experts. *Trichograma*, different wasps, and spiders and fungi like *Metarrhisium, Beuveria*, and *Paecilomyces* application has been initiated. Similarly to check pathogens of crops use of cultures of *Trichoderma, Pseudomonas* and *Bacillus* also was in progress. Selected cultures of such microbes from SAUs and other Institutions were mass cultured and formulated by biopesticide companies that reached crop fields through extension network of State Agriculture Department. Some leaf-decoctions like neem leaves boiled in water, seed oils of neem, karanja, leaf oils of citronella were brought in emulsions with water or formulated into granules and were used for management of soil borne and other diseases. These technologies remain to be popularised.

In fact the philosophy of maintaining undisturbed the pest-predator or pathogen-inhibitor balance in nature as it exists in crop field, in this pest-disease management programme is the key. Over and above diversity of crops and varieties, use of organic and natural manures and products, use of tolerant varieties, plowing fields in summer, and use of natural products like cattle urine, kerosene, tobacco, garlic, neem decoctions etc. are integrated in this programme.

Since crop produces are invaded in market, godowns and transports, by different pests and diseases like rats, birds, monkeys, snails, jackals and fungi etc. the programme needs to be linked with needs of time and locality depending on regular scouting of produces be it in fields or after harvest. Recently elephants are destroying paddy over vast area. State Forest Dept, 2008-05 Report has claimed that in the year 2004-05 elephants have destroyed crops worth Rs 90.0 lakh. As a management programme farmers erected stage's (*'Maacha'*) on tree-tops beside paddy field to guard and signal arrival of elephant groups to call villagers with torch (*'Masal'*) in hand to scare away the elephants.

15. Cultivation of exportable fishes

In the districts of South 24-Parganas, East Medinipur and North 24-Parganas, shallow wetlands of brackish water (*'Bhedi'*) were used to cultivate for quite long time getting the *'seeds'* of tiger-prawn (Bagda) (*'kathi'*) from rivers in still southern area. Practically during early seventies coastal brackish water from high tide flooding low *aman* lands were seeded with this fishlings (Tigerprawn) that grew in this water. Thereafter during pre-monsoon farmers harvested the prawns, puddle the land and transplanted 'aman seedlings' – a kind of prawn-paddy rotation. Govt. of India to regulate coastal agriculture enacted like "Coastal Aquaculture Authority Act, 2005" and thereby created an authority who recorded each of these prawn farm (*Bhedi*). Such registered farmers were entitled to bank loan as also compensation after any coastal hazard affecting them. Prawn or fish producers could get enlisted their registered farm with Sea-food Export Organisations to reach better market.

Tiger prawn farmers require to contact Fishery Extension Officer of their Block or Asst. Director of Fisheries, Brackish water at Barasat, North 24-Parganas or 'Captain Bhedi', Kolkata or Kanthi, East Medinipur and Export Inspection Council of India certifies the produce to be free from antibiotics or pesticides to become exportable. The state order no. 603 has provided that prawn can not be kept soaked in water. 'Marine Products Export Development Authority (MPEDA), West Bengal Region has been created to supervise and control all these activities.

16. Crop insurance

Weather-based Crop Insurance Scheme was launched in India in 2000 AD. Farmer on insuring his crop shall receive compensation when the crop is destroyed for lack of suitable environment to grow and produce due to natural calamities like hailstorm, flood or drought. The scheme is valid for both kharif and rabi season crops and a deposit of premium of Rs 500 for each acre of crop in the name of the farmer is required that is shared @ Rs 187.50 each by State and Central Govts and rest Rs 125 by the farmer. The compensation received by farmer is Rs 5000 per acre. For renewal of the scheme every year the State Govt. has to apply by depositing an amount determined. In West Bengal usually small and marginal farmers participate in the scheme provided the State Govt. renews the scheme. So far upto 2010 State Govt. spent a maximum of Rs 3 crore in a year.

12.4 Ready to eat food culture

(a) With the entitlement and partipation of a larger section of villagers as pattadars and bargadars the village economy and purchasing power of rural people increased slowly. Urbanisation at a faster rate, growth of service sector in areas extended to rural backdrop, development of roads, transport and communication system, though not satisfactory, led increased number of markets and capacity building of existing ones making them vibrants. Alongwith in the cities, towns, census towns, rail stations, bus terminus, all categories of education institutions, recreation centres new space evolved serving 'ready-to-eat'.

About two decades back one professional organisation was engaged to survey and analyse the prospect of development of kinds of food markets in Bengal. Their report contained an important observation that – Bengali housewives have no faith in the quality and freedom from germs of prepared, ready to eat foods in market. It appears that the basic difference of food habit and food culture in east and west is difficult to overcome. Contradiction between few hundred years old western food culture and thousand years old eastern food habit was actually the obstacle. For example, Bengali housewives can not imagine serving even hermetically packed frosen milk to family members without boiling it that westerners drink without hesitation.

Street food culture in Bengal has never been strong enough except for one exceptionally widespread and very popular culture of '*Telebhaja*' (Deep fried in mustard oil) using different vegetables dipped in '*Beson*' (pulse powder) paste, deep-fried in mustard oil and served very hot to consumers standing around. This is mostly an evening snack and is a very old culture of Bengal that brings from high intellectuals to persons moving in cars out of their abode.

(b) Categories of 'Ready to Eats' in Bengal

Many of ready foods are known in Bengal that are quite ancient and used for long time. Dishes like '*Alur Dom*', *Ghugni*, '*Alukabli*' are prepared fresh and served for which boiled potatoes skinned and boiled peas are kept ready for final preparation before serving as 'snack' ('*Jalkhabar*'). On the other hand different kinds of '*Nadus*' made of fried '*muri*', '*chira*', '*khoi*', '*Badam*', '*Til*' etc. are mixed with '*Gur*' (*molasses*) cooked and made into round, hard '*nadu*' that are ready snacks to eat, or to be carried in some kind of temporary packets. At this stage it may be mentioned that in preparation of such ready foods' some food materials like '*akher guder chak*', '*Gur*', sugar, '*Patali of Date syrup*', on the one hand and '*mudi*', '*chida*', '*khoi*', '*Til*', groundnut etc. are used in preparation of '*ready-food*' described above.

(c) Traditional 'Ready to Eat's

Traditional ready to eat items like '*Kachuri*', '*Singhada*', '*Telebhaja*', '*Jilapi*', '*Fuchka*', '*Pampad bhaja*' etc. are available at a particular time when the consumer has to reach its cooking place – a shop or a street stall. These are not packaged but obtained fresh at the shop. Sometimes preparations like *'Alur Dom'*, *'Ghugni'*, *'Parota'* etc. are cooked in house and brought to sale point in a container (*'Handi'* or *'Gamla'* and boiled at sale point also to allow consumers enjoy the hot dish.

(d) Packaged ready food

Some food items like *'Biscuits'*, *'Cakes'*, and snacks like *'Chanachur'*, *'Chidabhaja'*, *'Badambhaja'*, *'Badam Takt'* etc. are very common and available with vendors on trains, and in streets having no compulsion of consuming fresh. Besides the packaged *'Mudi'*, *'Jam'*, *'Jelly'*, *'Honey'*, *'Tal Candy'*, *'Packaged Chanachur'*, different fried nuts, different dry sweets like *laddoo*, etc. are usually collected from two kinds of shops namely *'Stationery shops'*, or *'Grocery shops'*. Packaged *'Ghee'* (in small bottle) and *'Dahi'* (in earthern pots of different sizes are also there.

(e) Packaged Beverages

Carbonated water in different brands were available since long; being made available in new packages with new flavour and tastes. *'Squash'* became available in sixties in bottles followed by bottled plain and flavoured milk, and 'fruit juices' in tetrapack since eighties of last century.

Some of these food items became available in both packaged and unpacked condition (loose) and important examples are rice, *'Aata'*, etc. and even articles like 'tea' (beverage made from) is also available in 'packaged' and loose condition. Introduction of *'aluminium foil packing'* has modernised and simplified carrying of cooked food of different kinds keeping them ready to eat.

(f) Transformation : Packaged from unpacked

Since the last two decades of last century most of the major food and related items are being gradually made available in packaged form from loose forms. From sixties or even earlier the concept of 'Departmental Store' was evident in major cities including Kolkata. Along with food commodities like rice, *'aata'*, flour, sugar, pulses, cooking oil, table salt etc. appeared weighed and packaged form both branded and unbranded. Table salt was possibly one item having its loose sale totally disappeared. Smaller packages of spices and many other items related to food pushed in the greater food world of Bengal and all these spread to different corners of Bengal.

(g) *Stall, restaurant, eatery and 'dhaba'*

In small to large towns street shops were quite common in Bengal of olden days selling *'telebhaja'*, *'Jhal-mudi'*, *'Chanamix'*, etc. while shops, generally attached to sweet shops sell *'Kachuri'*, *'Singhara'*, *'Jilipi'*, etc.

'Dhaba' is a major-road-side food shop, generally opened in forties and fifties in Bengal mainly by *'Punjabi'*s serving truck drivers and helpers getting food and rest during their long journey.

Food stalls in small, medium and large cities developed over decades mostly to serve snacks and preparations like Bread toast, 'French' toast, 'Omlet', Moglai parota, different rolls, *'Kabiraji'*, *'Dimer devil'*, etc. that attracted evening consumers since long. South Indian dishes namely *'Dhosa'*, *'Masla Dhosa'*, *'Idli'*, *Meduvada*, etc. was served in stalls since seventies of last century.

12.5 Newer Technologies

In fact some of these technologies to be listed now are not exactly new technologies but are being applied in a newer way. Scientists, farmers, and people interested in agriculture are, while working or experimenting in fields experienced some new ideas and methods that has been accepted by larger sections of farming community. Some such technologies are being mentioned now.

1. *Zerotil*

According to the philosophy of *Masanobu Fukuoka*, tilling of land for cultivation has been reduced to minimum and that has reduced soil erosion, cost of cultivation, time and labour to till land etc. keeping production unaltered at least in some cases.

2. *Soil solarisation*

Long term practice of plowing land in summer is the origin of this technology. Land is plowed in summer, made weed-free, soaked with little water and then covered with transparent sheet of polyethylene. Solar radiation passes through this sheet to reach soil inside and turn into heat that can not come out of the sheet resulting in 6-7°C rise in temp inside. As a result the soil borne weed seeds, insects and pathogens are killed. J. Katan, reports that in 10 years (1976-86) the new technology is being used in at least 24 countries.

3. System of intensification of rice (SRI)

Mukerji, 1901 has possibly for the first time suggested a method of cultivation of transplanted rice that is in principle similar to one that is now known as SRI. In 1983, *H. Laoneli* tried a method he called '*System* of Rice Intensification, (SRI) in which only three-four kg paddy seeds sown in seed-bed producing two-leaf seedlings (in 12 days in Kharif and 15 days in Rabi season in Bengal) that are transplanted singly in 25 cm (10") spacing on a puddled (having no standing water) land. The method requires less quantity of chemical fertiliser and more organic manure. However, extensive weed growth requires to be controlled with paddy weeder.

4. 'Poyra' cultivation

'Poyra' or *'Utera'* cultivation is one old technology being popularised and extended since eighties of last century. Five to seven days before harvest of Aman paddy commonly *'Khesari'* or *'Grass Pea'* (*'Gaimung'*) seeds were sown by broadcasting and paddy was harvested five-six inch from soil level, for *'Khesari'* growing on them. This conserves soil moisture as well as omit land preparation saving some time in the crop rotation. *'Poyra'* cultivation is possible with crops like mustard, blackcumin, hemp etc. in place of *'Khesari'* (N.R. Das, 2006). It has been determined through experiment that in West Bengal *'poyra'* crop can be grown in at least eight districts.

5. Boro rice planting in deep water

Farmers developed a need-based technology of rice transplanting from a floating boat putting a mud-ball at the roots of rice seedlings and dropping them from the boat into the water to reach soil at the bottom.

6. Protection of Boro seed bed seedlings from cold injury

Boro seedlings are raised in hard winter. Due to soil getting cold, seedlings turn red. As protection measure the bed is covered with water (flooding) over the night or covered with ashes.

7. *Manual pollination of cucurbits*

Obtaining the idea from agricultural scientists, in the morning farmer takes male flower and touches the female flowers with it to increase fruit setting. Later they started taking the pollen in clear water and use a dropper to pollinate.

8. *Selection of new varieties by farmers*

Agril. scientists in the second or third phase of crossing varieties, in the selection of a better variety asked farmers to see plants bearing panicles and use their wisdom to select.

9. *Rope scaffold on ponds for growing creeper cucurbits*

Seeds are sown on bank of pond and the growing creepers of bittergourd, snake-gourd, ridged gourd etc. are guided to grow on the rope-scaffold. This space-utilisation design is common in South 24-Parganas.

10. *Regulating flower initiation in guava*

Farmers of Baruipur, North 24-Parganas trained long branches of Guava, removing leaves, bending the branch and binding them to soil with rope. This induced flower at a time as desired by growers.

11. *Inviting light and air within mango orchard*

Dept. of Pomology, BCKV scientists succeeded in reducing pest and disease pressure in a Mango orchard. Prunning and cutting branches at several points to create '*air tunnel*' in the thick of mango-canopy is the wayout.

12. *Microtuber production for potatoes*

Crossing artificially beween two select parent lines, the resultant hybrid seed (TPS) is sown to produce plants and microtubers on them. Production of '*minituber's* from such plants (pieces containing one leaf and one microtuber is done in air-conditioned tissue-culture space.

13. *Production of hybrid rice seeds*

On crossing between selected parent lines, the F_1 obtained gave much higher yield. Concerned Chinese breeder trained Indian farmers in the technique of hybrid-seed production. Hybrid rice seeds are produced in South India successfully and BCKV and State Agric. Dept.'s joint effort may yield hybrid rice seeds.

14. Hybrid vegetable seed production

Hybrid varieties of vegetables e.g. tomato, cabbage, cauliflower, bottle gourd, snakegourd etc. have been produced in India. Using chosen parent lines hybrid seeds are being produced. These varieties are high yielders and very often tolerant to tropical climate particularly higher temperature resulting possibility of their cultivation over wider time period.

15. High yielding varieties

HYVS are created through AICR projects of the crop concerned in multi-state efforts. Such varieties of crops like paddy, wheat, maize, barley, jute, sugarcane, soybean, pulses, oilseeds, vegetables, flowers, and fruits has transformed the production scenario of the country as a whole including West Bengal. Besides hybrid varieties some crossing and selections for generations also have produced some good varieties.

16. Microbio fertilisers

Commonly called 'biofertilisers' some microbes that grow on roots of leguminous crops like *Rhizobium* is grown in mass and applied as seed or soil treatment to enhance growth of the N-fixing bacteia forming nodules. Others like *Azotobacter, Azospirillum*, Phosphate Solubilising Bacteria (PSB), Cyanobacteria, Mycorrhizae are important groups of microorganisms mass-cultured *in vitro* or *in vivo* to be used as biofertilisers.

17. Microbiopesticides

Number of virus, bacteria and fungi are identified and are in use to check insect pests and pathogens of crops. The microbes that are usable or in use in Bengal are *Trichoderma, Metarhizium, Pseudomonas, Bacillus subtilis* and *thuringiensis, Beauveria, Paecilomyces* and also some viruses like Nuclear Polyhedrosis Virus (NPV).

18. Use of microorganisms in composting

To speed up composting different organic material mixed with cowdung, moisture, aeration and incubation under cover, microorganism culture like bacteria, actinomycetes, aspergillus etc. are mixed.

19. Microorganisms in jute retting

Retting of jute sticks tied in bundles, submerged with weight in flowing water body surface is often sprayed with cultures of *Aspergillus, Sporotrichum* and *Chostridium felsinum* to speed up retting.

20. Infield mass culture of Trichoderma

Prepared cowdung manure (15-20 kg) is mixed with 200 g of *Trichoderma harzianum* culture and covered with a wet gunny bag for two weaks to get the entire compost mass full of *Trichoderma* growth. The multiplied culture is then applied to the soil around the collar of the affected plant.

21. Culture of Azolla, its use and conservation

Azolla is a water fern that grows on water in a pond in shady places, where they usually spend hard scorchy summer. They naturally multiply in monsoon particularly under tree shades. Besides their use as animal feeds, they are used as manures (for having N-fixing bacteria *Annabaena* in their leaves) for paddy and in transplanted rice field applied @ five kg/acre. It grows very fast and covers the entire field in one week that is puddled in prepared land with paddy-weeder to contribute nutrition and OM to paddy plants.

22. Energy (electricity) generation from rice husk in rice-mills

In Barddhaman, West Bengal in eighties of last century with Santipada Gon Choudhury's technology, electricity is generated in more than 70 rice mills incinerating accumulated rice husks to run the mill.

23. Rice bran oil production

Fresh rice bran obtained after polishing rice grains in rice processing mills are subject to solvent extraction to get rice oil – a non-oilseed oil that has good demand. This production process is on in different oil mills in Barddhaman in nineties of last century.

24. Seed production of carp fishes

Mostly in North 24-Parganas carp fish is injected with required hormone in the beginning of monsoon and the fish is released in shallow water in the confine of a nylon mosquito-net to allow releasing eggs that very quickly metamorphoses into fishlings. Later mother fish is taken out and fishlings are allowed some growth before selling.

25. Seed production of cat fish and others

Injecting male and female fishes with required hormone, sex-organs are scissored out and made into squash in water and the two waters are mixed to get the cat-fishlings that are sold to growers.

26. Cultivation of different uncommon fishes

From the seventies of last century new fishes namely silver carp, grass carp, *Cyprinus, 'Pangus',* Hybrid catfish and *Pabda* cultivation started and first four are appreciated in Bengali market while hybrid catfish and *Pabda* has not been liked by Bengalis. Production of brackishwater fishes like *Parse, Bhetki, Topshe* and '*Bagda*' (Tiger prawn) has increased in '*Bhedi*' fisheries. Similarly sweet water pond-fishes like *Maurala, Gule, Bele, Leta, Shol, Tengra, Chanda* are being produced in larger volume for having a good market.

Ornamental fish culture has also spread through production of variety of ornamental fishes along with development and spread of aquarium-industry etc.

27. Milk production

After independence a large Governemnt Dairy farm was established at Haringhata P.S. Nadia. Initially a programme of upgrading of indigenous breeds of cows of Bengal was taken up with Haryana bulls. But during four decades of its running the Dairy Farm became sick and gradually cowsheds were vacated and lent to private milk producers. Regarding the programme of upgrading Jersy and Holstein were brought and cross breeds of indigenous cows (F_1) were the target. Using 'frozen semen' technology *Deshi cows* were artificially inseminated to get improved cows till eighties. Finally decision to use '*Sindhi*' and '*Shahiwal*' breeds for improvement of '*Deshi*' breeds has been taken up.

In the last decade of last century village women were inspired to form cooperative groups each rearing two to three cows, selling the milk to co-operative system that ultimately reaches Milk Unions at districts and Dairy Plants of Federation centrally at Mother Dairy, Dankuni, Metro Dairy, Barasat and Govt. Dairy, Belgachia who have homogenisation, pasteurisation and packaging plants ultimately increasing milk production in Bengal though bill not sufficient for opening milk processing plants.

28. Production of meat and hide

One quality breed of goat of Bengal is '*Black Bengal*' that is famous for its meat and skin quality. This breed due to in-breeding for long period has slowly become smaller in size. Animal breeders have taken up a programme of survey and selection of larger sized members among the animals and use them in breeding so that its original size is got back.

Slaughtering of cows being permitted in Bengal, production of beef and hide in Bengal is quite high leading to good development of leather industry and export of hide and beef though their quality improvement is required.

29. Pig rearing

Pig rearing was mainly done by tribals in Bengal since early days. Later programme of Dept. of Animal Husbandry was to popularise white, large 'Yorkshire Breed' and a farm was established at Haringhata along with one '*Bacon Factory*'. Later after its close down one or two small factories were established by private interested groups. In last two decades changing its policy with Department has been promoting local breed '*Ghungroo*' black skin but large in size and prolific breeder.

30. Introduction of 'Khaki Campbell' Duck

This breed having ability to live with small quantity of water, producing larger number of eggs and being hardy in health was introduced all over Bengal from hills to coast. It has already made an impact on egg production.

31. Rhode Island Red and white leghorn breeds of poultry

These two breeds RIR and WLH were introduced possibly since sixties in Bengal and has been largely accepted by commercial and also small growers for their high rate of production of meat and eggs. Large dip-liter farms have grown in Bengal. Produces of local breeds i.e. eggs and flesh having better taste however gets better prices in Bengal markets and for other rearing advantages remains popular among villagers.

32. Other animals and birds introduced

Since nineties of last century some animals mainly birds were introduced in Bengal. These birds are '*Koel*' (small bird), Turkey, Emu (large bird) that has been admired by people at large, producers and consumers. Animals like buffalow, horse and ass were however not new introductions their number in the state being small. Unlike many other countries pet animals like cats and dogs, though exist in large numbers are never sacrificed for consumption in Bengal.

Rearing of one indigenous breed of sheep in Bengal is a long time practice in south Bengal mainly in Sundarbans but only for milk and meat. Use of wool from this animal was not in practice excepting some attempts under BCKV for developing techniques for its use commercially.

12.6 Changing weather and agriculture

For quite sometime due to global warming, weather all over the world is changing. The change is felt over last two decades. The average rainfall has reduced up to 29 per cent. India has 32.7 per cent land area eroded and 24.78 per cent of land has turned into desert. (Current Science, 2006, 22nd Nov. issue). This has greatly affected western India but eastern India particularly West Bengal has also been affected. Excessive chemical use in agriculture has affected environment. Continuous use of urea and DAP has developed some amount of acidity in soil and inspite of expert recommendation its correction with lime application has not been done to the extent it was required. The technology of minimum tilling of land is also not being followed. Irrigation using minimum water required or microirrigation techniques has not been popularised.

Decline in duration of winter in Bengal has resulted in reduction or 'no increase' in productivity of crops like wheat, pulses, oilseeds etc. Chemical agriculture over last five decades has in effect reduced organic manure use in agriculture and temperature rise has enhanced oxidation of soil OM process particularly in tropical areas. Direct effects of change of weather has effected cyclone, flood, coastal flooding, drought and such others in increased numbers. An account of cyclonic storms etc. in Bengal coast has been published (Sing, 2002). It showed that upto 1994, 59 whirlwind storms, seven serious cyclones, 14 floods and three earthquakes occurred in Bengal coast. All these caused crop loss and destruction often in years interval and those in 1762, 1865, 1921, and 1942 led to four famines in the area. Evidently extremely destructive cyclonic catastrophes have increased in frequency since middle of 20th century. Along with high rainfall and flood high rise of sea water caused salinisation of extensive agricultural land that prevented any agricultural activity for years together. However West Bengal Government for last few decades started giving relief incuding seeds, seedlings 'minikits' containing seeds, fertilisers and pesticides that has brought back normal agricultural activity of farmers so that production is not hampered.

12.7 Co-operative and agriculture

'Co-operative' is a kind of organisation of number of individuals joining hands with a pledge to work together all having equal rights and responsibilities. Usually a co-operative helps one to be self-sufficient and often take up different production, processing, marketing and services programme. Rabindranath explained that the co-operative ('*Samobay*') does not permit individuals to be clever, win and ride over others but to progress jointly. Cooperatives have succeeded in agriculture, animal farm, milk production and marketing, fish-culture and marketing, bee keeping and honey marketing, flower and ornamental production and marketing etc. both in the state and the country. Co-operative Banks, Credit Societies provide some capital for agriculture and others though they remain weak. In this country and more so in West Bengal, Nationalised Banks are shy giving loans, and money lenders ('*Mahajans*') charge exorbitant rate of interest. Cooperative banks with Government support could make farmers free from all these. The philosophy of 'small drops make a ocean' followed in cooperatives could do away middlemen and profiteers from agriculture and farmers' life – both in their production, processing and marketing programmes. In the context of financial crises worldwide cooperatives can prevent harmful contract farming and such others and play a positive role in social change particularly in economic depression worldwide.

The primary agricultural cooperative societies (PACS) formed after independence mostly failed for their lack of setting target, corruption, management incapability and such other reasons. Before this Sir Daniel Hamilton of Scottland reached '*Gosaba*' in Sundarban in early 20th Cent. and devoted his might for village improvement in such a remote area and made co-operatives his primary agency for development. Rabindranath at the later part of 19th century selected two areas of Bengal in east (*Silaidaha*) and west (*Surul*) and inspired people to constitute cooperatives for village reconstruction. His activities in *Surul*, Birbhum was pushed forward by Leonard Elmhirst and others. In both places cooperative grain godown, paddy marketing, rice mill, credit society, healthcare and primary education centres were organised in cooperative system.

In nineties of last century one such non-functioning PACS at '*Gnotra*', Nadia was revived by some agricultural scientists of BCKV through adopting seed production programme and transforming the village into a '*Seed Village*' producing quality paddy seeds. This became a model for running PACS with commercial success as also a Quality Seed Production village. Later at the beginning of 21st century the leader of same scientist group, Dr P.K. Chattopadhyay, organised another PACS running a cold store, at Tarakeswar; Hooghly to produce quality potato seeds and their storage and sale.

In some of the large water bodies ('*Khal*', '*Bil*' etc.) in Bengal, fish production cooperatives were organised in different districts of West Bengal. These could be turned into large fish farms with great commercial success, provided they were run with that objective, commitment and sincerity absence of which failed to best utilise such water-body resources of the state.

Since eighties of 20th century, with some Government initiative, following the NDDB model as implemented in Gujarat ('*Amul*'), primary milk producing cooperatives were organised with village women, who produced milk rearing cows. This milk production and supply helped develop milk Unions at district levels like *Bhagirathi* (Murshidabad), *Ichhamoti* (North 24 Parganas) etc. in 13 districts with primary processing capabilities. Processed milk of the Unions were collected by Milk Federation at state level for final pasteurisation, homogenisation, packing at Govt. Dairy, Belgachia, Mother Dairy, Dankuni and Metro Dairy. Barasat are marketing milk to consumers in a large area of the state. The primary need of milk has thus been met but Bengal is yet to produce sufficient milk to build up processing factories to produce milk powder, baby food, butter etc. to fulfill the states requirement.

In 2002, Y.K. Alagh, ex-member, Planning Commission recommended and one additional provision (IXA Clause) was introduced in Company Act that provided that Cooperatives can act as 'Company' with suitable plan and proposal. Thus in addition to existing co-operatives, acting as companies being engaged in trade and commerce, new cooperatives may be constituted to participate in commercial and trading activities.

12.8 Agrobased multi-functional projects

Procuring agricultural land that is used for agricultural production and also processing of some of the produces and marketing has been linked with other activities, developing resorts etc. It has been a new trend. In the districts of West Medinipur, Purulia such organic farms with orchards, vegetable and spice growing, fish culture, cattle etc. rearing and processing of their produces along with rest house and resort development for tourism have been commercially successful. Later established orchards have been partially transformed to accommodate tourism etc. in North 24-Parganas has also achieved commercial success.

12.9 Agricultural extension through targeted project implementation

Central Ministry of Agriculture and Indian Council of Agricultural Research (ICAR) has adopted one policy to help State Govts. to establish at least one State Agricultural University (SAU) to take the responsibility of agricultural education, research and extension education for the state or the earmarked area of the State, leaving for the State Agriculture Department the entire agricultural extension work. In fact the responsibility of agricultural marketing (network building and implementation), building network of ordinary and cold storages, encouraging people to develop requisite transport was to be vested with the Dept. or by establishing a separate Dept. of Agricultural Marketing, and organisation for export of fishes, animal products etc. This policy is being followed by most Indian States and the first SAU was established in UP at Pantnagar in the year 1960. In West Bengal first SAU – Bidhan Chandra Krishi Viswavidyalaya was established in 1974 at Mohanpur, Nadia but unfortunately the research responsibility was not transferred from State Agriculture Department. The State retained the Adaptive Research works under its own care along with its responsibility of agricultural extension work all over the State.

The extension network in West Bengal is organised under 340 Development Blocks each having one or more Agricultural Development Officer (ADO) formerly AEO and subordinate staff. Block is a common place having Livestock Officer, Veterinary Surgeon, Co-operative Inspector, Lady Social Education Officer, Panchayet Inspector for extension work in respective fields. Recently after 'flood' or 'drought' to promote agriculture a new procedure of distribution of seed, fertiliser and pesticides in '*minikit*' has gained popularity and in many other occasions like 'new variety seeds', 'new crop seeds' etc. it is followed. Some specific targeted projects are now briefed.

A. 'Lab to Land Project'

Launched in 1979, small and marginal farmers are selected including farm-labour who are trained in local but improved agricultural practices, with the object of increase of income through increased production of such very low income families. This was done through field demonstrations. Based on 'where there is will there is way' – philosophy small farming practices like vegetable cultivation, poultry bird rearing, fish cultivation etc. were encouraged particularly for those growers who remained so long untouched.

B. Krishi Vigyan Kendra (KVK)

One KVK was established in 1974 in *Puducheri* but its recognition as National Project was only in 1983. The country was notionally divided into number of zones and in the Zone-II, West Bengal was placed. As per the rules of having one KVK in each district, 17 KVKs were established in West Bengal. Of these KVKs (generally established under SAUs), West Bengal University of Animal and Fishery Sciences controlled three KVKs at Bhagabangola (Murshidabad), Ramsahi (Jalpaiguri) and Ashoknagar (North 24-Parganas), five KVKs controlled by Uttar Banga Krishi Viswavidyalaya (UBKV) at Kalimpong (Darjeeling), Poondibari (Coochbehar), Chapra (Uttar Dinajpur), Majhian (Dakshin Dinajpur) and Ratua (Maldah), three KVKs under BCKV at Jagatballavpur (Howrah), Chunchura (Hooghly) and Gayeshpur (Nadia). Besides one each are under control of Palli Siksha Bhavan, Visva Bharati (Birbhum), Ramkrishna Ashram, Nimpeeth (South 24-Parganas), CADC, Sonamukhi (Bankura), Seva Bharati, Jhargram, West Medinipur, '*Kalyan*', (Puruliya) and at CRIJAF, Budbud (Barddhaman). The experts in agriculture in these '*Kendra's* forward and train farmers in modern technology of agriculture, help farmers in application of such techniques in farmers field. The KVKs act as communication between technology developing Institutions and the farmers in respective districts.

C. Frontline Demonstration (FLD)

This project started functioning since 1997-98. Newly discovered technologies in crop production and crop protection is demonstrated through field experiments in farmers' field. The objective is to train farmers and agricultural extension officers in newly discovered technologies suitable for respective agroclimate. At least two to four ha farm land at a stretch is identified and all the farmers within that area trained in selected technology or package of technologies providing only the special inputs required from the project fund. This project helped in development of '*leadership*' as also made subject matter specialists and extension workers aware about the technologies.

D. Institute Village Linkage Programme (IVLP)

In 2002, CSWRI, Aviknagar made an assessment of the relationship of 90 ICAR research institutes and 45 SAUs with villages. They tried to estimate the influence of such Institutes that could be extended on the socio-economic conditions of the villagers. This ICAR-project studied the correct selection of farmers and villages on the one hand and extension of appropriate technology for right farmers and the result of the survey appeared hopeful and positive.

E. Village Adoption Scheme (VAS) and Lead Bank

In 1968, as per recommendation of D.R. Gadgil, 'Lead Bank' project was started to adopt a village and extend support to expedite its development. State Bank of India also started village Adoption Scheme, both being closed down finally. In 1975, Regional Rural Bank Project was taken up to help the neglected section of a village through extending loans but did not take a comprehensive shape. National Bank for Agricultural and Rural Development (NABARD) in 2007 revived these programmes and proceeded for all out development of 400 villages. Some other nationalised banks also started adopting villages in village adoption and total development scheme.

F. National Agricultural Technology Project (NATP)

Project activity started in November, 1998. After formation of World Trade Organisation (WTO), Govt. of India jointly with World Bank started experimenting on location-specific research, technologies generated thereof and extension of these. Out of these research and their extension to farmers in increased speed and taking decision about technologies at district level to make them more effective and economically sustainable correct one was selected. Another objective of the project was to develop non-government extension-structure wherever possible. To reach this target 24 Agricultural Technology Management Agency (ATMA) were established in selected districts, and in West Bengal it was established at Narendrapur Ramkrishna Mission. Besides in West Bengal and four other state's State Level Agricultural Management and Extension Training Institute (SAMETI) were developed to ultimately cause Human Development Department to work for the same purpose.

G. Agricultural training of SAUs

Over a long period of time trainings in agriculture are going on like farmers' meeting ('*Krishak Sava*'), workshop (two-three days), camps, and still longer courses. Trainings are organised for professionals of other sectors like fishermen, animal rearers, '*Kabiraj*' (medicinal plant), fertiliser dealers, Bank Officers, NGO-people, silk farmers, bee keepers, lac growers and others, mostly by experts from SAUs, Regional Research Centers, KVKs and Dept. of Agriculture. Training courses of longer duration (one to six months) are also common. Trainings for 6-18 months in certificate or diploma courses are mostly for sponsored candidates. Dept. of Agriculture has number of Agriculture Training Centers (ATC) in West Bengal that were previously known as Gram Sevak Training Centres.

It is now well known that at Central Engineering College (now BESU), Shibpur one year training course in agriculture was introduced in 19th century and Dept. of Livestock and Animal Husbandry used to offer training in animal husbandry and veterinary science at Belgachia in 20th century. Lok Siksha Parishad at Narendrapur runs different training programmes in agriculture. SAUs in West Bengal started, besides regular graduate and post-graduate courses under their Directorate of Extension Education training programmes since 1974 and a full fledged Farmers' Training Centre has been established at Kalyani, subsequently KVKs taking up the responsibility of trainings in the regions concerned.

In the field of crop protection trainings in Integrated Pest Management (IPM) starting from the efforts of State Agriculture Department, continued in an intensive manner in SAUs and other agricultural Institutions in West Bengal. Training in mushroom seed production for a longer duration and cultivation for short duration were taking place in Dept. of Plant Pathology in BCKV and UBKV. Besides trainings in Vermicompost production, biofertiliser production, biopesticide production, liquid manure production, hybrid seed production, flower harvesting, commercial rearing of animals, carp fish seed production, cat fish seed production. Macrobechium seed production, bee-keeping, silk insect rearing, etc. training required infrastructure and technical skill. Popularising SRI rice cultivation among farmers is being done by State Agriculture Dept.

SAUs organise summer school, winter school etc. and refresher training courses for teachers in different disciplines.

12.10 Agricultural Marketing

Due to weak and imperfect storage and marketing network in the country and in West Bengal also, a part of produces of all kinds are perished as also the farmers do not get reasonable prices for their produces. National Commission on Agriculture in their report (1976) recommended for one regulated market for every five km space that has not been implemented.

State of West Bengal has 2918 market most of which are private owned and run. In the towns, cities and municipal areas 350 daily markets are running.

Under the Marketing Board of the State there are 28 major markets, 200 submarkets and only 46 regulated markets. 'Agrinet' of Agricultural Marketing Directorate has created 100 market information centers and 22 Food Processing and Training cum Market Production Centre. Again 'Department of Food Processing Industries and Horticulture' has established five Export and Agro-Processing Centers and outlet. Fishery Department's '*Benfish*' runs separate markets. Animal Resources Development Department has created some 'Sale Counters' of meat and milk based products and the Milk Federation has established 'Mother Dairy Booths' in all the large and medium cities and most small towns that are also used by private milk business makers e.g. '*Amul*'.

Forest Department has not created any such 'sale points' excepting a few at Bidhan Nagar and other places to sale Eucalyptus oil etc. Most other products of forests are sold right on the spot around the forest concerned. In the mean time in 1994 Govt. of India signed "General Agreement on Tariffs and Trade" (GATT) and accordingly became a member of World Trade Organisation (WTO) established in 1995. As a result in the first step 715 agricultural commodities are permitted free export-import. The situation was very grave for Indian Farmers since they are not in a position for hard unfare competition with highly subsidised commodities coming from abroad. Farmers are compelled to sale their produce at lower prices. On another context, markets having no Govt. agency to purchase farm produces at Govt. declared Minimum Support Price (MSP) compelling farmers to sale their produce to dishonest '*Farias*' engaged by private mill owners. Forward marketing and advance booking of farmers' produces are also anti-farmer. Another deceiving practice is contract farming that is not so evident in West Bengal.

12.11 Rural people dependent on agriculture

Qualitative development of human resources of a country or a state has profound influence on agriculture and other fields also. In 2011, 77.08 per cent of people are literate and 99 per cent of children goes to school in West Bengal. In 2010, 10.5 lakh students appeared in Secondary and 4.26 lakh appeared in Higher Secondary (12 class) examinations. The population rise is 17.77 per cent in 2001 and 13.93 per cent in 2011. In 1977, 53,509 patients were treated in Government hospitals and in 2010 it is more than a lakh per year. The death rate was 7.4 per cent per thousand in 2001 and 6.2 per thousand in 2011, child death reached 35/thousand, and 141 mother's death per lakh were much-better than national rate. Under Indira Awas Yojona more than 1.51 lakh poor people have their house and number of people below poverty line has also declined. All these has positive influence on agriculture.

Spread of service sector and small and cottage industries in rural areas usually lowers the population dependent on agriculture. In West Bengal due to increase of income of rural people, the service sector and small and cottage industry sector has grown absorbing in their turn a large section of rural people, so long a congesting burden on agriculture. Over last few decades the number of small and medium industries has increased to 25.13 lakh employing 58.31 lakh people. Similarly for same reasons of income increase a faster urbanisation created many and better paying jobs in growing towns, and census towns.

12.12 Women and agriculture

Women of a farm family has been actively participating in relatively lighter works in addition to home-making in Bengal since beginning of agriculture. It followed an excellent planning of the farmer and his women family members. Usually farmer does clearing of land, plowing, laddering, sowing, harvesting, application of fertilisers and pesticides etc. In carrying harvested crop, wife participates. Besides the operations that required completion in one or two days like transplanting, carrying seeds and fertilisers to field, harvesting, threshing, winnowing are some more operations where farmer's wife takes a major share. As long as paddy husking was done in '*Dhenki*' it was exclusive job of women. Primary processing of produces for storing was also women's exclusive job. These include frying in sand paddy or rice to produce '*Khoi*' or '*Muri*', parboiling of paddy and their drying in sun, boiled rice turned into '*chira*' by pressing in a '*Dhenki*' etc. Husbandry of animal folk i.e. goat, chicken, ducks, cattle etc. received major participation of women. Milking of cow, and preservation of it by boiling and '*Khir*', '*Chhana*' and sweetmeats in addition to all cooking job are exclusively done by women. Recently jobs like crossing (pollination), harvesting of flowers, making of garlands, and even their sale have been identified as girl's job. Similarly kitchen gardens growing vegetables, manuring and irrigating them lifting water in a pitcher in her '*Kankh*', i.e. however a hard job (being done in South 24-Parganas).

Success of agriculture in Bengal is no doubt a success of farmer's family in which women play a comparable role. Women are path finders in multi-various processing from needle and thread work on clothes, excellent '*jari*' work, and many other delicate beautification of dresses that are difficult to be described.

It may be mentioned that in northern and western India hard job like dragging plow is often done by women, that never happened in Bengal.

12.13 Younger generation in agriculture

The normal process of transfer of family agriculture from parents to new generation has been modified in different ways during modern times of Bengal agriculture. During first three decades since fifties the trend was generally the comparatively less educated son stays with the family and takes over agriculture from parents. During next three decades with the spread of education and relatively more income generation, the farmer's family faced problem of persons to take over agriculture, educated son taking a job elsewhere. That's how in a family-scale man-power was declining in agriculture. Side by side the youth from farm labour (*'Kshet majur'*) families has been trying to enhance their capabilities through education, awareness and activities in agriculture or non-agriculture sectors while others continue to do job in agriculture. Those who became aware and enterprising are trying to do something remunerative e.g. a youth developing a small organic farm in Kalna, Barddhaman area in eighties, and another in East Medinipur cultivating without any chemical input (for being poor to purchase) using vermicompost and spraying leaf retting liquid manure. Some others brought *'Khaki Campbell'* duckling from Bangalore and started duckery, and someone mixed tourism and picnic spot in fruit orchard in North 24-Parganas. There are persons in Medinipur engaged in agricultural machinery business and one or two in Hooghly engaged in input sale business.

From the end of seventies few young boys and girls developed nursery, fish culture or fish seed production enterprises. Recently people are finding ornamental fish culture, spice farming or flower production remunerative. Village women are rearing hybrid cows to sale milk to cooperative system. Younger women are forming groups (SHG), purchasing paddy, getting that milled and selling rice. Some others are engaged in making spice powder, or weaving cloth or making baskets of different kinds like *'Khalui'*, *'Dhama'*, *'Chupdi'*, *'Saaji'*, *'Dhuchuni'*, *'Kunke'* etc. or weaving mat and mattress with *Tagetes* or *'Sitalpati'* to earn some money. Making of different decorative handicrafts from agro-produces is traditional.

12.14 Traditional knowledge and indigenous technology

Traditional knowledge and indigenous technology (TTK) is being selected and its re-application in agriculture is introduced in eighties of 20th century in Bengal. The high chemical fertiliser use has not been practiced in this state may be due to resource-poor state of Bengal farmers. But whatever has been done has lack of balance between nutrients (may be very low imbalance compared to the condition in many other states) that resulted in many problems. In this context wise farmers decided to follow the methods and techniques followed by his parents and grand parents. But as per need of farm, time and logically applicable in present time. Side by side agricultural experts are also advicing in same way.

For cultivating land with 'plow' lengthwise and breadthwise, laddering (farmer standing on the ladder if necessary), drawing heavy wooden plank to break clods, are all traditional techniques. In case of small seeds like mustard, sesamum etc. laddering twice-one before seed casting and one after is an indigenous knowledge. For creeper-vegetables or large space requiring plants like papaya instead of plowing the entire land, farmers prepare '*Thupi*' i.e. around (1' to 2' dia) worked land, apply and mix manures and sow seeds. On river beaches similar '*thupis*' are made mixing OM with sandy soil and sowing seeds of crops like water-melon or even groundnut. In case of potatoes, brinjal, chilli and tomatoes are planted at wider spaced ridges ('*Bheli*') or subsequent soil-dressing ('*Kanimati dhorano*') is an exclusive traditional technology. Seed storage methods like paddy in earthen pots but vegetable seeds folded in newspaper piece and put in inside (lower surface) of thatched roofings. Conserving grafts of fruit plants with a prepared-soil ball ('*Guti*') covering its roots in dug channels under a deep tree-shade selected on an upland ('*Haapa*') is indigenous. To enrich soil, every dry season the silt from a pond is collected and put in farm land is a long tradition. Similarly sweepings of cowshed ('*Goalghor*'), cowdung turned into manure, or cow-urine ('*Gochona*') soaked straw are also put in farm land before plowing under.

The human faeces or dead bodies of animals deposited in trenches in a remote place ('*Bhagad*') ultimately produces good manure that is also used to build up soil fertility. Applying cowdung to arecanut or coconut plants supply surface roots of such plants get nutrients but tradition of 'table-salt' application to coconut plants is a negative tradition excepting the explanation that 'Na' releases K in soil to be used by coconut. Application of starch (*'Fen'*) from cooked rice to bottle gourd or application of used tea-leaves to flower and vegetables have also been put before questions.

Many indigenous technologies of crop protection are still in use in Bengal. Application of water from smoking device (*'Hunko'*), ash mixed with kerosene, or pulling rope soaked in 'Kerosene' over crop canopy, spraying of neem-decoction or tobacco decoction has been in practice for long time. Erecting *'Kaktadua'* (bird scarer) was double purpose providing space to birds from where they picks up insect pests on crops. But fixing one bamboo-peg or a scaffold in the field was also a common practice for birds stand both in days devouring insects etc. and owl in the night to consume rats. Planting *'Ocimum'* plant in field to release odour that scared away pests.

As post-harvest protection measures covering surface of potatoes with 'brick dust' removed moisture from surface that lowered chance of bacterial infection. This was an ancient practice in Bengal. Using solar radiation and fire in suitable methods to dry and preserve grains or slices of potatoes, mango (*'Aamsi'*), grinding such dried materials (*'Aamchur'*) or drying in layers-mango juice to make leathers (*'Aamsatta'*), drying seeds of jackfruit, cowpea, pea for storing and consumption later are all traditional practices. Using high concentration of salt, *'Gur'*, sugar that helped preservation are also practiced for long time. *'Khoi'*, *'Mudi'*, *'Chida'* or parboiling of rice are also traditional practices. Preparation of excellent quality of pickle in oil or *'Gur'*, *'Morabba'* preparation, or preparing *'patali'* or candy boiling saps of Date palm, Palmyra palm are also ancient culture of Bengal. Traditional practices also include collecting honey from 'hive' in forests scaring away the flies with smoke by burning water-soaked straw or turning milk into *'khir'* by boiling or into *'chhana'* adding citrus juice were methods for short term preservation.

Fishes were mixed with turmeric paste and table salt that helped early Bengalis to preserve different fishes like *'Ilish'* (*'Nona Ilish'*) or other fishes (*'Shuntki'*). There were innumerable method followed in Bengal for animal food preparation and animal healthcare, harvesting fruits, storing fruits for ripening and many others that are essentially value addition to the produce.

12.15 Modern Technology in Agriculture

With the advancement of knowledge and science modern humans are equipped in many ways and methods for working in a much finer way and in sharp techniques. Slowly some such techniques are coming for use in agriculture. Popularisation of use of computer has opened up the prospect of video compact disc (VCD) use to make farmers in all remote areas aware of modern farming techniques through demonstration movies. They can see and learn the visual identity of pests, diseases and other disorders of crops along with specific recommendations for correction for each as experts suggest. Again use of cell phone (mobile) for easy, distant contacts have helped modernise agriculture particularly in marketing or transport sector. All these have spread in rural areas of West Bengal also quite fast and satisfactorily.

Remote sensing, GPS, GIS use, land levelling through use of laser beam, application through mixed liquid as per separate requirements of every square-meter of levelled land and finally site specific and precision farming at least partially make it possible in Indian context. Perhaps excepting remote sensing, our position is yet not in a stage when laser beam levelling, computerised fertiliser and water spraying as per requirement of every unit of land in 'grid' can be applied in farmers' field.

A. Remote sensing in agriculture

Remote sensing is a modern technique of 'sensing' characteristics of an object that are land, crops, plantations on land or fishes etc. in water with quantitative and qualitative information. Forests and other vegetation are estimated as also soil physical, soil moisture, soil mineral conditions of land, crop growth and maturity, pest and diseases on crops and pollution of land or water, surface and ground water position of an area and after necessary co-relation forecasting of the situation is made using '*detectors*' placed on balloons or aircrafts or satellites.

Remote sensing gives transparency to our awareness about environment and weather change. It helps in flaw-less survey of land, crop fields etc. In fact analysis and interpretation of all information obtained through RS from land provides accurate guidelines on economic, social and statistical aspects and enables to take correct and dependable decisions.

In India RS use was started in 1970 taking IR-photographs with a '*Hassel Blad*' camera. In India through experimental '*Bhaskar I and II*' projects Indian Remote Sensing Satellites – IRS-1A in 1988 and IRS-1B in 1991 were launched. Through this modern technologies land use, management of fallow lands, use of water resources, areas under crops and their productivity, agriculture planning on the basis of agroclimatic zones, estimation of sea-resources, etc. are made and used in development programmes of the country. All these studies were being conducted by concerned Departments in collaboration with Dept. of Space. In addition to Central Remote Sensing Centre, 22 State RS Centers have been developed.

In case of agriculture and food (i) determination of area and production of crops, (ii) measurement of aerable and dry areas and (iii) measurement of saline and alkaline soil area are in progress. However making of maps of fallow lands, determination of area having ground water, detecting fishing area in seas have been in progress and area of application of this technology is being made wider with time (ISRO, 1995).

B. Geographical positioning system (GPS)

Geographical or Global Positioning System was started in 1973. Satellite placed in one orbit around earth sends message in all seasons about time and position of any object on earth's surface. The programme was initiated by four satellites and the GPS-Receiver on land by USA. In India IRNSS-regional center is expected to start functioning since 2012. This system while functioning will prepare farm-plan, field map, collection of soil sample, and even directing the tractor in field, scouting of crops, production estimate etc. jointly with GIS.

C. Geographical Information System (GIS)

This technology is capable of imaging and collecting all kinds of information, their conservation, analysis, control, demonstration and supply to all interests. Drawing maps, and statistical analysis of informations and data helps to clearly understand all detail aspects and context of agriculture. It also shows the inputs to be used in a 'farm' and what production can be received from that-all that helps to understand success and profit position of the farm.

D. Land leveling through 'Laser' use

Maximum success in crop production in a farm is achieved to maximum extent by best leveling of land, since this provides equal amount of moisture and nutrients to each of the lakhs of plants in the field allowing each of them to grow equally reaching maturity at same time giving finally maximum production. One 'laser-beam' controlled leveling system can bring the highest slope in the field within ± 2 cm. Using ox-drawn or tractor drawn plow, ladder and wooden plank leveling is achieved partially provided the land is levelled before every crop cultivation. On the land since after harvest of one crop level of the land is lost to some extent for the present traditional practice is followed. Moreover the indigenous practice of laddering before and after sowing even in case of large-seed crops will be helpful.

E. Application of irrigation water and nutrient in modern spray technique

On analysis of nutrient statuses of each small unit of land as seen in grid in computer screen, fertilisers are brought in solution to be sprayed on the soil according to its specific need. The entire programme is computerised right on the moving tractor. The liquified fertiliser (slurry) is stored in a tank on the tractor, application from which is controlled at the outlet in the ranges from full to one fourth quantity. Computer controlled release of nutrient and controlling tractor speed the smaller units are supplied nutrient as per their determined requirement.

Both D and E are applicable in large farms since farmers of 100-1000 acres farm land cannot see and read the '*hunger*' of each corner (units) of one's land excepting use of a computer. In our country small and marginal farmers know every corner (unit) of his small farm and if made aware, he obviously can take corrective steps for moisture and nutrient application in all corners of his field.

F. Site specific farming

Land and soil in different areas of farm always differ in some or other characters for natural and human intervention reasons. Its level and nutrient content (fertility) varies. Studying and noting these spatial variations correctives are arranged accordingly particularly in cases of soil moisture and nutrients. This procedure can be adopted by a farmer if he is given the clarification. In fact in Bengal many experienced and wise farmers practice this farming and often called – 'a farmer who knows his land like his own palm'.

G. Precision farming

PF means a farming in which all the portions of land are provided with right quantity of water and nutrient as required by the land portion (from soil analysis for 16 elements) in right time and maximum possible production is obtained. First of all the fertility status of every part (unit) of the farm land including slope and level, physico-chemical status is determined using GPS, GIS system. The level of the entire land is first brought within ± 2 cm using tractor mounted '*Laser beam*' level system. Then water and fertiliser in slurry is applied with a computer-driven application system as per 'E'. Such a precise farming system gives maximum production per unit area.

In India in some states in southern part scientists conducted projects on PF, with funds from GOI. In Bengal too research Farms at Birbhum and east Medinipur attempts for PF has been made. However, the need and feasibility of that has been questioned. But instead of making leveling of land equipment dependent and applying right quantity of fertiliser in right time depending on farmer's knowledge and experience, double-laddering and such other practices could be the answer for the country with small and marginal farms.

13

Conclusion

13.0 According to the provision of laws in regard to heir of property including land, agricultural land of a family is continuing to be divided and sub-divided in generations in the country. Side by side in Bengal at least female members are being deprived of landed property till sixties or seventies of 20th century by-passing the legal provisions. However fragmentation of holding continued.

Secondly, partition of India (Punjab and Bengal) to earn independence has increased pressure of people on land due to massive migration of Bengalis to West Bengal from the then East Pakistan. Alongwith over a long period of time the growth of sectors like industry and service has been unsatisfactory in the country increasing pressure on agriculture.

Over last three decades (eighties of 20th to 1st of 21st) land reforms vesting ceiling surplus land of people their and distribution among landless villagers has fragmented holdings but provided security of existence to landless. Along with registering names of '*Bargadars*' (share croppers) with the land they cultivated made their stay on the land for successors also secured.

13.1 In another side the size of 'Bengal' has reduced in number of times due to socio-political changes and the course of events thereof. Side by side population of Bengal has increased.

Bangladesh has appeared with its sovereignty and culture as a separate country. Earlier identity of Bengali's has been recognised in Tripura. In Assam, Jharkhand, Delhi, Andamans some places in south India or Nagaland this human community is living with their characteristic culture and contributing their creative might.

In the field of agriculture also they have shown their capacity to overcome different adverses – both natural and created to move forward. Is it possible to earn livelihood by cultivating less than 2 ha agricultural land ? Agricultural experts are in deep search and research in answering this question. In agricultural economics in India one commonly discussed issue was positive and negative sides of 'fragmentation' or 'consolidation' of holdings. Many differences and divisions cropped up from this issue. In the midst of all these some pragmatic agricultural scientists, economists and wise and experienced farmers started serious thinking about any way-out from this dilemma. Compared to the farming in wests on thousand hectare or hundred hectare farms, can the one two hectare farms in 'Bengal' support livelihood of a family? There have been unending debate or discussion on this small and marginal farm agriculture's capacity to produce food or to earn enough to take charge of livelihood of a family. Pragmatic, optimists started with examining the geographic positional and the climatic advantage of Bengal over other places. In case of cropping intensity-how much increase is feasible, or combination of different farming in mixed farming– growing food crops, oilseeds, sugar and fibre crops, vegetables, flowers, spices, medicinal plants, narcotics, fruits etc. or rearing animals like cattle, goat, duck, chicken, pigs, sheep or in water body fish, prawn, crab or rearing insects like bees, silk, *tasar* or 'eri', *lac* insects in most profitable combination(s) for a specific area has been the goal.

13.3 The soaring price of chemical inputs of agriculture compelled wise farmers to think of suitable substitutes (if any) and small and marginal farmers with very small or no capital are out to find best substitutes in organic manures etc. transforming their long experience of compost from refuses and sweepings or cowdung manure. They are experimenting with vermicompost, vermi-wash, phosphocompost, enriched compost, supercompost or leaf-retting liquid manure for spray with the objective of minimising chemical fertilisers without sacrificing yield.

'Bengal' has achieved self-sufficiency in food only in nineties of 20th century. Landless getting land, '*bargadars*' receiving right to '*barga*' land for cultivation, spread of minor irrigation and widespread 'Boro rice' and vegetable cultivation are the main contributors. In the next phase Bengal farmers emphasised increased income generation and to start with (in nineties) they picked up vegetable cultivation and in some places flowers. Bengal has long history of growing jute as cash crop. In Hooghly and Barddhaman potato was also cash crop over long period of time. Introduction of vegetables and flowers often with short duration, flexible time period and variable sowing and harvesting dates favoured farmers to enhance their income getting appreciative market for their produce. However regarding introduction of tuberose in Nadia in seventies the consideration of short duration was not there but harvest and marketing the produce helped them.

13.4 Another important change with time is decline of number of persons in farmer's family due to spread of education taking some members away for better job or shifting to job in service sector in a nearby developing town or for some other reasons. Compared to service in agriculture that is irregular in a year and low rate of payment prompted them to opt for jobs mostly in service sector that are regular paying higher wage. The service sector is fast spreading in West Bengal for reasons of income-increase of villagers leading to their increased and wider consumption. In fact in the first decade of this century the annual sale and purchase in villages was 30-40 thousand crore. The supporting statistics is number of service units increased from 23.25 lakh (2001-03) to 33.5 lakh in 2006-07. Again the engagement of 3 crore 35 lakh in the country 13 per cent is in West Bengal (highest 14 per cent in UP) and employment of 22 lakh 32 thousand (63rd NSS, 2007) people in 2006-07.

Urbanisation all over the State also enhanced progress of agriculture. Number of towns that was 378 in 2001 has become 909 in 2011. Besides Census Town no. increased from 255 to 780 and municipalities from 123 to 129. This has also reduced man-power in agriculture. Census 2011, showed decline in village number in Bengal and the rate of population increase in villages has come down to 7.37 per cent. All these created a situation that felt to change agriculture system further. Since 1990-91, farmers stared to replace paddy and vegetable with banana, guava, mango etc. In north Bengal many farmers started planting tea, selling leaves to existing tea gardens (bought leaves), with processing unit. Objective was that in absence of any member to take over farming, aging farmer wanted to run the farm this way.

13.5 Agriculture of the state is run by small and marginal farmers. Their agriculture was 'subsistence' two decades back. Agriculture was their livelihood and to secure their existence. After land reforms their capability and economic condition improved through agriculture. Thereafter since nineties of 20th century their agriculture started turning toward a kind of 'commercial agriculture'. A very slow all out transformation of the farmer and his family position was taking place. The kind of commercial agriculture practiced in large farms of farmers with big capital is altogether different from this commercial agriculture. This is a new type of commercial farming on small landholding and small or zero capital that is unique in West Bengal for reasons of all out support from State Govt. During last two decades of 20th and first decade of 21st centuries this farming is taking shape. The elected Panchayeti Raj is also a strong support for this farming for many reasons. It appears that its care through Govt. support has to continue for few more years so that it produces a sustainable method of commercial small farming. This support in the forms of subsidy on inputs and assured reasonable market for their produce that will not only help these villagers to be established but also contribute a sable development of rural area in Bengal.

13.6 Bengalis are now self-sufficient in food. It does not necessarily mean that poors and backwards in all corners get enough food. it all depends on their economic strength. Bengalis are capable of procure variety of foods from rice to fishes via vegetables. Intake of fruits and milk-based sweets has spread to villages. Spread of education, awareness and health consciousness have pushed up their food taking.

References Consulted

Land surface, rivers and weather :

1. IAASTD-report, 2004, International Assessment of Agricultural Science and Technology Development; Summary, pp. 126; Net.
2. ISRO report, 2009; Current Science, November.
3. Chakrabarty, Ramananda and Bijan Bihari Mandal, 1983; 'Sasyotpadaner Mul Tatwa'; *Bengali*; West Bengal State Book Board; pp. 672+
4. Basu, Ashok Kumar, 2002; 'Paschimbanger Nad Nadi', '*Bengali*'; Mitra o Ghosh; pp. 90.
5. Bassam, AL, 1981; The wonder that was India; Rupa & Co.; Kolkata; pp. 572.
6. Mandal, Krishnakali, 1999; 'Dakshin 24-Parganar Bismrita Adhyay; *Bengali*; Nabachalantika; Kolkata; pp.127.
7. Roy, Sankarshan, 1979; 'Bhutatwiker Chokhe Paschim-bangla', *Bengali*; West Bengal State Book Board; pp.166+
8. Habib Irfan; 2002; Prak-Itihas : 'Bharatbarsher Manusher Itihas-1', Bengali translation; NBA; pp. 87.

Origin of living organisms, human arrival, Paleolithic, Neolithic, Heliolithic and Iron Age :

1. Chattopadhyay, Bhaskar, 2003; Gaurbanger Itihas o Sanskriti; 1st Part; B*engali*; Progressive Publishers; Kolkata; pp.134 +

2. Child, Gordon; 1930; What happened in History; pp. 230.

3. Nene, YL; 1966; "History of Indian Agriculture"; Ed. Asian Agri History Foundation; Sekandrabad.

4. Bandyopadhya, Rakhaldas; 1914; 'Banglar Itihas'; *Bengali*, 1st Part; pp. 230.

5. Basu, Tapas; 1995; "Bangladeshe Krishir Bibartan; Krishak Samaj-o- Sahitya"; *Bengali*; Pustak Bipani; Kolkata; pp. 229.

6. Balkundi, HV; 1996; in "History of Indian Agriculture"; Ed : Asian Agri History Foundation.

7. Mukerji, NG; 1901; "Handbook of Indian Agriculture"; Thakerspink and Co.; Calcutta; p. 622.

8. Roy, Niharranjan; 1949; 'Bangalir Itihaas, Adiparbo'; *Bengali*, Desh Publishing; Kolkata; pp. 788+.

9. Sinha, Gopalchandra; 2009; "Bharatbarsher Itihash" : Prachin o Adi Madhya Jug" *Bengali*; Progressive Pub; Kolkata; pp. 1010+.

10. Sur, Atul, 1986; 'Bangla o Bangalir Bibartan"; '*Bengali*' 'Sahityalok', Kolkata; pp. 438+.

11. Habib, Irfan, 2004; "Sindhu Sabhyata" (*Bengali translated*); NBA; p. 117.

12. Habib, Irfan, 2005; "Baidik Sabhyata o Louhajuger Agoman"; (Bengali translated); NBA; p. 104.

Maurya, Gupa and Pal Era :

1. Debbarma, Debal; 2010; "Kingbadontir Khana"; *Bengali*; Nababharati, Kolkata; p. 69.

2. Pramanik Paramananda; 2011; 'Sharadiya Jnan-c-Bigyan', *Bengali*, Kolkata; pp. 543-45.

3. Bhattacharya Sukumari, 1998; "Beder Juge Kshudha-o-Khadya"; *Bengali*; 'Chirayata Prakshana'; Kolkata; p. 120.

4. Mazumdar, Girija Prasanna and Banerjee, Suresh Chandra; 1960; '*Krsi Parasara*'; Asiatic Society, Kolkata; No. 285 : 1590.

5. Maitreya Akshoy Kumar; 1912; 'Goud Lekhamala'; Bengali.

6. Habib, I., 2006; 'Maurya Juger Bharatbarsho"; *Bengali*; NBA; p. 200.

Sen, Muslim and Mughol period :

1. Thakur, Abanindranath, 1945; "Banglar Brato"; *Bengali*; Visva Bharati; p. 79.

2. Datta, Ramesh Chandra, 1874; "Banglar Krishak Samaj"; *Bengali*' Dipayan, Kolkata; p. 188.

3. Habib, I., 1985; Mughol Bharater Krishi Byabastha; *Bengali*; K.P. Bagchi & Co., pp. 486+.

4. Sen, Sukumar; 1965; Bangla Sahitya Itihas; Sahitya Academy; *Bengali*; p. 338.

English Rule and Bengal Agriculture :

1. Uliyanovoski, R; 1985; Bharater Krishi Byabastha : Dui Biswajuddher Madhyabartikale; *Bengali*; Manisha; Kolkata, p. 261.

2. Chakrabarti, Sudhir; 1996; "Paschimbanger Mela o Mahotsav"; *Bengali*; Pustak Bipani, Kolkata; p. 216.

3. Chaudhuri Fakruddin Md; 1940; 'Grihastha Darpan'; *Bengali*; Basumati Sahitya Mandir; pp. 300+.

4. Dash, Asitava; 1998; 'Swadhinata Sangrame Bharat; Tarikh Abhidhan' *Bengali*; Patralekha, Kolkata; p. 137.

5. Bose, Tarun; 1998; In "History of Agricultural Education in Bengal"; Ed. BCKV; pp. 127-145.

6. Mandal, B; Sen Gupta K and Trivedi, N; 1998; In "History of Agril Education in Bengal", Ed; BCKV; pp. 33-48.

7. Mitra, Manmathonath (ed. Nikunjabehari Dutta); 1925; 'Sabji Chaas'; *Bengali*; Bharatiyo Krishi Samiti; Kolkata, p. 112.

8. Mitra, Sudhir Kumar; 1952; "Hooghly Jelar Itihas o Bongo Samaj"; *Bengali*; Mandol Book House; Kolkata; pp. 680+.

9. Mookerji, NG, 1919; Handbook of Sericulture; p. 201.

10. Mukherjee N. and Ghosh, T.; 1998; In History of Agricultural Education in Bengal; Ed. B.C.K.V., pp. 55-58.

11. Mukhopadhyay, U. and Mukhopadhyay, S.; 2003; 'Hazar Jinish'; *Bengali*; Basumati Sahitya Mandir; Kolkata; p. 208.

12. Roy Niharranjan; 1947; Prachin Banglar Path Ghat; *Bengali*'; Viswa Bharati Patrika, 6 : 1.

13. Shastry, H., 1947; "Prachin Banglar Gaurab"; *Bengali*; In '*Lok*', 2007, Ed. Pranab Sarkar.

14. Sarkar, Pranab; 2002; Ed. 'Bhanglar Hat'; *Bengali*; '*Lok*'; p. 560.

15. Sarkar, P.; 2007; Ed. 'Sekaler Pathghat'-2; 'Swadesh Charcha: Lok'; *Bengali*; p. 587.

16. Samanta, Basantakumar; 1987; Hitakari Sava, Stree Shiksha o Tatkalin Bongo Somaj; *Bengali*; Sahityalok; p. 159.

17. Haats and Bazars of West Bengal; 1992; Krishibiparan Bivag; Paschimbanga Sarkar; p. 206.

Agriculture in Modern times :

1. ISRO-Report, 1995; Parliamentary Committee Review Report; ISRO-SP, 74-75; Bangalore; p. 61.

2. Ghoshal Kalikrishna o Adityachoudhary, N; 1997; "Paschimbange Veshaj Udvider Chaas'; BCKV; p. 44.

3. Das, Aniruddha, 2005; "Bharater Krishi Niti-o-Bij Bil"; *Bengali*; PBVM; Kolkata; p. 32.

4. Das, NR; 2006; Rainfed Payra / Utera Crops in India; Kalyani Publishers; p. 182.

5. Dasgupta, MK; 1998; In "History of Agricultural Education in Bengal"; Ed. BCKV; pp. 70-77.

6. Nayban, G; 2001; "Sahaj Kathay Bigyan Vittik Chasbas"; *Bengali*; Ananda Prakashani; p. 358.

7. Mukherjee, N; 2005; "Choto Chasi, Jaiba Dhan Chas"; *Bengali*; "Jana Vigyaner Iistahar"; Sharad Sankha; pp. 43-45.

8. Mukherjee, N. and Khatua, D; 1998; In "History of Agricultural Education in Bengal"; Ed. BCKV; pp. 194-196.

9. Mukherjee, N, 2011; "Sabjichase Paschimbanger Chashider Ebong Rajyer Samriddhi", *Bengali*; Nadia Samabay; April-June; pp. 11-13.

10. Sing, Sukumar, 2002; "Sundarboner Itikotha o A-sarkari Unnayan Sannstha"; *Bengali*; Mass Education; p. 184.

11. Sen, Amartya, 2000; 'Jiban Jatra o Arthaniti; *Bengali*; Ananda Publishers; Kolkata.

12. Hajra Pranab; 2006; Bharatbarse Sabji Bij Uttpadaner Chalchitra o Paschimbange Tar Samvabana"; *Bengali*; 'Krishi Bhabna'; Samiksha, 2006; pp. 67-75.

Note : References have been used also in chapters other than where they are listed.

Index

D

E

G

S